Understanding Your Child's Entertainment

By Leonard Suib and Muriel Broadman

MARIONETTES ONSTAGE!

Understanding Your Child's Entertainment

Muriel Broadman

HARPER & ROW, PUBLISHERS
New York, Hagerstown, San Francisco, London

To Jonathan Henry Lobl
who began it all

UNDERSTANDING YOUR CHILD'S ENTERTAINMENT. Copyright © 1977 by Muriel Broadman. All rights reserved. Printed in the United States of America. No part of this book may be used or reproduced in any manner whatsoever without written permission except in the case of brief quotations embodied in critical articles and reviews. For information address Harper & Row, Publishers, Inc., 10 East 53rd Street, New York, N.Y. 10022. Published simultaneously in Canada by Fitzhenry & Whiteside Limited, Toronto.

FIRST EDITION

Designed by Eve Callahan

Library of Congress Cataloging in Publication Data

Broadman, Muriel.
    Understanding your child's entertainment.
    Includes index.
    1. Performing arts and children. I. Title.
PN1590.C45B7   790.2   76–5114
ISBN 0–06–010481–3

77 78 79 80 10 9 8 7 6 5 4 3 2 1

Contents

Foreword

Entertainment plays an important part in the life of a child. To the extent that it is selected with judgment and care, entertainment contributes to his or her social, intellectual, and emotional development. It may, of course, serve purely as escape or diversion, which, when well done, is an equally valid reason for its inclusion. Entertainment may go beyond fun, however, when substance is provided. Content and the posing of questions contribute to a child's experience by giving information, a chance to gain a better understanding of himself and others, and perhaps even the first consciousness-raising on social issues.

Young people are curious about the world they live in and they are eager to explore it. Too often we underestimate their intelligence as we overestimate their experience. The arts have always been an important means of discovering and learning; today, perhaps more than at any other time in history, we need what the arts can provide.

In *Understanding Your Child's Entertainment* Muriel Broadman covers children's theater, television, film, puppetry, dance, opera, mime, animation, radio, recordings—in short, every experience in the performing arts and public entertainment directed toward, or available, to the young. If this seems like a comprehensive survey of the field, it is. Yet the result is far from superficial treatment; it is a frank and penetrating view of the arts and the media as they engage the attention and influence the attitudes of children.

The author's years of experience as a previewer and critic of children's entertainment provide her with a wealth of information. With keen perception she identifies the positive values and negative aspects of what she has seen. Unfortunately, there are more of the latter than of the former. Her lively style and sense of humor enhance a readable text that keeps one absorbed until the message has been thoroughly delivered. Muriel Broadman makes it clear throughout the book that she is expressing a personal point of view; yet the obvious sense of her arguments wins us to her side.

She examines such controversial subjects as audience participation, violence, the protagonist in a children's play, and age level programming. Equally engrossing, but less often treated, are racism, sexism, attitudes toward age, anti-intellectualism, cruelty, and death. She supports her arguments with compelling examples, citing plays and using names where necessary. There is guidance here for the most sophisticated adult and "required reading" for the lay person.

Muriel Broadman's key word is "enjoy." Unless a child enjoys an experience, he or she will get little from it, edifying as it may be. This, however, does not mean that everything a child seems to enjoy is good. A child's reactions are certainly to be studied but the critical judgment of a ten-year-old is unformed, hence the need for supervision and help in selection. A second key word is "respect." The performance that respects the audience, be it adult or child, will honor its humanity and its intelligence and will reject condescension, cheap humor, the assuming of a background that it does not have, and obvious preaching.

She expresses belief in the folk and fairy tales as material that meets the deeper needs of children as well as appealing to their love of fantasy. In discussing the relevance of subject matter to the lives of children, she acknowledges their interest in the present. She makes it clear at all times that she is not a psychologist or an educator; but she has come to many of the same conclusions expressed by writers in these fields.

Her final chapters deal with the establishment and organization of a children's theater. Based on the principles that she has outlined in this text, a community could avoid many of the common pitfalls. While Muriel Broadman may not ingratiate herself with the producers and purveyors of children's entertainment, they will do well to listen to her. She writes with candor and honesty, but above all with a caring concern.

NELLIE MCCASLIN
The Program in Educational Theater
New York University
New York City
October 1976

Introduction

This book is about the content of entertainment for children. Of necessity, whatever conclusions I've reached and set down are personal ones, arrived at by over twenty years of watching entertainment and audiences in the United States and abroad. My position is that of critic and parent—not educator, psychologist, anthropologist, or folklorist. My involvement in children's entertainment and my standards derive mainly from three sources:

1. An apprenticeship of more than ten years on various committees of Region 14 of the Children's Theatre Conference (CTC), now the Children's Theatre Association of America (CTAA). This organization initially guided my understanding of children's entertainment as a constructive force.

2. The tens of thousands of young people composing the audiences I've observed, who have taught me so much about entertainment for them.

3. My son Jonathan, who has educated me to recognize children for what they are, to appreciate their current level of development, neither condescending to them nor making unrealistic demands.

It would be difficult to choose which of the three has contributed most. Without the live audiences, much of what I learned from CTC would have been empty theory, but without that theory, my comprehension of their entertainment could have been without a basis in principles. Certainly without close proximity to an individual child, in this case my son, I'd have lacked an intimate awareness of a child's capabilities and the incentive to continue my preoccupation with children's entertainment.

As an example of what I learned from CTC, and to help those adults who want to appraise entertainment and to import good professional theater for young people into their community, there are in the Appendix two questionnaires developed by a committee on which I served.

Audiences have taught me to accept their judgment regarding what they dislike, and to query and evaluate what they applaud.

What I've learned from my son is that I mustn't expect a mature reaction from an immature human being, and that I have no right to impose my interpretation of an event on someone seeing it through different eyes. A case in point: When Jonathan was just under three, we were together one afternoon in the living room. I left for a moment, and as I entered the hallway, out of his sight, I tripped over my long housecoat and with a crash that shook the walls measured my full length supine on the floor. The shock and the pain made me want to weep and I was able to keep from screaming only by holding the thought that I must not frighten the baby. Jonathan came out to investigate and found me on my back being terribly brave. He stood over me with tears welling up.

"Don't cry, darling," I managed to gasp. "I'm not hurt. Just let me lie here till I catch my breath and then I'll get up and be fine. I'm not hurt, so don't cry."

"That's not why I'm crying, Mommy," he said. "I'm crying because I didn't see you do it. Do it again, Mommy!"

That took my remaining breath until I realized this was a thoroughly reasonable reaction from a three-year-old. It was only one of many lessons he's taught me over the years.

What ideas I have put down in *Understanding Your Child's Entertainment* do not always accord with those of some of the members of CTC/CTAA who have been my mentors, or with the responses of some children's audiences, or with some of my son's opinions. They are *my* convictions, developed through viewing some three thousand live productions and audiences and an uncounted number of films and TV programs for boys and girls. I hope these ideas will enable adults to understand better what entertainment is doing for and to their children, and what its potential is.

Acknowledgments

The author thanks Jerry Lesch and Arlene Blaker, who read sections of the manuscript and made suggestions for inclusion of material. Most of all, thanks are due Jack Leskoff for permission to quote his review, and for his unfailing moral support while the author was preparing this book, when it was sorely needed.

1. Your Child's Entertainment

———⸱⟨∞⟩⸱———

As the days of childhood slide by one by one, they seem endless to boys and girls. But those of us who have watched children grow know how illusory this is. We know these endless days make up short, short years, and how little time there is for children to learn what they must to make their way through the world with some degree of competence and happiness. What is "entertainment" doing to enrich their present or to help them prepare for their future? According to Action for Children's Television, children younger than five spend three to four hours a day in front of a TV set, and they will have spent more time there than in school by the time they've been graduated from high school—four thousand more hours on the average than the eleven thousand hours they'll have put into their classes. Most children go to the movies with some regularity also, and many attend live theater, either productions designed for young people, or adult fare with their elders.

Part of the TV programming children watch is designed for them: *Sesame Street, The Electric Company, Zoom,* and the like, and the run-of-the-mill Saturday-morning kiddie fare.

However, estimates have been made that most of this TV time is spent on programs not designed particularly for children,* and while some parents insist that children leave the TV at 9 P.M. or earlier, many boys and girls, surreptitiously, or openly with the consent of parents or baby-sitters, view TV until past midnight.

Since such a great portion of children's lives is consumed by entertainment, it's important to see what it's giving them. What are they learning about this earth? . . . Its past? . . . Its present? . . . Their role on it now and in time to come? What are they learning of the philosophies and arts that have created some degree of order and civilization out of personal and social chaos? What are they learning about their own feelings? . . . To accept them? . . . To control them? . . . To live in them? Are your children getting value received for the investment of their time and your money? Are they being short-changed or otherwise ripped off?

This is what *Understanding Your Child's Entertainment* is going to explore. We are not so much concerned with which medium delivers this entertainment—the television screen, the movie theater, the puppet stage, the living stage, the circus arena—as we are with what remains with your children when it's over.

Does this mean all entertainment for children must contain factual information or models of admirable behavior only? Perish the thought! Just as the adult realm of entertainment encompasses *Hamlet* to *Hellzapoppin, cinema vérité* to a carnival side show, so young people may enjoy material that ranges from profound to frothy. The key word is *enjoy.* No matter how important the message you may want to get into a child's head

---

*CBS has estimated that the Saturday-morning children's programs represent no more than 9 percent of their total viewing. The remaining 91 percent of their viewing time is spent on adult or family fare, news, etc.

through the conduit of entertainment, if the child doesn't take pleasure in the experience, forget it. Nothing will go through. Watch an audience of boys and girls in a school auditorium when a boring play is being presented. There are two basic reactions: they fidget restlessly, disruptively, or they sit quietly with glazed eyes, eons remote from the events onstage.

There is no reason why children can't be served up a production that is pure fun and nothing else. They crave amusement, and legitimately so. But if *all* their entertainment is amusement and nothing else, they are being as starved emotionally and intellectually as they would be physically if fed a diet of nothing but candy, junk food, and sugared soft drinks. As children need protein to make their bodies grow, they need ideas to stimulate mental and emotional development. Entertainment can make a valuable contribution to the next generation of adults by conveying enriching ideas to young people in forms that will excite their minds and enlist their involvement.

But before we discuss what entertainment—theater in its broadest sense—can mean to your children, we should think about what theater means to you. If you turn to the stage, the screen, or TV merely for escapist diversion, there is no reason why you should expect it to be more for your children than a mindless baby-sitter, something, at best, innocuous to watch when there's nothing else to do.

If, however, you use the theater as a forum for the exchange of ideas, for a new look at familiar situations, or for insights into the heart, as well as for amusement, then you will be interested in considering the diversified roles entertainment plays for your girls and boys.

Children are like the rest of us in that we all are influenced by every aspect of our environment, including entertainment that ostensibly has no ideas. Even a brainless animated cartoon or action flick may or may not convey the impression that life is important and to be cherished, or that a good end justifies any means, or that one may take the law into one's own hands when other channels of justice fail. . . . Other factors contribute to the impact of impressions that make up the totality of concepts children grow by. Their homes, neighborhood, family, peers, schools, religion, economic status, toys—all these preponderate overwhelmingly in the scales, as against the weight of entertainment alone. Yet the values entertainment impresses on children are reinforced by many of the attitudes children absorb from the general society—the news, table conversation, peer pressures, for example. The circumstances, too, in which children view entertainment lend authority to its messages. A TV presentation enters the home, speaking directly and intimately to its audience, programming their responses. When a play comes into the school, it is with the implied or explicit imprimatur of principal and teachers. When children attend the theater or the cinema, usually the price of admission comes from the parents and it is with their consent, expressed or tacit, that the show is offered. In addition, the presence of large numbers of other children, alone or supported by adults, lends increased respect to the medium.

Once upon a time there were adults who believed that what they saw in print—no matter what—must be true. Now many, if not most, children are convinced that if they see it on TV or in the theater, it must be so. What does all this add up to? An influence entertainment has far beyond what even the enormous amount of time devoted to it would indicate.

Remnants of the Protestant work ethic are still to be found here and there, holding that the theater is at worst sinful and at best wasteful frivolity, but this attitude is giving way in some quarters. Several studies* have shown that there is an improve-

* Among these are two by the New York State Department of Education:

1. In 1970 the School Program Evaluation Bureau made a statistical survey (conducted by John Heim) of 63 New York State school districts (roughly 9 percent of the

ment in school grades where children become involved in performing arts programs. These studies are among the reasons state legislatures have been taking more seriously the whole subject of the arts for young people and allotting more money for theater activities through state education departments and arts councils. Federal funding through a number of sources is also more readily available. Those of us concerned with entertainment for young people applaud this support.

We regret, however, that theater arts must still achieve recognition through the back door, so to speak, entering on the coattails of more "respectable" subjects, such as reading and math skills. It's unfortunate that theater for children, again in its broadest sense, is not appreciated for what it most truly is —one of the great humanizing forces of our culture. The "creative artists"—playwrights, choreographers, and composers— give their ideas, their concepts, to the performing artists— actors, dancers, and musicians—to bring to life and transmit to the audience. There is no other means of communication so direct—body to body, mind to mind, heart to heart—as from the performers to the audience. Through no other medium can the participating spectators stand so easily in someone else's shoes or feel from inside someone else's skin. We say "participating" because being an audience is an active, not a passive, experience. Being receptive to ideas and emotions is a positive

---

total number, an unusually large percentage for sampling purposes) and found a small but significant increase in reading and mathematics scores in schools with performing arts programs over schools without. Evidence suggests that the increase would have been more marked had a uniform definition of "performing arts program" been used, but the schools were allowed to define this term for themselves and the average percentile of improvement was lowered by including schools paying lip service only to the qualifying criteria.

2. In 1971 the Division of the Humanities and the Arts, as it was then known, initiated a project involving a consortium of nine schools, coordinated with staff from Divisions of Reading Education, Evaluation, Federal Programs, etc. This was a summer curriculum stressing the performing arts and evaluating their influence on communications skills. Statistical results showed improvement in vocabulary, oral language, poise, self-confidence, et al.

state, as a radio or TV set must be turned on in order to receive signals from the transmitter. There is no better way in which to develop insights into relationships, empathy with other living creatures and their ideas and mores, and respect for their right to be what they are.

Whether the theatrical medium is the stage, TV, or film, each has its place and fills a different need. When we consider the theater to be a form of art and learn discernment in its disciplines, we have learned something about standards of quality that can be applied to other arts. All art leads to enrichment of experience, to stimulation to explore familiar paths more deeply or to strike out in new directions—to a greater understanding of life. Any form of genuine art deserves encouragement for its own sake, not merely because it contributes to a practical result in another field.

How well prepared are boys and girls to develop standards of appreciation in theater, to develop—to use an overworked and sometimes meaningless word—taste? The answer is subjective and depends in great part on your own feeling about children.

Some years ago I had an argument about this with a great lady of children's theater, a producer-director, who questioned an article I had written for the *New York Herald Tribune.*

"Surely," she said to me, "you don't mean it when you say, 'Children have no taste.' "

"Of course I mean it," I replied. "Taste is judgment, and judgment has to be learned through experience."

"In adults," she insisted, "but not in children. Don't you know every child comes into life pure and is undefiled until his tastes are debased by the world?"

I didn't know it, and she floored me. She had had over a generation of working with young people, whereas, except for my observations of young audiences, I had had no professional contact with them. But the memories I held of my own child-hood and that of my friends were clear and didn't corroborate her position. Moreover, dearly as I loved my own child and an assortment of nieces and nephews, I couldn't reconcile my knowledge of their discrimination with her stand. Indeed, I had been, and still am, appalled on many occasions by children's approval of entertainment where my kindest assessment of it is that it's rubbish. Then I must remind myself of what I wrote so many years ago: It's not that children have bad taste. Rather, they have no taste at all. Standards don't exist until there is sufficient experience to enable one to make comparisons. An inexperienced audience will applaud anything that moves, as long as it moves fast enough and, perferably, falls on its prat.

Audience reaction to entertainment can be very revealing, and must be understood if we are to have any comprehension of what it means to children.

I've known many instances where audience reaction has been completely misunderstood by the cast of a stage production for young people. Typically, the show had been an insulting bore. Throughout, applause had been minimal and there was an un-dercurrent of mumbling and foot-shuffling. However, at the final curtain there was a thunderous outburst of clapping, whis-tling, and stamping. The cast accepted this as an ovation and left in a state of euphoria, to spread the word the children had adored them. They couldn't have been farther from the mark. Anyone observing the children as well as the production could gather that they had been trapped in fidgety misery for an hour. The curtain meant release. *Whee!* Now they could stand, yell, or do anything to let off pent-up steam. At the first sign of permission from their teachers or chaperones, they struggled into their coats. Or if they were too impatient to get away, they snatched up their outer clothing and dashed for the lobby, climbing over seats to reach an aisle.

All kinds of tests have been devised to determine children's reactions to entertainment. Film organizations have been ingenious in developing methods to record responses moment by moment. Perhaps the best known of these is the use of seats that record the degree of activity of the small buttocks on them. The bounces, wriggles, and squirms are registered on a tape and compared against the film strip to check where the children were quiet and where they weren't. Conclusions are largely drawn that the children were most involved when most energetic.

My own observations lead me to mistrust these conclusions. I don't agree that a child's interest must necessarily be equated with physical movement. Children are as individual in their reactions as adults, and they can express involvement as idiosyncratically. Some will jump up and down. Some will hug themselves. Some will clutch their neighbor's arm, or the arms of their seat. Others will freeze, as if by their lack of movement they are creating a vacuum every detail of the production will rush in to fill.

When one observes an audience of children, the first factors to learn to evaluate are the kinds of noise they make and the quality of their silence. Do the whistling and shuffling mean boredom and inattention or are they indicative of response to tension engendered by the production? Does a silence mean lack of interest, or involvement so great the audience is afraid to stir lest any part of the scene escape it? There are clues to clarify these possibilities, aside from one's own opinion of the show. The most obvious of these clues—and for me the most infallible—is the degree of activity on the part of the bathroom brigade. During the course of the show, how many children dash down the aisles to go to the boys' or girls' rooms? If many, they don't particularly care about the program. If few or none at all, you can be sure they are engrossed to where they would rather wet their pants than miss five minutes of the performance. Almost as certain a measurement of interest is the number of young people patronizing the candy counter or soft-drink machine *during* a performance. We have, sadly, trained our audiences to be virtually unable to use their eyes and ears unless their jaws are also in use. Theatergoing and TV-watching seem to be synonymous with snack time, but if the show is sufficiently fascinating, boys and girls will—temporarily at least—sacrifice eating for viewing.

There are times when an audience leaves no doubt about its reactions. If the onstage happening does not engage their attention, children can make the proceedings in their seats more entertaining than the formal presentation. A subdued rumble of conversation, hooting, shuffling, and coughing mark the onset of trouble. If the production is unsuccessful in breaking through this rumble, it can swell to an uproar in which scuffling can break out among the boys and girls, printed programs turn into airplanes that sail across the house and onto the stage, and full-voiced talk and laughter drown out the actors' attempts to be heard. Children may even crawl under their seats to avoid paying attention to the stage. And of course, during this bedlam at least one wise guy will, for the edification of his peers, heckle the actors or comment audibly on the screen's doings.

The audience-watcher must consider *why* the chaos. Is it truly the fault of the production in being of poor quality, or are there other factors? Is the age for which the production is geared the same as that of the audience? Is it possible that the theater situation itself is not conductive to order and attention? Are there no adults, or too few, to nip destructive behavior in the bud, before it gets out of hand? Can it be that either the seating arrangement or the sound system is such that the audience becomes irritable due to difficulty in seeing or hearing the performance? Circumstances may hold the production to some degree guiltless for not giving the children what they want.

Which brings us to what children want from entertainment and what they don't want.

What they want above all else is a story. Though a magician or other vaudeville or circus act may be thrilling, unless a child has a special interest in the subject matter (like wanting to be a magician or an animal trainer), an occasional such performance suffices. But if one story or group of tales is presented, audiences seem always willing to come back for more. They enjoy abstract dance or puppet novelty acts, but they are happiest if some part of the dance or puppetry program is built around a story of some kind, even something as simple as an Aesop's fable.

They want the presentation to respect their intelligence and to respect the story. Boys and girls may not think about it in those terms, but they are uncomfortable and resentful when they feel condescended to.

They want the story to be one they're already familiar with, in many instances. (See Chapter 3, Familiarity, for comment to the contrary.) On TV, in films, and in "recognition" shows like *Disney on Parade,* they look forward to finding new stories with familiar characters.

They want to believe in the world the theater creates. Even though some part of them knows they are watching actors or puppets or animated cartoon people, they want to suspend this knowledge for the duration of the program, and afterward remember only the persons the players were creating, and their adventures.

They want to laugh. Children's audiences love all kinds of humor—word play, slapstick, funny situations.

They want to be able to participate vicariously but fully in the events they are watching, to share the protagonist's struggle and eventual triumph. Whether the struggle involves the skill of a juggler or Aladdin's rescue of his princess, it must be about something the audience can be made to consider important. They want the conflict embodying this struggle to be established early and grow to a satisfying climax.

They want action, not talk. They want to see something happening that entails visual excitement—pratfalls, chases, fights, magic. They want to see Gretel shove the witch into the oven, not be told about it. They want to see the Beast threaten Beauty's father, not hear Father describe his adventures to his daughters.

They want something to take away with them to remember or think about—a bit of hilarious stage business, a new idea, an insight into history. . . .

What don't children want?

They don't want to be patronized, condescended to, or otherwise humiliated.

They don't want babyish material. Babyish is anything that's too young for whatever age they happen to be. A ten-year-old could be embarrassed to have you think he was enjoying Goldilocks; he would make it clear he was only at the performance to escort his little sister.

They don't want to be preached at or moralized to in the guise of entertainment. They'll accept more obviously educational material in a presentation on school time than they will otherwise, but they are suspicious of and hostile to sugar-coated education as theater.

They don't want to be bored or discomfited by mushy love scenes. Many children loathe seeing adults playing children's roles. (This attitude is different in those countries, such as the USSR, where adults are given special training in children's parts and this specialization is a respected art.)

Most hate the insertion of songs into stories, particularly when the music stops the action dead and contributes nothing to enhance the play's dramatic values.

We'll go into these likes and dislikes in greater detail later.

Suffice it to say now that adults who select entertainment for young people should be aware of these preferences. Aware, yes. But how far should we take these likes and dislikes into consideration in evaluating a production's worth for our children? Speaking for myself only, I trust their dislikes completely. Children have as much right as anyone else to be offended by being bored, confused, or insulted. I should never think of recommending a show a young audience has disapproved. It's not as if I were insisting children take medicine for their own good. This is *entertainment* we're discussing, entertainment for their pleasure. Regardless of what else of value it embodies, without enjoyment "entertainment" is an affliction.

Do I have the same confidence in children's likes? No. Children can approve a production for reasons that have little to do with it, or that I consider ill-founded or inadequate. Here I place more reliance on my own experienced mature judgment.

As an example of audience enthusiasm that was unrelated to whatever intrinsic qualities the play possessed, there was a musical *Pinocchio* in which the players were all children from six to twelve years old. The script was devoid of all dramatic values. There was little perceptible talent in the young cast, who sang and pranced around vigorously in gaily colored costumes. The performance was put on in the round—that is, on a low platform in the center of a large room, with the audience surrounding it in three concentric rings. The innermost circle of children sat on cushions on the floor, with two rows of seats behind. Even in the outermost circle of seats no child was out of touching distance of the players. The lights glared down on the little stage and a live rock band pounded insistently off to one side. The audience was entranced, applauded wildly, and left the theater aglow. But the reaction would have been similar for any show where the proximity to the actors and lights was the same and the music so loudly contemporary. Move the innermost ring of seats ten feet back or transfer the production to a proscenium stage that creates a physical barrier, and audience reaction would have been as limp as the production was uninvolving.

Another example: I've sat through I don't know how many deplorably written productions in which clichés and physical excitement are substituted for craftsmanship. A frightened actor leaps for safety into another's arms, they back into each other, the cast chase each other up and down the aisles and across the seats. . . . The characters and point of the story become irrelevant. What matters is the furor into which the audience is whipped. The more inexperienced the children are as an audience, the more easily they can be manipulated into virtual hysteria. They leave the show often overstimulated, remembering only the pie in the face, the pratfall, or the pursuit through the house. They've been reached, but only in their muscles. This kind of play, where the story line and characterizations are merely an excuse for the physical high jinks, is unacceptable to me. In Chapter 2, Respect, we'll go into why, but now let's just say that no matter how the audience cheers and claps, my thumb is down.

There can be other reasons why children will endorse a show I can't go along with. A character may be so personally charming the audience overlooks gross discrepancies in the play, or the jokes come like machine-gun bullets and for their own sake, destroying the texture of the production.

Children don't always appreciate that they are being taken advantage of. As their guardians we are responsible for exercising judgment they are too immature for. We don't let our children gorge on foods we know will sicken them, or let them sunburn to a crisp no matter how good a time they're having on the beach. Likewise, we don't want them to fill their time with so-called entertainment that directly or by implication feeds them ideas we think are dangerous or merely wastes their time.

In evaluating any commodity or service we must know something about it, and this is where we go from here—to consider what makes theater a truly valuable experience or one that is at best innocuous and at worst pernicious. The topics in this book—respect, relevance, humor, and the rest—don't fit neatly into pigeonholes. They will all come up time and again in different contexts, so that while a subject will be treated extensively under its heading, much that pertains to it can be found elsewhere as well.

"How much TV should my children see?" is asked me every now and then. I must remind people I'm a critic of entertainment for children, not a pediatrician or a psychologist, and not qualified to answer. All I can reply is that different authorities give various answers. Arnold Arnold in *Violence and Your Child* (Award Books) believes that only occasional special programs should be permitted and the TV set locked the rest of the time. Action for Children's Television (ACT) in *The Family Guide to Children's Television* by Evelyn Kaye (Pantheon Books) is more flexible and gives a number of suggestions on how much TV and in what circumstances. These run the gamut from none at all to unlimited viewing.

This is a question better discussed with your doctor or your child's teacher. If your child seems tense or overtired without cause, or fearful without reasons that satisfy you, mention this in your discussion, and see if their advice doesn't help.

2. Respect

————◦∞◦————

Whenever children's-theater people assemble in convention, someone is sure to mention a comment by Stanislavsky, the father of modern Russian theater. He was asked if there is any difference between theater for children and theater for adults. "Yes," he replied. "Children's theater must be better." Stanislavsky understood that adults can be expected to have the maturity to be critical of their entertainment, to evaluate its message or story treatment or other important element, and to question any part of it that their experience has taught them is false or misleading. Children, on the other hand, are in the process of developing standards and have insufficient knowledge to judge between the valid and the meretricious. They are betrayed by their lack of experience into acceptance without discrimination. Therefore, it follows that if one respects young people enough to assume some degree of responsibility for the standards they are groping toward, one must give them work that has integrity and competence.

Not everyone feels the same about theater for young people. Ten years ago I attended a reception after a performance for adults and someone said to me, "You're a bug on children's theater, aren't you? There's a young man here who's in children's theater too. He's an actor. Do let me introduce you!"

So I met the young man, charming and personable, who told me he had just concluded a season with a production unit having several plays in its repertory. He asked if I was familiar with the company, which I was, and whether I had caught his performance, which I had.

"Hey," he said, "wasn't it a gas? How did you like the show?"

This was a purely social occasion, so I said, "For that time of year you had a great house, didn't you!"

"Yes," he said. "We all had a blast. But how did you like the show?"

"My," I said, "didn't the children get worked into a frenzy!"

"Yes," he said. "But how did you like the show?"

"Well," I said, back to the wall, "I thought it stank."

"How can you say that?" he wanted to know. "It was marvelous."

"All right," I said. "The script was episodic and went sideways instead of ahead. Within the outlines of the plot the situations were incredible and the ending unrealistic. The director couldn't decide whether he was doing a straight fairy tale, a burlesque, or a morality play. The actors were half-rehearsed and kept making in jokes throughout the whole performance. The vocabulary was at times too simple for a four-year-old, or elaborate enough to trouble Webster. The costumes bore no relationship to the story or each other. The scenery looked as if a good sneeze would bring it down. And having given the whole production earnest and prolonged consideration, I was unable to find one valid reason for its having been put on."

The actor just stared at me. "My God," he said finally. "You care! You really care! Imagine anyone caring about a kid show!"

This attitude is all too typical of the regard in which purveyors of much children's entertainment hold their audience. The proliferation of "kiddie shows" on stage, on film, and on TV makes this obvious. There's all the difference in the world between a kiddie show and children's theater. The former can be anything—a Christmas gift of vaudeville routines to the children of labor-union members, a puppet show in the park, a Saturday-morning TV cartoon, a stage musical, a film made for the juvenile matinee crowd. . . . So can children's theater. The difference is in the degree of respect for the audience, or the lack of it, that the presentation embodies. Theater for children regards its audience as young persons, immature but developing human beings. They are entitled to entertainment geared to their intellectual and emotional understanding in an honestly written and directed production crafted to the same high professional standards as adult fare. A kiddie show considers its audience to be not children but kiddies—a species somewhat less than human, to be legitimately manipulated, who may be programmed to reach a pitch of feverish physical excitement, who are unaware of any distinctions between quality and trash, and who will sit patiently albeit uncomprehendingly through campy jokes aimed over their heads at adults. Kiddies' entertainment can be made up of situations with neither motivation nor logic, and the kiddies will approve as long as the music blares, the activity is frenetic, and the pratfalls frequent. The kiddie show doesn't care, even when it appreciates that its condescension amounts to contempt. It proceeds on the basis that the kiddies won't know they've been defrauded and that their parents will neither know better nor care if they do.

Theater for children—including films and TV—is entertainment that in some way enriches the young people who come in contact with it. It can be as airy as dandelion fluff, but a child should come away having experienced the excitement of expert theater. What the difference boils down to is that real theater aims at filling the hearts and heads of children; kiddie shows aim to fill their time.

The kiddie show's lack of respect or, in positive terms, contempt for the audience is so interwoven with contempt for the material in such cases that they are inseparable. The thinking goes like this:

Children have little, if any, feeling for beauty. Therefore, the beauty in this story is not sufficient to involve them.

Children have no comprehension of depth of character or subtlety of relationships. Therefore, the subtleties in this story can be eliminated.

Children are not capable of compassion/magnanimity/sensitivity, etc. Therefore, the emotions inherent in this story are not dramatically viable.

Children are not interested in/cannot deal with serious ideas. Therefore, serious meanings in this story can go.

Children want humor and action above all. Therefore, anything in this story can be sacrificed without substantial loss for slapstick, camp, word humor, chases. . . .

Children neither know nor care about the distinctions among periods, so it doesn't matter about anachronistic or illogical episodes, costumes, or set styles.

Children don't appreciate technical craftsmanship, so if there are problems in providing good direction, acting, lighting, costumes, and sets, let's not worry about it.

The result of this attitude is that bright colors, broad acting, and slapstick are the basis of the kiddie show, with a song and dance or a chase through the audience thrown in whenever it's necessary to recapture waning attention. All surface, no substance.

Now, theater for children certainly employs bright colors and slapstick when a production requires them, and, unfortunately, acting broader than it need be. It even uses music and chases where they are justified by the internal logic of the production. But—and it's a big but—all these are to support the plot, characterizations, mood, and other elements of any good play, not to replace them.

Many dramatized stories for children are based on original themes, but the largest number are drawn from traditional literature, well-known classics, fairy tales, or other "titles." Why? Because a name like *Pinocchio* or *Snow White and the Seven Dwarfs* will always attract an audience to the theater or the television program, no matter how well or how badly it is produced. Children are eager for dramatizations of favorite stories, and parents are nostalgically enthusiastic about having their sons and daughters enjoy what they loved in their childhood. These familiar stories are commercially safer for the producer than unknown material, and they can be selected for production even when the producer, the adapter, and the director cordially detest them.

Classics and fairy tales have endured for generations, even for centuries. Obviously, their longevity means they have something children find likable, perhaps even important. But the adapter's lack of respect for these stories is clear when the productions show that no attempt has been made to discover the factors that have made them endure. Or if there is an understanding of the essence of a story, it is ignored or sacrificed to what the adapters feel is more important—the easy laugh. Any emotions inherent in the original material are eliminated or distorted to avoid affecting the emotions of the audience and to allow humor to take over. Likewise, much new, modern dramatization emphasizes gags, particularly campy ones, to a degree where the audience has no belief in anything it purports to tell.

Sometimes with full respect for the audience, but insufficient respect for the material, a playwright can come a cropper. I'm remembering a talented woman who was active in New York City as a writer/producer of children's plays in the late fifties and early sixties. She presented a series of productions each season. It was her idea that each play would exemplify a different theatrical style so that by the end of a series the audience would have had a miniature survey of world drama. In a typical season, one fairy tale would be performed as a Japanese Noh play, another would be treated as a Restoration comedy, a classic would be done commedia dell'arte, and so on. The lady had a highly developed theatrical sense and as a theory it was highly commendable. Unfortunately, the realities were that she had to select popular titles to lure audiences into the theater, and she had to impose her stylistic treatment on stories that did not always take kindly to it.

As a case in point: the Grimms' story *The Brave Little Tailor.* She determined that it would be done as an American minstrel show. Everyone knows the story.

> A little tailor was so pleased at having killed a number of flies with one swat, he embroidered and donned a sash with the legend "Seven at one blow." He went off to let the world know and took service with the king, who, like everyone else, believed the "seven" to be men. The tailor tricked two evil giants into slaying each other and was rewarded with the hand of the princess and half the kingdom.

Our playwright transformed the king into an old julep-drinking Kentucky colonel type. She changed the castle to a mansion with (as I remember) Doric columns, complete with Spanish moss and an air of decay, and set the whole thing on the edge of a miasmic Louisiana swamp. The princess became a man-hungry belle who had been rung too often. She had designs on the little tailor, but he was enamored of a po' relation who lived with the man-trap and her daddy, doubled as maid of all work, and had second sight. The colonel sent the tailor off into the swamp to kill or capture two giants who were responsible for a crime wave in the neighborhood. These turned out to be escaped (I never could figure out why) end men from a minstrel show, who regaled the audience with an authentic routine before the tailor tricked them into tying each other up. As his reward, he chose the po' little relation, while the daughter of the house settled happily for one of the end men.

Now, any child who loved *The Brave Little Tailor* and expected to find him at the theater was in for a jolt. The changes, not only from natural location but in style and viewpoint, were so drastic as to make it virtually another story. Young children, certainly, would be able to draw only the barest analogies between the two versions, and the new one would surely suffer by comparison.

And this was a treatment that took the children seriously, even while it used the material as little more than a vehicle for the playwright's (inappropriate) ideas. When the children, too, are not respected and jokes are inserted that appeal primarily to adults, ignoring the basic audience, a play makes even less sense to young people.

One of the ingredients of respect is understanding. No matter how fond of children we may be, without some knowledge of childhood we can't be truly respectful of their needs, potential, and present limitations. We can have kindly feelings for a turtle, a hamster, a kitten, a canary, or a horse, too, but unless we respect these creatures for what they are, taking the sometimes considerable trouble to learn about their requirements, we can, with the best of intentions, destroy them by giving them love and care in ways that are meaningful to us, but not to them. More than one pet has been hugged to death.

To sentimentalize about children and children's entertainment can be a common mistake of well-meaning persons. People who think of children as "cunning, adorable cherubs" and design entertainment for them accordingly are transferring their own adult emotions onto immature human beings, who are not sentimental about themselves and who, like as not, cringe at the epithets.

It's easy to forget that children of six, seven, or eight have been on this earth only a short while. Whatever happened before they were born is a blur until they can sort it out. Until a child develops a sense of the past, five years before he was born, or fifty, or five hundred, or five thousand has no clear definition for him. When I was little I asked my mother if she knew Christopher Columbus and Abraham Lincoln, and it was a long time before I understood why she laughed. Adults, as part of the maturation process, order the past more or less neatly in their heads. Along with this they may select one particular era or another to regard with nostalgia, because it is adventure-filled, or courtly, or luxurious, or quaint. If those in children's theater value quaintness in a period—say, the one depicted in the old Kate Greenaway drawings of little boys with hoops and little girls with pantalets—there is a tendency to want to pass its charm along to today's children via a dramatization. It doesn't work. Or if it does, the show holds together because it stands on its own feet, the nostalgia being only an incidental contribution. What do children have to be nostalgic about? If there is some fond memory from when they were three or four it would be a very personal one. It would have nothing to which they could relate onstage through notions of "quaint" that are from the adult's past, not theirs.

By the time most children arrive at the first grade, they have seen enough toys, picture books, and TV and film programs to identify several types of clothing and architecture: armored

knights and castles; cowboys and bunkhouses; The Three Musketeers and plumed hats and dungeons. . . . Even though they
may be vague about the periods these swashbucklers belong to,
children do have a pretty good idea that they can't all be put
into the same story. If one respects children, one doesn't confuse them by suggesting anachronistic combinations, unless the
boys and girls clearly understand that actuality is being
spoofed.

There is yet one more manifestion of the lowly opinion in
which children's audiences are held—the length of shows. Stage
productions designed for preschoolers and first-graders are often forty-five minutes long; for second-graders up they generally run an hour, give or take five minutes. These durations are
to some degree governed by the length of a school assembly
period, but even more important in establishing these times as
customary is the concept that children's attention spans and
physical limitations won't permit them to sit still longer. At the
movies, children can run in and out for popcorn to release their
energies when the films run two hours or more. Watching TV
at home, they roam around and raid the refrigerator during
commercial breaks, or if they prefer the commercials, during
the program proper. Children, it is said, don't have the ability
to sit quietly and concentrate on one thing for a protracted time
span. There's no generalization to cover all children from two
to twelve, but I've seen four-year-olds in Leningrad sit enthralled through puppet shows that ran ninety minutes, with
one brief intermission. In Istanbul I watched elementary-
school-age girls and boys at a matinee of a four-act musical
Cinderella that began at three o'clock and ended at six; there
was no evidence of impatience on the part of the audience.

When I've mentioned these situations to teachers and theater
persons in this country, they say that "foreign children are
brought up differently" and are subject to and respond to differ-

ent expectations of behavior. That may be, but I've observed children in the United States give their attention without restlessness to a two-and-a-half-hour ice show or a three-hour circus, each with one intermission. And I still recall with anguish an international martial arts demonstration in Madison Square Garden. After four hours of kung fu, t'ai chi, aikido, kendo, and more, much more, I staggered out into the early evening, leaving behind me several hundred boys and girls six or seven years old and up who refused to go home until it was all over. The next day I was informed that they had held out three hours longer, until the bitter end. And how many parents have had the experience of going to the local movie house to drag out forcibly children who were sitting through a double feature for the second time? To me the message is clear—our children can sit still for more than an hour if they want to. If they can't, it just might be that what they're looking at isn't worth more of their time.

When a production lacks respect for its children, sometimes it manages to keep the young people unaware of this. But some shows—particularly for the stage—make it obvious to the audience from the onset and raise invisible hackles at once. It's like this:

A performer enters dressed as a clown, a fairy, or Humpty Dumpty.

PERFORMER (*Coming from the back of the house through the audience, prances across the stage):* Hello, girls and boys!
AUDIENCE (*Silent, except for a few treble voices calling back):* Hello!
PERFORMER *(More loudly):* Hello, girls and boys!
AUDIENCE *(Now knows what's expected. Choruses obediently):* Hello!
PERFORMER: I can't *hear* you! Hello, girls and boys!

AUDIENCE *(Shrieks):* Hello!!

PERFORMER: Now I hear you! My name is Rooty Patooty [or Shirley Elf, or whatever]. What's your name?

AUDIENCE *(Unintelligible babble).*

PERFORMER *(Cupping ear):* What was that?

AUDIENCE *(Babble becomes a roar).*

PERFORMER *(Beams):* How do you do. How do you do. *(Cavorts around the stage, waiting for the responding din to die down. Comes forward.):* Do you know why you're here?

AUDIENCE *(Mumbles).*

PERFORMER *(Points to child):* Why are you here?

CHILD *(Smart-aleck type):* To see a play, you crazy clown, you.

AUDIENCE *(Thinks this is very clever and roars).*

PERFORMER: That's right, to see a play. How many of you have never seen a play before?

AUDIENCE *(Show of hands: about three-fourths of house. Ad-libbing of a somewhat hostile nature).*

PERFORMER: How many of you *have* seen a play before?

AUDIENCE *(Show of hands: about three-fourths of house. Most of the hands belong to the same children. Remarks tend to be more jeering).*

PERFORMER *(Ignores the obvious and proceeds with prepared patter and glazed eyes):* Who knows what a play is?

AUDIENCE *(Wildly waving arms to attract performer's attention):* Me, me, me . . .

PERFORMER *(Staring blankly ahead with fixed grin):* That's right, girls and boys! A play is a story that's acted out instead of being told. Do you know what story you're going to see now?

AUDIENCE *(Most call out):* Rumpelstiltskin! *(But a few wise guys yell out):* Pinocchio! . . . Snow White!

PERFORMER *(Continues imperturbably):* Yes, we're here to

see *Rumpelstiltskin.* This is what the story is about. . . .
(And tells the whole tale in synopsis.) Now, if there's any-
thing you don't understand, I'll be back later to explain it.
Goodbye for now, children. *(Somersaults off the stage.)*
AUDIENCE *(Mixture of applause, catcalls, whistling, stamp-
ing).*

When it starts out this way, it continues downhill, arousing
in the children the same contempt for the production the production has for them. It also kills the play. Why show it when
it's just been related?

When it comes to any kind of entertainment for young people, critics seem often to suspend their judgment. Theater for
children is reviewed by different, more tolerant standards than
theater for adults, and this in itself is indicative of the contempt
in which it is held, except as a moneymaker. Even parents fall
into the trap: "Well, to tell the truth, I was bored stiff, but after
all, it's only for the children, so it was fine." How can we have
the temerity to presume that what is dull for us isn't just as
insufferable for younger human beings?

There are distinguished exceptions to these positions, but
although there are films, TV programs, and several kinds of
stage production that show concern and loving craftsmanship
in every aspect, they are relatively rare in the entertainment
produced commercially. Rare, that is, in the United States. In
other parts of the globe (e.g., the USSR, other iron-curtain
countries, Spain . . .) children and entertainment for them are
of enormous concern to parents, educators, psychologists, theater professionals, and governmental bureaus. Not only is the
same level of respect accorded theater for youth as theater for
adults, but in some countries children's theater is considered
more important, due to its capabilities to influence growing
minds. In the Netherlands, for instance, the government subsi-

dizes theater for children more heavily than theater for adults. In the USSR, a children's playwright earns 30 percent more than a writer for adults. In these and other countries, entertainment of a trivial nature is offered to children, but the greatest number of presentations by far are works of substance by major writers.

Good entertainment is good entertainment for anyone. It goes without saying that for young audiences there will be subject matter beyond their intellectual comprehension or emotional maturity that should be avoided, and that sex and violence should be treated sensitively. And that the style of the presentation should be clear enough for the children to understand what is going on and why. But much engrossing entertainment for adults is as fascinating for children. Take *The Miracle Worker,* the story of Helen Keller and her teacher Annie Sullivan, both as a play for the stage and as a film; only preschoolers are too young to be caught up and inspired by it. There are many others equally popular: *On Borrowed Time, Lili, Harvey.* And abroad, where children's theater is taken seriously, the reverse is often true: adults in considerable numbers, unattended by young people, go with pleasure to shows designed for boys and girls. In the United States I have seen puppet shows and musicals for children play successfully to "golden age" clubs whose members were by no means in their second childhood. Those productions that cover virtually the entire age span of mankind share above all other factors one that is essential: respect for their audiences.

There is one more aspect of respect I want to cover briefly. This pertains to the way performers sometimes treat the children they invite onstage to participate in the show. An old-time magician, for example, will invite boys and girls up to "help" him perform a trick, whereupon the children become the helpless butts of his humor. He uses the children onstage to encourage those in the audience to laugh at rather than with them, for the purpose of demonstrating how clever he is. The "helpers" are in an agony of shame. They don't know how to leave so they stand there, more and more wretched as the performer turns them around, pushes them into position, and generally makes them ridiculous in their own eyes and those of their peers. This can be unpleasant at best; for a sensitive child it can be traumatic. This situation is not what the children paid their admission for. It is unforgivable.

One more example, from a Noah's Ark play that will be referred to again. When it came time for Noah to send the animals into the ark, the narrator invited children from the audience up onstage one at a time to imitate an animal for the audience to guess at. The "animals" then entered the ark. One child came up, dropped to all fours, and "roared," and the audience had no trouble identifying him as a lion. Another lumbered across the stage and with only slight difficulty he was recognized as an elephant. The third child jumped up and down but no one could guess what he was. The child wanted to tell, but the narrator said, "You came up here to have them guess you, and they'll do it if it takes all summer." Humiliated, the boy kept jumping up and down miserably while the audience shouted names of various animals. Finally the narrator conceded, "We can't waste any more time on you. What are you supposed to be?" "A gorilla," the boy replied. "Okay," the narrator said. "Now we know. Now get the hell off the stage." I must confess I've never seen another instance of audience participation quite like it.

3. Familiarity

In the preceding pages we've touched on the point that children, particularly younger children, are eager to see dramatizations of stories they're familiar with. The better they know the story, the more enthusiastic they are.

If bedtime stories are part of the nightly routine with young children, the story they select, as often as not, is one they have heard a dozen times. And woe betide the narrator who omits an episode or rewords a significant phrase. The children know the story verbatim and their pleasure lies in listening to it just as it should be. Each word must be in its proper order, as if the tale were a ritual incantation. And frequently the younger the child, the more insistent the rigidity.

Children come to the theater to find in a new medium characters for whom they have already developed affection and situations they know well. They are regaled by what the author/director of the play has done to the characters and situations in fleshing out a sometimes slender story for dramatization, but they are happiest when the additional detail confirms the characterizations and the plot they expect. The ritual formula may be elaborated on, but not distorted. The dramatization that follows the plot closely increases their sense of security. Children don't welcome drastic script alterations that have Goldilocks chase the bears with a broom, set their house on fire, or otherwise alter the result of her trip to their cottage. Young audiences will complain that that's not the way it really happened, or be confused and accept the dramatization as an alternate version they don't care for as well.

Preschoolers can be entranced by enactments of *Little Red Riding Hood, Goldilocks and the Three Bears, The Three Little Pigs, The Three Billy Goats Gruff,* and other simple stories they know well. It's interesting to note that in each of these there is the element of repetition that builds simple suspense. In the questions Little Red Riding Hood asks the wolf, in the adventures of Goldilocks, the pigs, and the goats, repeated with minor variations each time and building to a climax, small children find reassurance of an orderly world in which everything will come right in the end. Adapters and directors have a tendency to forget that while *Goldilocks* may be a creaky antique to them, it's fresh and vital to a child who loves it and has never seen it acted out before, and this is true of other old tales as well.

Children in the lower elementary school grades like more complex narratives, but again, they prefer stories they've read over and over or have had read to them at bedtime. *Cinderella* is an outstanding favorite. So are *Jack and Beanstalk* and *Rumpelstiltskin.* Perhaps another dozen or so make up the bulk of nearly all fairy tale adaptations: *Snow White, Sleeping Beauty, Hansel and Gretel, Beauty and the Beast, Rapunzel, Puss in Boots, The Brave Little Tailor, The Golden Goose, The Frog Prince, Aladdin, Ali Baba.* . . . Young children are also partial to classics with an element of magic: *The Emperor's Nightingale, Pinocchio, The Wizard of Oz, Peter Pan.* . . . As children grow older they like adventure stories where magic does not necessarily come into play: *Tom Sawyer, The Prince and the Pauper, Robinson Crusoe, Swiss Family Robinson, Robin Hood, King Arthur, The Ransom of Red Chief,* and so forth. It's interesting to observe that girls will attend all these, but boys are frequently reluctant to go to a show with a girl as the protagonist. Some boys need to be all but dragged to a performance of *Heidi, Alice in Wonderland,* or *Little Women.* They may enjoy themselves hugely once they are there.

Aside from the fact that children like the stories to be faithful in spirit as well as in detail to the familiar source, there's another reason why these should retain their fidelity. As almost any children's librarian will confirm, the classics aren't read by children these days as in the past. Some, like *Alice in Wonderland,* when read at all, are frequently read not as their authors set them down but in condensations or versions twisted to conform to motion pictures made from them. It's possible that the stage, screen, or TV dramatization may be all a child ever gets to know, so that it has the responsibility to give him at least a fair approximation of what the original story is all about. I'm acquainted with a man in his twenties who has flatly refused since he was twelve to read any of the splendid *Robin Hoods* and *King Arthurs* he had on his bookshelves. He had seen episodes of both serialized on TV, inane and full of senseless bloodshed. To this day he's convinced that idiotic violence is all these two great collections of tales have to offer.

Some stories can be transposed to another time and place without destroying the familiarity that young audiences look to them for. O. Henry's *The Ransom of Red Chief,* for example, the story of two bungling kidnappers and their bratty "victim," is as popular in Romania and the USSR as it is in the United States, and it is almost irrelevant whether the scene is laid here or elsewhere, at the turn of the last century or today. Even if children are aware that O. Henry had set his tale in another age, this scarcely matters to a story line and characters that are so instantly identifiable they can make such transitions with only minor adjustments.

An outstanding example of successfully transplanting a story is the way the Gingerbread Players and Jack, a company specializing in musicals for children, has handled its adaptation of *The Frog Prince.* From a spot in medieval Europe, the tale has been moved bodily to contemporary New York City. The king's castle is now an embassy on Fifth Avenue; the king represents his country in the United Nations. His daughter loses her golden ball down a well in Central Park, and the princess, as in the original story, must take home with her the frog who recovers it. In due course, after adventures that parallel the traditional ones, the frog becomes a prince and he and the princess live happily ever after. Throughout, the element of familiarity remains unimpaired. The play has weaknesses, but the transposition of location isn't among them. There's one more factor I like: in order to alert children and parents alike to the change so that they won't expect the story in every familiar detail, the name was changed to *The Princess and the Frog.*

What about satirizing familiar stories? How do children react? That depends. On the age of the child and on the particular story. A four-year-old at a puppet production of *Goldilocks* or Mother Goose wants to see it straight. He loves the story or the verses and finds comfort in the accuracy of the details and the sympathy implicit in the presentation. A burlesque only baffles him and even though he may laugh at it, he may be disappointed and somewhat uneasy.

On the other hand, children of eight or ten have usually long outgrown their attachment to such "baby" material as *Goldilocks* and Mother Goose and may relish a satire on them. However, if *Snow White* were to be satirized, or another tale this age range is still close to emotionally, the boys and girls might go along with the jokes, though resentful at having their favorites mocked.

Show biz appreciates the charm the familiar holds for boys and girls and cashes in on it. Major spectacles like circuses and ice shows always try to include at least one number based on fairy tale or Mother Goose characters young children recognize affectionately. *Disney on Parade* builds its entire extravaganza on characters young people can identify from Walt Disney movies. Touring shows of lesser magnitude feature characters from Saturday-morning cartoon programs.

Those who put on TV series for children understand this desire for the familiar. In creating a series the producer takes care that while episodes differ in details, they adhere to a basic formula the audience comes to expect, and the core of the cast, the identity figures the child looks for, are always there, no matter how perfunctory their appearance.

In a magazine-format or variety game show where the content of the show or the panelists or contestants change frequently, a "host" is introduced. If it is a series presenting dramatic or documentary segments, the host may become part of the program. On the CBS *Children's Film Festival* the hosts are Kukla, Fran, and Ollie, who set the mood for the film to be shown and come on again at station breaks and commercial times. They not only provide the young audience with identification figures, but afford continuity to the program and bridge and explain cuts in the film. Whether part of the time it takes to present them couldn't be put to better use is open to question. Films originally made to run for up to ninety minutes are cut to about forty-five to fit into the TV "hour." Perhaps a portion of the hosts' time allotment might go to restoring some of the cuts—but that's another matter. Now we're talking about recognition of familiar hosts.

In other formats the host interviews guests, sets up demonstrations or features, and may become involved in the main action of the program. Captain Kangaroo is the lovable grandfatherly host of one of the better programs of this type. In a game show the host presents the contestants and panelists, explains the rules, and conducts the game.

Parents may grind their teeth when their children turn the TV dial for the umpteenth time to the annual presentations of *Frosty the Snowman, Rudolph the Red-Nosed Reindeer, The Grinch Who Stole Christmas,* and *The Wizard of Oz*—the MGM film with Judy Garland, Ray Bolger, Bert Lahr, et al. And to the Charlie Brown specials for virtually every occasion on the calendar. And all the other seasonal specials that return year after year as regularly as the holidays they celebrate. Boys and girls will glue themselves into position for reruns of *I Love Lucy, Father Knows Best,* and other situation comedies they have seen over and over. Parents will say, missing the point completely, "But you've seen that four times already!" Which, of course, is precisely *why* they want the fifth time.

It can come as a surprise that children actually enjoy many of the commercials they see on TV and become fond of the characters who appear in them regularly. Indeed, I've seen boys and girls leave the television set during a program, only making sure to be back in time for the commercial message.

While children are drawn to familiar material, this doesn't mean that original stories aren't welcome from time to time. For very young children who might not be able to comprehend a new tale the first time they see it, a story they already know well extends the limits of the production's intelligibility. With older audiences, mature enough to understand any new story clearly presented, this is not a factor. New stories based on episodes from the lives of famous men and women are often attended without resistance—musical biographies of Christopher Columbus, Pocahontas, Ben Franklin, Abe Lincoln, or Harriet Tubman are among successes with young audiences, but there again the element of familiarity exists: the children already know the person the play is about.

It seems odd to me that parents and youngsters alike will investigate a new title on TV or on films, but hesitate to attend a stage show bearing a name they don't recognize.

Recently a survey was made by Claire Jones, director of creative dramatics and children's theater, Oklahoma City University, questioning children about whether they prefer to see onstage dramatized stories that are new to them, or old familiar ones. The responses were strongly in favor of new material (46 for familiar, 397 for unfamiliar). Interesting. Especially in view of the fact that many groups who import professional theater for children into their communities find it virtually impossible to sell tickets to their young people for productions with a name they've never heard of.

Most professional theatrical companies playing to children won't keep non-"titles" in their repertory because there's so little call for them. One explanation offered by those who support the results of the Oklahoma survey is that shows are not booked by children, but by adults who are conservative in their tastes and nostalgic in their selections. However, in communities where new stories are introduced onstage, more often than not, the boys and girls just don't come.

What does all this boil down to? While one must avoid sweeping generalizations that may be inapplicable to many individuals, it would appear that many children, particularly younger ones, are cautious about new experiences and find a kind of security in staying with material with which they are already comfortably familiar.

4. Credibility

When children attend the theater or watch TV, they want to believe in what they see. If they're watching a contest or a game, they want to think it's on the level. They want to be truly baffled by a magician, thrilled by the daring of an acrobat, frightened by Dracula, awed by an earthquake, touched by an act of compassion. When they're looking at a dramatized story, they want to suspend their awareness of their environment, enter an alternative world, and participate vicariously but fully in its activities. This world, for a time at least, must exist in its own reality so that the people and animals who inhabit it may also be real.

Whether the story is a classic, or an old fairy tale, a musical biography, a play of contemporary life—whatever it is, it must persuade the audience that it happened, or that it could have happened, or that it's happening now. Without conviction in its possibility, there's no reason for boys and girls, any more than for adults, to involve themselves. There is no sense in getting worked up over something that could never exist.

There are exceptions to the desire for credibility. When a famous comedian like Danny Kaye or Carol Burnett dresses up like Scrooge or the princess of *The Frog Prince,* neither is trying to convey conviction. He would be using Dickens's *Christmas Carol* and she the old fairy tale as a vehicle for a comedy routine in which all values are subordinated to the expression of the star's personality. Children understand this, and whether or not they find the burlesque of a favorite story as funny as adults do depends on their degree of familiarity with the source material and their emotional involvement with it.

Credibility may be achieved by having each part of the production interlock with the others, like a jigsaw puzzle. In two *Christmas Carol* films based on Dickens's story, one starring Alastair Sim as Scrooge, the other with Reginald Owen in that role, everything contributed to a believable whole—costumes, hair arrangements, sets, dialogue, and fine acting and direction.

The Paper Bag Players—one of the best companies anywhere performing for young audiences—achieve credibility using the opposite approach. Generally there are onstage no more than four actor/dancers; their musician/composer plays his electric harpsichord off to one side. In every one of their revue numbers they all—men and women alike—wear similar basic shirts and trousers. When they alter a costume, it's by adding a skirt, shawl, hat, or train made of newspapers, wrapping paper, or a cardboard carton. The set pieces are made of the same familiar, unpretentious materials. The "Bags" make no attempt to achieve realism, but their audiences believe in *them.* Their revue segments are hilarious and contrived through an intimate acquaintance with the way young people think. At their best, the Paper Bag Players are fresh and perceptive. Because they are completely honest, and devoted to high artistic and professional standards, the "Bags" can persuade children to believe in the most unlikely situations and characters. What audiences recognize and accept is a kind of inner truth, as real as any other kind theater presents.

To create an atmosphere of credibility, many carefully coordinated facets must be assembled into an indissoluble whole. We need characters who are consistent in their own actions and in their relationship to one another. We need an environment which our characters can live in and be part of, and which supports the demands of the plot. We need a story that has its own internal logic, from which it doesn't deviate. We need direction that gives artistic form to these facets and cements them together.

Let's think about what makes up a believable character. Adapters of fairy tales may have a hard row to hoe in this area, because except to indicate that this character is good and that one evil, very little is set down about what they were—merely what they did. If a playwright can flesh out the two-dimensional figures most traditional material contains, that's all to the good. However, since children are more concerned with what their characters do rather than with internal subtleties, what the playwright does not have his characters do can be as important as the other way around.

Here are some false characterizations and relationships that notified the audience right off the bat that it wasn't to take anything seriously—a very different matter from not believing in a funny situation, an amusing character, or a hilarious joke. There was a puppet show of *The Pied Piper* in which the mayor of Hamelin Town spoke with a baggy-pants-comedian type of German accent. Why not, since Hamelin was in Germany? Because, among other reasons, he was the only one in the cast with a foreign accent. All the rest were German too, but they spoke standard American. This is analogous to *Pinocchio*s set in Italy, as rightfully they should be, in which only one or two of the actors use Italian accents, for comic effect.

The Prince Street Players perform a musical *Emperor's New Clothes* on TV and on stage. The empress is a raucous woman, as brassy as the musical instrument she carries and blasts on before she sings, "You've got to blow your own trumpet, you've got to toot your own horn." A vulgar characterization, impossible to believe as empress, wife, or human being.

An *Emperor's Nightingale* staged off Broadway had me hopeful when the curtain rose on a throne room in ancient China, but hope fled rapidly. One of the royal pages kicked his majesty in the seat of his royal robes. A big laugh from the audience, naturally. But that was it for the play. This was an emperor, divinely ordained, with the power of life and death over his awe-stricken subjects. He could, conceivably, be assassinated, but kicked in his regal derrière? Never!

Then there was a dreadful little marionette production of *Aladdin.* One moment of genuine excitement occurred when the puppet Aladdin rubbed the lamp and a real, live six-foot man appeared. The difference in scale was overwhelming and one could honestly believe that the apparition was a genie—until he whipped off his turban, leered at the audience, and announced that he was the genie with the light-brown hair. Funny? Of course. But oh, the poor play . . .

Perhaps you're familiar with a Rodgers and Hammerstein *Cinderella* that reruns with some regularity on CBS-TV, an opulent production with big stars all over it—Lesley Ann Warren as Cinderella, Stuart Damon as Prince Charming, Ginger Rogers, Walter Pidgeon, Pat Carroll, Celeste Holm, and many, many more. There are too many factors amiss to go into here, but at the heart of the problem is an unbelievable Cinderella. It's not the fault of the actress, poor girl. She can't help it that while every other woman at the ball wears an elaborate medieval headdress and long trailing sleeves she has to arrive, barearmed and bareheaded, in a dress that looks as much Victorian as anything else. Or that she has to sing a song in her own little corner about her dreams of an African safari—a girl out of the Middle Ages who had never been more than a day's journey by horseback from where she was born, and who wouldn't have known about Africa if it fell on her.

There was a scene from a *Prince and the Pauper* in which the Prince learns of the death of his beloved father, Henry VIII. Does he weep, look sad or even thoughtful for a moment? Not at all. He merely says, "Now I am the king." And that reminds me of puppeteer Bil Baird's *Pinocchio*. In this instance the Blue Fairy has been transformed into a social worker who must break it gently to Pinocchio that the father he loves has been drowned. "Well, kid," she says, "he went down three times and he came up twice." Utterly heartless and utterly phony.

There are more, so many more, but there's no point in flogging a dead horse. As long as playwrights put together stories for children without respect enough to develop honest, convincing characters, they will have audiences who are not convinced.

Building a credible atmosphere requires imagination, intelligence, and art on the part of everyone involved in the production, but it is the *sine qua non*. Opulence, fast pacing, and hilarity are no substitute—even on those relatively rare occasions when they are supplied. A living environment is necessary for living creatures, but this carefully crafted environment of the theater is fragile. A mere crack, and the outside world rushes in to destroy it and those who dwell there. Particularly where magic comes into play is a believable background important.

To make clear why this is so, let's examine the magic in a story from *The Arabian Nights,* the one in which the caliph must decide which of three suitors is to receive the hand of his daughter. At the end of a specified time and in a distant land, the three young men meet and display the gifts they hope will gain them the princess. One prince brings forth his magic glass that shows whatever its owner desires to see. The princes look on the face of their beloved and she is revealed to be dying of an incurable malady. In haste the three mount a magic carpet, the gift of the second prince, and travel with the speed of an eagle a day and a night to reach her side. Just before she gasps her last, the third prince administers his gift, the elixir of life, and the princess is restored to health and chooses her husband.

Now, two hundred, one hundred, even fifty years ago, a child would have been breathless with wonder before these three miracles, for after all, what's magic but the accomplishment of the impossible? But to a child who has been reared with TV, what's remarkable about a magic glass? To a child who knows that a supersonic transport can span an ocean in a few hours, what's so special about a flying carpet? And what's so great about the elixir of life to a child who knows that 500,000 units of penicillin in the rump will cure nearly anything? To bring a sense of magic to today's children, they must be taken out of today and transported to a time and place where a magic glass, a flying carpet, and the elixir of life were truly magical. The awe such miracles evoked can be evoked again—but only if their age can be recreated.

Where magic is involved the scene must be set with particular care. In the old Moslem world of the caliph's daughter and the three princes, or Ali Baba, women in the marketplace would be veiled, the men turbaned; no one would be wearing platform shoes or a wrist watch; and street vendors might be hawking dates, but not the *Daily Bagdad News-Times.*

Even when magic is not a factor, environmental fidelity to a given era can help make or break belief in a story. In a musical called *Absolutely Time*, by Maximillion Productions, the men wear doublets and hose and the women long robes. But the princess receives umbrellas for birthday presents and the king goes from room to room in the palace on a scooter. In a puppet *Jack and the Beanstalk,* the giant in his kingdom above the clouds discusses bicycles with his wife. And I can't remember how many plays I've seen set in the Orient where the playwright thought it was oh, so clever to name his characters Chow Mein, Chop Suey, Foo Yung, Won Ton, and such.

A few years back, the New York City Center revived Franz Lehar's *The Merry Widow,* not specifically for children but as entertainment for adults young people could also enjoy. Sets and costumes impeccably reinforced the period—Paris, 1905—and the dialogue and music were schmaltzy but charming. Spectators were enveloped in the ambience of this other, more romantic era until a gentleman onstage, having a disagreement with his wife, ordered her to be silent or he'd send her home on the BMT subway. And there went Paris, Maxim's, champagne, and crystal chandeliers, and we were back in our theater seats watching a number of quaintly dressed players going through their paces onstage.

Anachronisms like these are the easiest way to demolish an environment's credibility, except for the equally easy gag that's too tempting for an author or director to resist, regardless of the consequences.

Credibility of environment is extremely sensitive in the area of music. The trend for some time in children's theater has been toward the production of musicals rather than straight plays, and now almost every story has songs interpolated, with dance sequences as well on occasion. In films and on TV, while musicals have nosed their way in, straight comedy or drama seems to be holding the line. Although a first-rate musical—like any other excellent play—will always be welcomed enthusiastically, too often music and dance have been inserted not to carry the story line, develop character, enhance a mood, or serve some other valid purpose, but to cover up the emptiness of the writing and the inadequacy of the direction. Indeed, it would appear that music is increasingly supplanting the formerly ubiquitous wild chase through the aisles and across the seats.

When one goes from one musical to another, it's apparent that the one characteristic they share is monotony. Almost always, the music and the movement have a kind of nondescript Broadway show-tune flavor—unfortunately the only flavor many of them possess. A prince in Tudor England, a woodcutter from the Grimms' Black Forest, a robot in outer space, a genie from the *Arabian Nights*— all, at the drop of a cue, slip smoothly or otherwise into interchangeable and irrelevant melodies and, perhaps, soft-shoe routines. Occasionally, with the assistance of superb players, banality is raised to bearable mediocrity.

Rock musicals are having something of a vogue these days, and children love the music. If they think about it, they must realize that Cinderella didn't twist with the Prince at the ball, and whether or not they are aware of it, the music has more reality for them than the story of which it supposed to be an integral part. If one is using the stories as an excuse to perform the music, and the audience comes prepared accordingly, this can be justified. But where the play is the thing, and music from a conflicting era destroys belief in its existence, music would better be omitted.

I'm not insisting that a tale set in Robin Hood's England be slavishly faithful to the actual musical style and instruments of the period, although I daresay it would lend verisimilitude to the total effect. But I have been present at a performance of *The Pied Piper* where the music carried a flavor of medieval Germany, and the result was a deeper conviction in the play. Of course, the children didn't know and wouldn't have cared how the musical effects were created, but without being aware of what was making this Piper's flute more magical than others, they responded by giving themselves over to the spell he was casting.

In the world of entertainment, as outside it, we are all subject to conventions we accept without consideration. The way music is treated is one such convention, in the adult theater as in theater for children. Children's entertainment emulates much of adult standards, within its smaller budget, even when these standards don't always deserve uncritical admiration. The music for *The Threepenny Opera, Finian's Rainbow,* and *West Side Story,* to list only a few, worked superbly to enhance the setting of their several locales. Then there was *Oliver,* a smash by box office standards, whose music did nothing whatever to convey the spirit of Dickens's London; or *The Rothschilds,* with music that couldn't have been less involved with Napoleonic Europe and the later nineteenth century. If one is sensitive to what such music implies, it can drag one from the scene it is purporting to enhance into its own alien milieu.

Speech patterns can be as destructive as poorly selected music to the credibility of a production. It's very difficult to believe in an Ali Baba of *The Arabian Nights* when every word from his mouth marks him as a native of Brooklyn or Boston or Atlanta. It isn't necessary to play a French prince with a French accent to place him in France. It *is* helpful if his speech is standard English—or American—which places him where the play script says he belongs, without the intrusion of another country (this one) or another time (now).

Likewise, if a story is set in the past, it isn't obligatory to sprinkle it with *thee*s and *thou*s. Standard language not sharply evocative of a particular era other than its own is satisfactory in most instances. On the other hand, if a playwright *wants* to use *thee*s and *thou*s, and knows how—something of a lost art these days—they can be deployed to good dramatic effect.

Now, given believable characters in a believable world, there must be a story for them that's also believable. This doesn't mean realistic, necessarily, because fantasy can be as convincing as literal naturalism. No, it means that a story must be built solidly and honestly, without tricks to camouflage its empti- ness. *Dr. Needle and the Infectious Laughter Epidemic* by Rich- ard Sanders is a sadly typical example of a kiddie show that it would take a pretty hard-up kiddie to suffer. Its script possesses respect neither for its audience's intelligence nor for itself as a theater piece, possibly because it may not have occurred to the author, producer, or director that this quality is in any way relevant. Inane songs, actors running up and down the aisles, pratfalls, audience participation—anything and everything to distract the boys and girls from awareness that they are being insulted. I tried very hard, unsuccessfully, to find one positive feature, just one, that would help me forgive all the rest.

Another kind of play demonstrates yet a different lack of respect for its young audiences, with consequent loss of credi- bility. This type may be put together with considerable skill, but to make a point, it twists all logic—stacks the deck, if you will —in favor of its bias. *The Cavern of the Jewels* by John Heuer purports to tell the story of a boy and a girl, their parents, an archbishop, and some forest creatures—a couple of gnomes, a water sprite, etc. The magical creatures are treated with love, with tenderness. The real people—the mother, the father, and the churchman—are caricatures; the boy and the girl, card- board cutouts. The three grownups are depicted as heartless, avaricious, hypocritical, lecherous, and ruthless, lacking even casual concern for the children. All this viciousness forces the children to abandon the world of reality in favor of the forest creatures. When Father dies and Mother frolics off with the archbishop, the boy and girl don't even look back. They escape into a never-never land where, like Peter Pan, they will never grow up.

Does this seem in any way familiar? Of course! It's the wish- fantasy of the flower children of the sixties. Show your parents and the establishment to be utterly despicable, interpret their every action as venal and contemptible, and what choice do you have? You flee to an all-embracing, all-loving cosmos, where you have no responsibilities but to love in return. You toil not, neither do you spin. You put behind you the hypocrisy of organized religion, etc., etc., and go off to find a new and purer faith. These ideas petered out in the seventies because they didn't work. But this play doesn't set up a fair fight. It rigs the results against its young audiences, who are too immature to realize that the premise is false and the conclusion a cop-out.

But we're talking about credibility. In *The Cavern of the Jewels* the audience could believe in the affectionately conceived forest people. The real adults were drawn with such venom few children could believe in them or relate them to any experiences.

We mentioned that children have sometimes only a foggy notion of the past, but this doesn't mean they are incapable of realizing something is wrong when a medieval Sleeping Beauty pierces her finger on a sewing machine needle, or a Gretel wears hot pants, or a character from *East o' the Sun* eats a banana. An audience will become involved only when it believes, and whatever diminishes belief reduces the involvement that is perhaps the prime reason for a production's existence.

5. Relevance

Relevance is a subject about which there have been more conflicting opinions than anything else in children's entertainment, with the possible exception of violence. Relevance is of concern not only to those involved in entertainment, but to those interested in other phases of children's life. Most obvious of the changes this concern has brought about is that in schoolbooks. Now white-middle-class-suburban Dick and Jane are out, and textbooks feature boys and girls of a variety of races, who live in cities and have problems normal to an urban existence.

In the entertainment media, relevance requires, to many critics of conventional entertainment, that a program deal with situations children can relate to out of their own experiences, or provide them with role models that will enhance their self-image. Stories should deal with contemporary situations and characters children can recognize and identify with themselves and their family, friends, and acquaintances.

It's hard to disagree with this in theory. The problems arise when the definitions of "experiences" and "role models" are established. It's my opinion that when we place a narrow construction on those terms we are denigrating the ability of young audiences to appreciate analogies in circumstances and in human relationships. This restricted view is all unwittingly as contemptuous of children as is the view of "kiddies."

Accepting the narrow view as axiomatic, we have as a corollary exclusively black role models and black themes for black children; Hispanic role models and themes for children of Puerto Rican, Mexican, Cuban, or other backgrounds where Spanish is spoken as a primary language; American Indian models and themes for our first Americans; WASP material for white Anglo-Saxon Protestant children. . . . There is surely no disputing that minority children—and in the United States we all belong to minorities—are entitled to identify with and fashion their dreams around heroes and heroines of their own race or culture. Particularly in the area of non-Caucasian or non-English-speaking minorities, it's obvious why parents feel their children need to see characters "of their own" on stage, in films, and on TV. It's true they have a right to feel sardonic about an occasional production supplying this lack that is supposed to make everything balance out for them. Compared with the deluge of "white," "majority" programming, the trickle of minority programming is like the fifty-fifty proportions of the old horse-and-rabbit stew—one horse, one rabbit.

My observations from twenty years of working with children's theater organizations of many kinds lead me to believe that trying for exclusivity in entertainment, denying the diversity of the rich ethnic backgrounds of our population, is cheating *all* our children. In predominately white communities, many parental groups book into their schools, churches, etc., only "white" entertainment. They want neither dramatic themes nor performers of minority cultures because, among other reasons, they think their children won't be interested in them. This is pernicious nonsense. I've seen white audiences entranced by puppet stories from folklore of every continent. They've cheered to the rafters when a black troupe performed dances of West Africa to pulsating, hypnotic drums. They've shouted *olé* to dancers from the Caribbean area. They've held their breath until Harriet Tubman found sanctuary with the escaped slaves on the underground railroad.

Not to include programs of this nature in a season of children's entertainment, on the presumption that white children can't identify with performers of another ethnic group, is to insult the intelligence of the audience. More, it is to deprive the children of the opportunity to learn something of another history or culture that could enrich their lives.

Likewise, I know inner-city schools and community centers that will book only "black" programs. Here the conviction is that their children are awash in the sea of the majority culture, with which they have little in common and small sympathy, and that they need to have their self-image reinforced by exposure to black role models, black history, black music, and black African civilization. We can certainly appreciate the need for this enhancement of self-esteem, but we can also question the doctrine that black children can respond only to black heroes/ heroines and black cultural examples. It seems a pity to deprive these children of *Pinocchio, Beauty and the Beast, Puss in Boots, Treasure Island,* and other stories they evidently enjoy as much as any audience does. Indeed, schools that sell theater tickets to children have told me that black children often prefer a well-known fairy tale or classic to a production featuring off-beat educational material of an ethnic nature.

Although other minorities frequently have difficulty in finding programming of the kind they want for their children, they are sometimes reluctant to supply them with so-called standard material. From time to time non-black ethnic heroes and heroines are portrayed sympathetically on TV and in films, but these are relatively few and far between. However, watch any audience of children and it's clear that while they may have a strong initial attraction to protagonists of similar background to their own, this attraction is not so important as their subsequent identification with characterizations, situations, or musical rhythms and dance which cut across ethnic lines to the heart of what is much more relevant—our common humanity.

Everyone wants entertainment to be relevant, but there's another area of dispute as to what relevance means. One group insists that stories for children should deal with contemporary themes, with problems that our children can identify with out of their own everyday problems. They want stories to be "meaningful" in subject matter in the sense that they portray realistically situations that are part of children's lives. Or contain useful information—e.g., material about outer space, causes of the American Revolution, the life of the bee, ecology, lives of famous persons. . . . Realism in! they cry. Fantasy out! Fairy tales must go!

Children are eager to believe in a world of fantasy where anything can happen. They'll go much more than halfway emotionally to meet a production.

There's a school of thought which holds that children in poverty-level districts need realistic story material that will relate to their everyday experiences and prepare them for life. But my observation of several school classes in such New York City neighborhoods suggests this is not the feeling of the boys and girls. They seem starved for tales of wonder and enchantment and resist stories that deal with the world they know. Fairy tales seem to relate more truly to their inner needs, and their imagination feeds on them and makes the grimness of their days more bearable.

The Oklahoma City University survey we referred to earlier asked children: "Which do you like better—plays about things

that could really happen or plays about make-believe things?"
Only 97 respondents wanted "really happen"; 324 wanted
"make believe." These figures substantiate my more informal
and smaller-scale inquiries. But the Oklahoma survey also
asked: "What kind of stories do you like plays to tell?" By far
the largest number of replies (126) were in favor of "funny
ones." In sixth place, with only 17 votes, were fairy tales. I find
it difficult to reconcile a three-to-one response for fantasy with
the small number of fairy tale votes. It might be that the children were given one choice. Perhaps a "fairy tale with funny
parts" might have brought a higher rating.

Fairy tales have been a sore point for a long time with those
who hold the view that not only are they old-fashioned and
outdated, but because they deal with princesses, castles, ogres,
enchanted frogs, and other fantastic people, things, and situations which bear no relation to a child's life, they can be in no
way relevant to his experience. Pure nonsense, they say. Worse,
even: they clutter up children's minds with make-believe rubbish and blur the distinction between truth and imagination.
Down with *Cinderella* and *Jack and the Beanstalk,* they insist,
and good riddance!

The opposite tack is often taken by those who remember the
fairy tales of their own early years and see no reason why their
children shouldn't find the same pleasure in them. They are
reluctant to burden young boys and girls prematurely with
ideas and facts of the real world. Let them remain children as
long as they can and revel in the fantasies of tales of magic.
They'll grow up soon enough and they can learn about the
problems of life then. Meanwhile, fantasy, yes! Realism, no!

Both sides taking such extreme views are missing the point
of what relevance is. Both are selling their children short.

Of course children are interested in plays about other children of today who have problems. Stories suggesting solutions

to these problems (getting along in school, decisions about right and wrong, future careers . . .) and standards of behavior, when well staged, will be welcomed, as will any play that's fundamentally good drama and is *relevant*.

I remember a 1966 television drama on the *Hallmark Hall of Fame: Lamp at Midnight* by Barrie Stavis. A study of Galileo, it was intended for adults, but because it began at an early evening hour, a ten-year-old presumed it was for children and planted himself in front of the set. The program didn't engage his attention immediately, but bit by bit he became involved in the story and characterizations and oblivious of everything else. During the commercial breaks, instead of wandering off as usual, he remained in the living room, bombarding his parents with questions. When was all this happening? Why wasn't Italy all one country? How did the city-states operate? What did the papacy have to do with freedom of thought? The Inquisition? The solar system? Copernicus? Separation of church and state? He was almost overcome with new ideas. Afterward he said, "That's the best children's program I ever saw! Why don't they have more shows like that?" The excitement the program generated in his mind provided the family with dinner conversation for months.

This is the kind of stimulation to the intelligence a good realistic play can provide. There are parents who feel that children shouldn't concern themselves with such serious matters, but much depends on the individual child. A six-year-old in the room with *Lamp at Midnight* paid no attention to it and played quietly. If this particular ten-year-old boy hadn't been ready for the ideas, he too would have ignored the TV screen. But he *was* ready, and the program opened doors in his brain which have stayed open to this day.

This doesn't mean that all dramas of a realistic nature will spark such an explosive response or that nothing but realistic stories will satisfy all a child's requirements. Fairy tales are more than the harmless diversion many parents regard with nostalgic fondness. They are, according to the child psychiatrist Bruno Bettelheim in *The Uses of Enchantment,* a necessary part of childhood.

> Children. . . . have found folk fairy tales more satisfying than all other children's stories. . . . They speak about his severe inner pressures in a way that the child unconsciously understands and. . . . offer examples of both temporary and permanent solutions to acute psychological difficulties. . . . Fairy tales have an unequalled value, because they offer new dimensions to the child's imagination. . . . The fairy tale. . . . confronts the child squarely with the basic human predicaments. . . . It simplifies all situations. . . . From them a child can learn more about the inner problems of man, and about solutions to his own (and our) predicaments in any society, than he can from any other type of story within his comprehension.

This is what is truly relevant in fairy tales. I'm not qualified to discuss the deepest levels of meaning buried in a child's subconscious, and what effect fairy tales have on them. What I can talk about is what the child finds relevant, what he can relate to, which is apparent to any adult who takes the trouble to learn why fairy tales have endured to comfort children over the centuries. If we can dissect some of these stories to find their message, we shall then be in a position to understand whether the child is getting a fair deal out of their dramatization.

We could begin with the most popular of all stories—*Cinderella.* About a thousand versions of *Cinderella* have been tracked down by folklorists. There is at least one version from every European country, besides many from African and Asian countries, and others from the culture of the American Indians.

Like most folk fairy tales, *Cinderella* was created over the millennia for adults more than for children, but it speaks to the needs of young people as well and they have made it their own.

The *Cinderella* our children know best is Charles Perrault's adaptation for the court of Louis XIV (from an earthy French peasant story), or Walt Disney's animated film modification of it.

Sweet, lovely Cinderella, hated by her wicked stepmother and sisters, is made into an abused household drudge. The family goes to the Prince's ball, leaving her in loneliness and misery. Her fairy godmother appears, clothes and equips her sumptuously, and sends her off to the festivities with the warning to be home by midnight. Cinderella falls in love with the Prince and forgets the stricture. She leaves late, escaping barely in time to avoid the Prince's seeing her rags. He finds one glass slipper, left behind, and searches throughout the kingdom for the only foot it will fit. He finds Cinderella and takes her to his palace to reign as his bride and queen and to live happily ever after.

The version collected by the brothers Grimm in Germany has elements that are typical of many Cinderellas in Central Europe:

Cinderella's wicked stepmother and stepsisters abuse her. A hazel twig she plants on her mother's grave grows into a tree, on which there is a white bird that throws down to her what she wishes for. When she is not permitted to go to a wedding at the palace with the family, the bird sends down a lovely dress. Wearing it, she is so beautiful the Prince falls in love with her, but she eludes him. She goes back the next day and again evades the Prince. The third day, he has the palace staircase smeared with pitch, so that when Cinderella flees, one golden slipper remains stuck fast. The Prince tries to find the owner of the shoe. One stepsister cuts off her toe to make the slipper fit. Two birds on the hazel tree warn the Prince he has a false bride. The other stepsister slices a piece off her heel to force the shoe on, but the birds warn him again. This time he finds his true bride. At their wedding, the birds peck out the stepsisters' eyes as a punishment.

A Jewish Cinderella in the Near East has some surprises for us, but adheres to the basic plot:

This Cinderella is named Rosy-Red. She was a happy little girl until her widowed father remarried and her grandmother, who had been caring for her, went away. The stepsisters were cruel to her, and as she grew, Rosy-Red became a slave. On one occasion she was sent to the well to draw water and a genie, charmed by her sweet voice, filled the bucket with jewels. Rosy-Red gave the gems to her sisters to make them kinder, but they falsely accused her of stealing. She fled into the forest, wearing magic red slippers she had had as a child. They guided her to food and water and then to a cave where she found her grandmother. One of her slippers became lost, and a handsome young man, the son of a chieftain, found it. He came seeking her on a richly caparisoned camel, with a hundred and one followers, similarly mounted. He took her to his home and made her a princess. The days of her suffering were forgotten and she wore the magic red slippers always.

Let's analyze these stories to pick out what they have in common. Not all the elements appear in each fairy tale, but enough do to qualify each as a Cinderella story.

First, there's Cinderella, abused and unappreciated.
Second, there's something she wants: to go to the ball, to win the favor of her family, etc.
Third, the magic enters: the fairy godmother, the tree and the

bird, a genie, or some other beneficent force. (Perrault's fairy godmother is a relatively modern, artificial creation for the court. Older, genuine folk versions utilize an animal embodying the dead mother's soul, or a tree growing from her grave, to protect her child.)

Fourth, the magic supplies her with what she needs to gratify her wish.

Fifth, in the process she loses something, usually a shoe (but in some tales, a glove or another recognition factor).

Sixth, her beloved searches for her, using the slipper or other talisman to identify her.

Seventh, Cinderella marries her lover and is elevated socially and economically far above those who had abused her.

And eighth (frequently missing), the evildoers get their comeuppance.

Why is this story so loved by children? Is it relevant today, with its princes or chieftains' sons, its fairy godmothers or genii, its magic slipper? What can today's child find meaningful in it? Well, let's see.

Let's postulate a little girl and call her Ella—about eight years old or so. She wants to go to a movie on Saturday afternoon, but her mother says no. "If I've told you once I've told you a dozen times that if you didn't pick up your room by today, you couldn't go out. You haven't lifted a finger all week. Your room looks as if a cyclone had struck it."

"But my sisters are going," wails Ella.

"They cleaned their room," says Mother.

"You love them more than you love me," accuses Ella. "You never let me do anything. You let them stay up to look at TV last night and you made me go to bed."

"They're older than you. When you're as old as they are you may stay up as late. Now march up to your room and get to work."

Ella goes off to her room, feeling martyred and miserable. A look at herself in the mirror doesn't help. Her face is puffy and streaked with tears. Her scraggly hair is plastered to her cheeks. She has a tooth missing and a scratch across her nose. A hole in her battered jeans reveals a scab on her knee, and her sneakers have seen better days. She is a mess. She'd like to hate her mother without feeling bad about it, so she fantasizes:

"She's not really my mother or she wouldn't be so mean to me. I must be adopted, or maybe she's my stepmother and they're my stepsisters and they're all nasty and unfair and they hate me." Ella knows that under her grubby exterior there's a very special, really great person. True, it would take a remarkably acute eye to discern her hidden loveliness, but somehow, something magical will happen to make her inner beauty apparent to the world. Then someone wonderful will recognize her worth and take her into a splendid life where she will be able to do whatever she pleases and every wish will come true. She'll be more important than her family and then they'll be sorry they were so cruel to her. So there!

Does a child think all this out on a conscious level? Perhaps; perhaps not. But all children have sometimes been at the mercy of those who are older and stronger than they. All children feel they are treated unjustly by adults, at least occasionally, sometimes often. They identify instantaneously, even automatically, with maltreated Cinderella, and if she is to triumph for them in her own victory over her oppressors—and theirs—she must personify the image they would like to have of themselves. Cinderella must be brave and enduring in her helplessness. She must have the intelligence and courage to use the magic when it comes, and to protect herself until her prince comes to the rescue. Identifying with her and admiring her makes it possible in their daydreams for children to wait until the prince comes for them someday.

What could be more relevant to any child, girl or boy? This

is certainly at least as relevant to a child's inner problems and fears as a realistic contemporary drama I saw in Moscow in which a young boy learns that he needs self-confidence to enable him to hold his own in his studies and to be on a par socially with his classmates. It was a good story, superlatively staged, and the audience liked it. But what it gave children was different from what *Cinderella* gives them, and I should like to see boys and girls have both. If they can only have one, I'd opt for *Cinderella*.

Cinderella has been performed as a play for puppets, animated cartoons, and live actors; by dancers, singers, and ice skaters; on the stage, radio, television, screen, and in the sporting arena; as a musical, an opera, a ballet, pantomime, and straight play. Whether it's been successful depends less on the medium than on whether that medium gives its young audiences what is important to them: the opportunity to identify with a believable and likable Cinderella, the satisfying wonder of convincing magic, and the exultation of participating in Cinderella's triumph over the persons and circumstances that had demeaned her. The Cinderella story works whether it is performed as a contemporary piece or as one from long ago; in a distant part of the globe or anywhere else. As long as the elements of the fairy tale are kept intact, the audience is not disappointed. Considering how much leeway this allows a scriptwriter, you'd think it would be virtually impossible to louse up *Cinderella.* Not so. The number of bad *Cinderella*s I've sat through is legion. Here are some horrible examples:

1. A play in which the most important role was assigned not to Cinderella but to her pet mouse. Cinderella was one of the least interesting of a weak cast. The audience of young children was convulsed with laughter when the wicked stepmother was frightened by the mouse. My sympathies were all with Stepmother. If a 130-pound rodent came after me, I'd run too.

2. Another stage production for which the story was substantially altered. The stepmother, widowed for the second time, was portrayed as a beautiful woman with two ugly daughters. She wasn't essentially a cruel woman, but her concern with her own problems and her own children left her indifferent to Cinderella's emotional needs. The invitation to the ball revived an old romance with the man who was now the Prince's chief courtier. The story, narrated by Britannia, a stately dame with trident and buskins, was set in late Victorian or Edwardian England. Britannia subsequently stepped into the play as the fairy godmother. At the end, Cinderella was engaged to the Prince, Stepmama had snagged the courtier, and a large Union Jack descended to cover the backdrop, while each of the cast members whipped out a tiny Union Jack to celebrate the betrothals. The young children in the audience were confused by Britannia and the flags, with which they were unfamiliar. One more sophisticated child asked, "Mother, why are they waving Canadian flags?" (This was before the maple leaf became the official emblem of our northern neighbor.)

But what genuinely upset them was that the wicked stepmother was to be happily married. It bothered me too. If the two beautiful women, one good and one evil, found desirable husbands, it follows that Cinderella was rewarded not for being good but for being beautiful. The two sisters were punished not for being bad but for being ugly. Adults may agree that this is sometimes the way the world spins, but it's an immoral concept for a child. And disheartening to a little girl who considers herself plain. I said as much to the author, who told me I had missed the point. The stepsisters got what they wanted too, whether they knew it or not: a new father. I doubt whether many little girls would feel a new father was as desirable an acquisition as a Prince Charming. And I don't agree that seven-year-olds need dramatizations of Freudian concepts.

3. An opulent ice-show extravaganza that included for children, as one of its big production numbers, a ballet based on the Cinderella story. The ugly stepsisters were played by male clowns dressed in ludicrous finery; most of the children in the audience didn't realize they weren't women until they lost their bodices and each hairy chest was displayed naked except for a set of pasties and tassels. All the audience—including the boys and girls—exploded into the laughter of surprise when the two swung their tassels like burlesque queens to bump-and-grind music, but the kids' belief in the story went down the drain. Already, at the ball, all the great ladies had skated in wearing elaborate headdresses, trailing voluminous skirts of brocade, satin, or velvet, with sleeves hanging to the ice, and all sequined, begemmed, and befurred. Since everyone knows that Cinderella enters wearing the most beautiful dress in the world, the children held their breath to see her appear and outshine that glittering assemblage. The suspense built as one elegant princess after another entered, and at last—Cinderella! The shock of disappointment was virtually tangible. In the accepted balletic tradition, she wore a simple sleeveless white satin bodice with the briefest of tutus and a chaste diamond tiara on her short hair. Granted that her garments gave her the greatest possible freedom of movement for the complicated skating she had to do, physically Cinderella was the least interesting and imposing figure in the arena. She should have been pure enchantment. She was a dull thud.

Enough. I don't want to create the impression that every *Cinderella* is a disaster. Several excellent versions come to mind, very different one from another, but alike in presenting Cinderellas that charm children and adults and give boys and girls what they look to *Cinderella* for. The Walt Disney feature film succeeds by these criteria. Along with animation up to the highest standards of the Disney Studios and singable music which advances the action, there are a host of new subsidiary characters that support and enrich the characterization of Cinderella without getting in her way. The magic is satisfying and the ending leaves the audience in a happy glow.

At the opposite end of the scale in size is a miniature hand-puppet *Cinderella,* written and designed by Larry Berthelson and produced by the Pickwick Puppets. Only twenty-five minutes long, the production is delightful—witty and charming both in characterizations and in stage business. The narration is faithful to its source and the magic is true enchantment. One example: As Cinderella flees at midnight and the Prince follows, he finds only a pumpkin at the foot of the long staircase. While he looks around desparingly, the pumpkin splits open, revealing a crystal slipper in its heart. An exquisite moment. The young audience is euphoric.

In another vein entirely is a children's version of Rossini's *La Cenerentola* called *Cinderella in Italy.* This has an entirely new book by Elizabeth McCormick, with English lyrics and musical editing by Dianys d'Arcy Frobisher. The opera has been cut to about an hour and it works for children as do few other young people's operas I've seen. The music and dialogue are clever and as fast-moving as the operettas of Gilbert and Sullivan. But for boys and girls, much as they may love the music, it's Cinderella they come for. The identification with her is as intense as it is in the other media, and her triumph is as satisfactory. The magic is handled in an original fashion that is, when staged properly, spectacularly effective.

It's safe to surmise that *Cinderella* will stay in the repertory of young people's favorites for generations to come. As long as children remain weak and helpless in relation to adults, her story will continue to comfort girls and boys and hold out hope for a future in which they will be dominant. And nothing could be more relevant than that.

Let's look at relevance in another fairly tale loved by children
—*Jack and the Beanstalk.* This story, too, frequently suffers in
the transition to dramatic form, for much the same reasons as
does poor *Cinderella.* Too seldom do those who produce it
think about why children, particularly boys, turn to it again and
again. We all know the tale as it has come down to us from
English folklore:

> Jack, a none-too-bright boy, is the sole support of his
> widowed mother. They are in straitened circumstances
> (some versions state as a result of the theft of their treasure
> by the same giant who slew Jack's father). Mother sends
> Jack off to sell their last remaining asset, their cow, who
> is also their friend. Jack is bamboozled into trading the
> cow for a handful of beans, which Mother throws away in
> frustration and despair. By next morning the beans have
> magically sprouted into a beanstalk, whose top rises above
> the clouds. Jack climbs it and discovers the giant who has
> been their ruin. By displaying great courage, Jack regains
> his family's treasure and escapes down the beanstalk. He
> chops it down, killing the giant, and lives happily ever after
> in luxury with his mother.

Now, as we did with a little girl and Cinderella, let us hypoth-
esize a boy of ten or so named Jack. His mother has given him
some job or other to do and Jack has fouled it up. She loses her
temper and scolds: "Jack, can't you ever do anything right?
You knew this was important and I was counting on you. How
could you be so stupid? I don't know why you did it and I don't
care. Just don't talk to me!"

Jack goes off in a confusion of emotions. He's resentful because his efforts are unappreciated. He feels guilty, but he'd
done his best. It had seemed like a good idea at the time, and
it wasn't his fault if everything came out wrong. He's miserable
because his mother is unhappy and disappointed in him, and he

doesn't want to admit to himself what he really knows—that just possibly he hadn't exercised the wisest judgment. So he daydreams, and the elements are clear:

Jack is entrusted by his mother with an important task that involves sacrifice on his part. He does something which appears idiotic on the face of it, as silly as swapping a cow for a handful of beans. Mother becomes angry and rejects his effort, but lo and behold! Magically, Jack is proved to have been correct. The magic offers him the opportunity to be a hero and overcome evil and danger. He returns, clad in self-righteousness, to be the man of the family. Now Mother will be sorry she misjudged him and was mean to him. Now he can provide for her better than his father did. Jack will bask in her gratitude and admiration and she will be dependent on him for the luxuries that will sweeten her existence (and her temper), and she will love him forever.

As with *Cinderella*, a child doesn't have to be conscious of all this reasoning. Every child has been in the position of doing something wrong through using poor judgment, and wanting to be vindicated. This is relevance, this identification with Jack, in every sense of the word.

So, how is it possible to spoil *Jack and the Beanstalk?* Very easily.

1. Most versions of *Jack* insist that the cow is the boy's only friend. When he must sell her, if he is not emotionally affected by her loss, if he hands her over to the peddler too casually or if he makes no attempt to reclaim her at the end, then the story is lost. Every child who has loved a cat or a dog or a hamster presumes that Jack should love his cow the same way. Jack's indifference, only too evident in so many *Jack*s I've sat through, defines him as a boy without feeling, with whom the children will refuse to identify and in whose difficulties they will not become involved.

2. The relationship between Jack and his mother, at the heart of the fairy tale, is not always defined adequately or sympathetically. Jack must be concerned about his mother's anguish. He can appear somewhat thick-witted and careless, but the audience must never doubt his good will. She must be shown to be shrewish and distraught only because of circumstances pressing on her harder than she can bear with serenity. The audience must never doubt her love for Jack. The result of lack of clarity is that the children may not like either Jack or his mother, or both of them, and that's what the story is about.

3. Another area in which *Jack and the Beanstalk* falls apart is its "violence." Many playwrights don't want to show their young audiences anything that might upset them, like a convincingly evil giant, or a subsidiary villain, equally but differently evil—a grasping landlord, say, waiting to throw Jack and his mother out into the cold. These writers are ingenious in the devices they invent to avoid both the evil and the violence with which the giant meets his fate. The giant/landlord/other villain appears fierce, but only because he has built a wall to protect himself from having his feelings hurt. Or he is unhappy because he has no friends to play with/share with/etc. Or he really wants to help humanity in his own way for its own good—not the way humanity would choose to be helped. Instead of being killed, the giant/etc. comes down the beanstalk/demands the rent/whatever, and reforms after a heart-to-heart talk with Jack, in the course of which they achieve insight into each other's emotional needs. Children *hate* this sort of thing. They understand better than their elders that if Jack is to be truly the hero with whom they want to identify, whose triumphs will be theirs as well, then he must face and conquer genuine evil. If the giant is in truth nothing but a bumbling overgrown puppy under his ferocious exterior, then Jack has really fought against nothing and his triumph, and that of the audience, is hollow.

The giant *must* be wicked and powerful, so wicked that when he meets his doom the children rejoice. There is something unsatisfactory in a giant who says, "Gee whiz, I'm sorry I played so rough. Let's all be friends." And shakes hands all around and goes off to live a purer life.

4. The ethics of the treasure must be taken into consideration. Regardless of whether the source material states that the giant's treasure had once been owned by Jack's father, it is important to make this clear. Unless Jack has established a prior right in the golden hen and the singing harp, he is no better than the giant who stole them in the first place—merely smarter. For Jack to have right on his side as well as cunning and valor, he must be reclaiming his own. Obvious? Not so you could notice it in some of the *Jack*s I've seen.

5. You may remember an hour-long *Jack and the Beanstalk* TV special, rerun from time to time. Probably because they had a star (Gene Kelly) for whom only the tiny role of the peddler was suitable, the writers padded the part, having him help out Jack when he got into more trouble than he could handle. This is one of the worst possible approaches to the story, for it diminishes Jack's heroism. The relevance in the situation is the audience's desire, and Jack's, to be heroes to their mothers, and Jack must manage without help or his mother will never appreciate how wonderful he is. And what is just as egregious, because it also affects the mother-son relationship, is that the star ends up a suitor for Mother's hand, with the strong implication that Jack will soon have a new and loving father. But Jack wants to provide for Mother and be the head of the household. A father is the last thing he would consider a reward.

6. Just one more way of damaging the story for the preadolescent—giving Jack a girl whom he'll marry at the final curtain or in the future when they're both old enough. The audience for *Jack* isn't interested in a love story. Children this age don't

want to impress a sweetheart; they want to be important to their parents. Girls like *Jack and the Beanstalk* as much as boys do. They've also been in the position of doing something for which they'd like to redeem themselves. The situation is as basic as Cinderella's, and children identify with it as readily, but only when the components of the essential tale are presented in undistorted form.

The theme of a boy rescuing his mother from peril or poverty, without the intrusion of a love story or assistance which weakens the youth's accomplishments, is found in many cultures. Here's a summary of one such folk tale from the Ojibwa Indians of Canada:

> A woman with her infant son on her back is captured by a grizzly bear, who imprisons her in his cave and makes her serve him and his five sons. When the boy reaches nine years, a water sprite appears to tell him he can save his mother only by escaping and growing stronger, and she shows him a way out. He joins two strong men, who shift all their tasks to him. As the boy performs them, he absorbs the men's strength and they become weaker. He defeats a wicked little imp, who offers him treasure and power, but the boy refuses, for he wants only to save his mother. In a fearful struggle the boy conquers a giant and the imp becomes his friend. The two men vainly try to kill the boy, and then flee. The boy returns to the cave and defeats the great bear, while the imp takes care of the five sons. The boy leads his mother into the wide beautiful world, builds a wigwam for her, and takes care of her always.

Although the "I told you so" aspect is missing, this is obviously a *Jack in the Beanstalk* type of story, with the same universality for children for the same reasons. Like that other universal fairy tale, *Cinderella, Jack* can be transplanted to virtually any setting and work dramatically, as long as the elements of the story are respected. But though I've seen it done as a puppet show, a straight play, and a musical, on stage, in TV, and in films, I can't remember one version that I consider satisfactory in every aspect, that truly served its young audiences.

Relevance runs strongly through other fairy tales that analysis reveals to have an important common theme, though at first glance they appear very different from one another. These share the idea of the weakling or dullard who turns out to be more successful than those who at the beginning seemed stronger and sharper—a comforting concept to a child, whether the more powerful, more knowledgeable ones are brothers and sisters, parents, classmates, or whoever. The less competent the child feels to cope with these others, the more reassuring are stories that promise someday the tables will turn. Typical is *Hop o' My Thumb,* an old favorite:

The youngest and smallest of seven brothers, Hop o' My Thumb lives with his family in the forest. His father, a woodcutter, is unable to feed them, and Hop overhears him planning with the mother to lose the children in the woods. Hop collects pebbles to mark their way the next day, and after the father abandons them, Hop leads his brothers home. The parents are delighted to see them, because in the interim they have received repayment of an old debt, and as long as the money holds out, all is well. Eventually, however, Hop overhears them planning as before, but this time he is locked in and can't gather pebbles. The next day he uses bread crumbs to mark the path, but birds devour them and the boys are truly lost. At night they find their way to the home of an ogre with seven daughters. All fourteen children are sent to bed and everyone falls asleep but Hop, who takes the crowns from the girls' heads and puts them on his own and his brothers' heads. The ogre comes in the night and kills the children without the crowns. Hop leads his brothers away, pursued by the ogre. Having stolen the ogre's magic seven-league boots and tricked his wife out of their gold, Hop eludes the ogre and takes his brothers home. The gold enables the family to live in comfort forever. The ogre dies in the forest.

The Golden Goose deals with the same theme:

The eldest of three brothers wants to cut wood in the forest, so his mother gives him rich food and wine to take with him. He refuses to share his lunch with an old man he meets, shortly afterward has an accident, and goes home. The same events befall the second son. Then Dummling, the despised youngest, goes off with a small supply of poor food, which he shares willingly when the old man appears. Dummling's lunch changes to a delicious meal, and the old man, to reward him further, tells him to cut down a certain tree and keep what he finds at the roots. This is a goose with feathers of gold. Dummling goes with his goose to an inn. One of the landlord's daughters touches the goose and sticks fast. Her sister touches her, and also sticks, and the third sister is caught as well. When Dummling leaves with his goose, all three girls have to run behind. The parson, the sexton, and two laborers join the unwilling procession. The king's daughter bursts into laughter at the sight—a girl who had never been able to laugh before and whom the king had promised to the man who could break the spell. The king sets Dummling three tasks, hoping thus to be enabled to break his word. With the help of the old man in the forest and his friends, Dummling performs the tasks and wins the princess. After the king's death, Dummling inherits the kingdom and lives for a long time contentedly with his wife.

Like *The Golden Goose, The Table, the Ass, and the Stick,* another German story, has its counterpart in many other countries. In this version the fairy tale deals with the three sons of a tailor; in others the father may have a different trade.

The tailor's three sons leave home, each to apprentice himself to a different master. At the end of a year the oldest is rewarded with a magic table that provides food on request. On the way home the table is stolen from him by a dishonest innkeeper. The second son receives for his payment a magic ass that can drop gold from its mouth; the same innkeeper substitutes another ass. The youngest brother is paid with a magic stick that will beat anyone on command. When the innkeeper tries to steal it, the stick drubs him until he surrenders what was stolen from the youth's brothers. The youngest returns home in triumph with all three magic objects and the three sons live happily with their father forever after.

Different only superficially is *The Princess on the Glass Hill,* from the Norse *East o' the Sun and West o' the Moon* collection. Again, with variations in the circumstances that let our hero conquer all obstacles, this fairy tale can be found virtually everywhere:

Cinderlad, the youngest of three sons, is held in low esteem by his family. He performs a task no one else has been able to do—capturing one at a time the three horses that have been ravaging their fields. He hides the horses and the armor they were carrying and keeps them secret. The king announces he will give his daughter to the man who can ride up to the top of a glass hill, where she will sit with three golden apples in her lap. After all the nobles fail, a mysterious copper-clad knight rides one-third of the way up, and as he turns to ride back down, the princess tosses him an apple. The next day a silver-clad knight comes when all have given up. He rides two-thirds of the way up before he turns and catches the second golden apple from the princess. The third day a golden knight appears, rides to the top of the hill and snatches the last apple from the princess's lap, before riding off like the other knights, too swiftly to be followed. The king commands every subject to come before him and declare whether he has an apple of gold. When Cinderlad arrives in his rags, he produces the three apples and stands revealed in the golden armor. The king gladly gives him the princess and half the kingdom, and if they have not left off their merrymaking, they must be at it still.

Hop o' My Thumb and the third son of the tailor demonstrate their maturity by being responsible for the support of their parents. Dummling and Cinderlad indicate their coming of age by acquiring brides and coming into their kingdoms. All four, the smallest or least thought of in their families, succeed where the stronger, abler brothers fail. Young children anticipate their own growth and importance through participation in the adventures of these once lowly heroes.

Stories of this genre seem to take well to adaptation for dramatic purposes. Possibly because the theme is not a subtle one and external rather than internal adventure is at the heart, these fairy tales often manage to avoid the distortions that devastate dramatizations of *Cinderella* and *Jack and the Beanstalk*. What is relevant on the printed page or told at bedtime remains relevant in the form of a play.

Snow White and the Seven Dwarfs is a fairy tale that will likely be just as popular several hundred years from now as it has been for the past several hundred. What is there relevant in this story?

Snow White is hated by her stepmother, a queen with magical powers. When the queen's magic mirror reveals that the queen is less beautiful than the young girl, Snow

White flees. She takes refuge with seven dwarfs, who protect her until the queen's magic locates her and enables the queen to put her into a deathlike sleep. The grieving dwarfs can't bring themselves to bury Snow White and they place her instead in a glass coffin, where she remains until a prince comes for her and she awakens to a new, secure life with love all around her. The evil queen comes to her wedding and, according to one story, falls ill of passion and dies; according to another, she dances herself to death in red-hot shoes.

If ever there was a story fraught with all sorts of psychological implications, this is it, but that's not what I want to discuss. What concerns us here are those aspects of the story children find relevant in terms they understand. Snow White is the identification figure, so she must be someone they can trust and respect. The crucial relationship is between Snow White on one side and the dwarfs on the other. They are her security, her surrogate parents, and they will be there until she marries and her prince takes over. Where most dramatizations of *Snow White* fail is in not convincing the children of the strong emotional bond between girl and dwarfs. If the audience believes Snow White loves the little people, and vice versa, it will love them, too, and relax, knowing she will be safe. Without this conviction, the children will be merely amused by the dwarfs and the point will be missed.

Of all the *Snow White* productions I've seen, only two were fully satisfying in this basic respect: the Walt Disney animated film and a musical staged by the Gingerbread Players and Jack and written by Elsa Rael.

Other aspects of a dramatization must be treated carefully for the full impact of the story to be felt. The queen must be convincing in her wickedness or there is no reason for the story to happen at all. The magic mirror must provide the enchantment that is the catalyst for the suspense. And the queen must be punished at the end if good is truly to overcome evil. At one time or another, I've seen all of these necessities violated. The queen has been merely a spiteful, petulant, vain fussbudget who became sorry for what she had done to the poor child. The magic mirror became a comic invention instead of an object of mystery and doom. And in one version, although the queen showed no sign of turning over a new leaf, she danced at the wedding with Snow White and her prince. The audience rebelled and had the drama not terminated at that point with a dropped curtain, I think the children might have got out of hand.

Besides being a story of good versus evil, something it has in common with many other fairy tales, *Snow White* serves to console children with the idea that even though they may seem to be forsaken and in peril, they can find protectors who will love them. This is an important concept for any child who feels insecure in an enormous world he doesn't understand.

A fairy tale in which the idea of good versus evil is not a factor but which supplies a protector to a forsaken child is *Puss in Boots*. Here it's a boy instead of a girl who needs help:

A miller dies, leaving his valuable property to his two older sons and only a cat to the youngest. The youth is in despair, having no means of livelihood, but the cat asks him for a pair of boots and with them forages for food. The cat takes gifts to the king on his master's behalf and persuades the king and princess the youth is a marquis. The cat tricks an ogre into turning himself into a mouse, which the cat kills. Puss turns over the ogre's vast holdings to the youth in time for him to impress royalty. The boy marries the princess and Puss "became a great lord and never ran after mice any more but only for his diversion."

The story could hardly be more different from *Snow White,* except for the protection coming from an unlikely source.

Snow White is sheltered until her prince comes to care for her forever. *Puss in Boots* presents a sexist difference in that although the boy is basically passive, merely doing what he's told, the cat enables him to marry a king's daughter and become powerful enough to be self-reliant from then on. Dramatizations that miss the point of the relationship between boy and cat and the youth's eventual maturity miss what is relevant for a children's audience. Children want the magic of the cat-ogre confrontation to be convincing. It's an exciting means to an end and, dramatically, the big scene, but it's not what's *relevant.*

Let's look at only one more fairy tale—*Beauty and the Beast:*

A once wealthy merchant lives in poverty, toiling with his six sons and six daughters in a desolate place. He leaves to investigate a possibility of recovering his fortune. Returning empty-handed, he finds shelter from a storm in a lavishly equipped but lifeless castle. He is fed by unseen hands, and as he departs he plucks a rose for his youngest daughter, Beauty. A frightful beast appears and threatens to kill him unless he brings back one of his daughters. The father agrees and is sent home with the rose. Beauty volunteers to go to the Beast. Left alone in the castle, Beauty finds much to occupy her time. Every evening after dinner the Beast visits Beauty, to talk with her for an hour and, before he leaves, to ask her to marry him. She refuses and goes to bed to dream of a handsome prince who begs her not to be misled by appearances. After a while, Beauty longs to see her family, and receives the Beast's permission to visit for two months. She overstays her time and is warned in a dream that the Beast is dying. She wishes herself back to the castle and finds the Beast close to death. Realizing she loves him, she consents to marry him. He is transformed to the prince of her dreams and they live happily every after.

This fairy tale is always popular. Why? Well, first of all, it's a particularly good story. It has action, suspense, a monster (and how boys and girls love a monster!), and more than a hint of mystery. There is good character development, with Beauty growing in intellect and compassion and becoming more than a cardboard cutout. But what is relevant? It's that one can discover beauty if one has the courage, integrity, and capacity to love that enable one to go beneath the surface, and since we all like to feel we have these qualities, we have the hope that something wonderful will let us use them to find happiness even in an unlikely source.

Every fairy tale which has endured has qualities that are relevant in that they reassure children about some aspect of their lives. As long as dramatizations of these stories retain those qualities, they will always find a responsive audience.

Classics also present children with relevance, and when these are being translated into theatrical terms, it's important to analyze what their peculiar charm is.

One of the most popular classics is Collodi's *Pinocchio*. Boiled down to its essentials, the story goes like this:

Old Geppetto receives a talking log and carves a puppet from it, which he makes his "son," Pinocchio. The puppet kills a cricket which is warning him to watch his behavior. Geppetto sells his coat to buy his son an ABC book; Pinocchio sells it for a ticket to the theater. The marionette master gives Pinocchio five gold pieces, which are tricked away from the puppet by a fox and a cat. He is saved by a Blue Fairy, his nose grows when he lies to her, and when he tells the truth, woodpeckers bring it down to its normal length. Pinocchio turns over a new leaf when the Blue Fairy "dies" of disappointment after he is duped again. He is "good" for a time, attending school regularly, until he cuts classes and injures a schoolmate in a fight. He is arrested, imprisoned, escapes, is caught by a farmer and chained, is chased by a dog, helps the animal and in turn is helped by it to escape from being eaten by a fisherman. Pinocchio again turns from duty to visit the Land of Toys (or Pleasure Island, according to an alternate translation), where he and his friend Candlewick are changed into donkeys and sold. Pinocchio's new master tries to drown him for his skin, but fish eat away his donkeyness so that he becomes a puppet again. He is swallowed by an enormous whale (or shark, depending on the translation), and he discovers Geppetto, who has been two years in the creature's belly. They escape and find the house of the cricket, restored to life. Pinocchio works hard to support his father and gives all his earnings to him and the Blue Fairy, who, he has heard, is in need. He finds Candlewick, who dies, and for Pinocchio's sacrifices, the Blue Fairy changes the puppet into a real boy.

What's relevant here? Several factors. There's the relationship between Geppetto and Pinocchio, which is the foundation for the story. This is a parent/child situation in which the child must learn to grow up for the parent's sake and for his own. It's the story of how a little woodenhead learns to become a human being through assuming responsibility, through sacrifice and courage. He follows the primrose path rather than the straight and narrow on his journey to maturity. Children anticipate seeing him turn into a donkey and enter the whale, but above all, they relish seeing his nose grow when he tells a lie. Although these episodes contribute dramatically, they're not the point: Pinocchio's struggle with himself and his final transformation are what are relevant. Children look forward to growing up to be responsible for their own lives, and not to be manipulated by those who are older and therefore wiser and stronger than they. They will be disappointed if the gimmick of the nose's growing is eliminated (this isn't entirely gimmicky, because dishonesty warps us one way or another), but what truly matters is Pinocchio's achievement of independent humanity and the hope it offers children that no matter how many and how serious are their childish, irresponsible mistakes, they will still grow up.

In Chapter 4, Credibility, we mentioned a typical incident in the Bil Baird puppet musical of *Pinocchio* that prevented belief in the story. That was just as well, because if the story had been credible, the final letdown would have been that much greater for the audience. In this show Pinocchio was a marionette enacting the role of a puppet. At the play's conclusion, Pinocchio remained a puppet, a conclusion he and Geppetto accepted happily. Had this *Pinocchio* been performed by an amateur company, I'd have guessed the ending was selected because the company lacked the skill to convince the audience a marionette puppet could change to a marionette boy. However, the Baird company has such proficiency it can create practically any technical effect it wants, and this nothing conclusion bewilders me.

Another *Pinocchio,* excellent in most respects, had an offbeat production with unusually strong relevance. This was an updated version called *Poppinocchio,* removed from nineteenth-century Italy to a big-city ghetto. Instead of Jiminy Cricket— the Disney nomenclature for the talking cricket—*Poppinocchio* substituted a knowledgeable, cool Reggie Roach, on the assumption that inner-city children don't know as much about crickets as about roaches. As Pinocchio's mentor, Reggie was unsuccessful in keeping him away from the friendly neighborhood pill-pusher, who induced the woodenhead and his friends to make jackasses of themselves. In the end, Pinocchio had the choice of becoming a selfless, unworldly, unrealistic man like Geppetto, or the greedy, corrupt, vicious characters who had betrayed and preyed on him. These were the only two types of humanity he had been shown. Neither alternative contented Pinocchio and he elected to remain a puppet until he could find a life style that would be right for him.

I attended several performances of *Poppinocchio* because I was especially interested in the audiences. These were made up mostly of children from day camps and settlement houses, from preschoolers to boys and girls of high school age. The small children had no difficulty in following the story, and its switch to a contemporary locale didn't bother them at all. What was more interesting was that sixteen-, seventeen-, and eighteen-year-olds, who would have been bored into disruptive mockery by a standard *Pinocchio,* sat through this version in rapt attention. They saw the analogies to their own inner-city lives and applauded the performance with a degree of enthusiasm I've seldom witnessed. Their approval extended to the ending. Mine is not so unequivocal. I feel that other, more rational, less extreme role models could have been presented to this ghetto Pinocchio. The ending would have been more viable had he chosen to be come a real boy, adapting himself to a healthy, constructive way of life—still *his* way, but more positive, more self-directed.

The Walt Disney *Pinocchio* has become a classic of its own. It carries through the story in its essentials, but it has added a number of attractive subsidiary characters who enrich the detail of the plot without overwhelming it: Jiminy Cricket, Pinocchio's conscience; Cleo the goldfish, and others. Delightful.

Another musical play, *Rainbow Junction,* produced by The King's Players, reminds me of *Pinocchio.* Here, enacted by a large cast of players taking the roles of puppets, are a number of marionettes who are unhappy at the way they are being manipulated by a wicked puppet master. They overcome him and take their destiny into their own hands, to live happily ever after as puppets in Rainbow Junction. To me this whole concept is a contradiction in terms, and there's nothing in it for children to identify with or find in any way relevant. If the characters are able to exercise free will, they can't be marionettes. If they remain puppets, by definition they can't be free agents.

And Now Miguel is a film that displays the achievement of maturity in a way analogous to the original *Pinocchio.* In it, a young Spanish-American boy, after a series of adventures, grows up enough to share the adult work of the men of his family—sheepherding. His family life is warm and supportive, and though the roles of the family are stereotyped, the picture works. Identification with young Miguel is strong in the audience; his goals are clear and desirable, his problems and solutions equally credible, and participation in his success deeply satisfying.

I must confess that Louisa May Alcott's classic, *Little Women,* has never been the favorite with me it is with many children. Its particular charm, except for the character of Jo, has eluded me. But I can find a marked likeness between this story and that of *The Waltons* and *Little House on the Prairie*, prime-time family TV series. *Little Women* also has a strong feeling of ideal home life, with wholly admirable parents and a variety of young people others can relate to. When *Little Women* has been dramatized, as stage play, film, or ballet, it has worked only if the aspects of family integrity are stressed.

The Waltons and *Little House on the Prairie* are solid hits with young audiences. What is relevant to today's children in a story of the 1930s depression or of sodbusting a hundred years ago? For one thing, the situations within individual episodes are well defined and appeal to a young audience's sympathies and sense of justice. For another, in the case of *The Waltons,* there are many children, offering the audiences identification figures close to their own ages. More important are the relationships. It doesn't matter that the stories take place on Walton's Mountain forty years ago. What counts is that here is an ideal three-generation family, every member of whom is admirable in some way. With all their idiosyncrasies, they love and respect each other and need each other to complete their lives. Despite the too short supply of money, Walton's Mountain bears a remarkable resemblance to a well-populated Garden of Eden. Here harsh words are repented, unkind or thoughtless deeds atoned for, and the growth of all the characters, from the youngest girl to Grandfather, the oldest, never ceases. They enjoy each other. In its relative isolation the family is united, not against the world but in limited participation in it.

Little House on the Prairie has only three children in the central family, all of them girls, but there is a good age spread among their male and female schoolmates. The parents, like the Walton parents, are protective, wise, kind, sensitive, loving, patient, etc. . . . Children want to believe in such idyllic families the way they want to believe in Santa Claus and the Tooth Fairy.

There may be a great number of such ideal families, who never turn out the lights without harmony and loving serenity enveloping their homes like the dark of night. I don't know very many, and I suspect most boys and girls don't either. I can't prove it, but I surmise that children find reassurance in these pictures of family life. They may be comforted when they have had an unappeased conflict with a brother or sister or a parent by the view that *The Waltons* upholds—that come what may, love is the bedrock on which the family stands.

All the stories discussed here have something young people can identify with, and there are many other fairy tales and classics as well as original stories that, with thought, will appear as relevant. When we educate ourselves to discern where relevance lies, we are able to find where it is not. The Saturday-morning kiddie shows, for instance. If you take the time to watch the programs, you may find that along with respect, relevance is conspicuous by its absence. Whatever excitement they contain is frequently artificial and based on the chase: the good guys are pursuing the bad ones because the latter have possession of something wanted by the former. Or vice versa. Or the latter are doing something the former want them to desist from. Or vice versa. Because the characterizations are as shoddily and superficially indicated as the barely contrived situations—not to mention the contemptible quality of the animation—no genuine involvement in either is possible. The attention of the audience is held by the familiarity of the characters, the visual movement on the TV screen, a succession of programmed laughs (with a prepared sound track to indicate where they should come), and the fact that there's nothing better to do.

When children are involved regardless of the medium, through identifying with the personae of a dramatization and with a situation that has meaning for them, none of these just-mentioned factors is necessary to hold them. Familiarity can reinforce relevance, honesty in presentation can make it credible, and humor can arise from and support the relevance a respectful treatment of the story substantiates. When these elements are present, boys and girls will watch because they can't tear themselves away.

6. Implications

They are the rare adults who, sitting with their children, sharing their enjoyment in a TV, stage, or film presentation, consider what the production is saying. Not what the plot purports to be about; perhaps not even what the dialogue is saying. The presentation may be telling a story that has nothing to do with the theme, but will remain in the mind after the production has been forgotten. Or the show may be saying what it means to say in such a manner that its well-meaning message becomes distorted or pernicious.

Because a show is "for kids," the people who put it together are sometimes more casual about its construction than they would be for a primarily adult audience. Even when they are conscientious in their efforts, sometimes they are so involved, so close to their production, they lose their objectivity in appraising their work and their ability to hear what it is saying.

There's nothing surprising in this, since entertainment designed for the adult market is subject to the same perils and disasters, and it's not unusual to find that the finished product doesn't convey its creators' original intentions. There's one important difference, however, between inadvertent messages for adults and those for young people. It can be presumed—with whatever degree of accuracy—that an adult audience has the maturity to comprehend whether the entertainment is merely the vehicle for a "message," whether it contains implications that, like red herrings, lead the audience elsewhere or that, perhaps not even remaining in the conscious mind, influence one's attitude on some almost extraneous matter.

Children, who may of course be influenced more readily than adults, are unaware that with or without any intention on the part of the producer to manipulate them, they are subject to the point of view, direct or indirect, the "entertainment" embodies.

Let's take some examples, important only because each is typical of many that unwittingly convey a message more important than the story they tell. Let's begin with a stage musical, *Who Am I?*, written by Seymour Barab. This is an adaptation of *The Goose Girl*, from the collection by the brothers Grimm:

> It's the story of a princess whose mother sends her to a far country to wed a king she has never seen. The queen gives the princess a talisman to keep her safe and a maidservant to attend her, and sends the two women off on horseback alone. The princess loses the talisman and falls under the power of the maid, who forces her to change places with her and swears her to secrecy. The wicked servant marries the king. The princess becomes a goose girl. Eventually the truth is manifested and the evil queen pronounces her own doom. The true bride comes into her own and lives happily ever after with her king.

Who Am I? updates the story by its Broadway type of music, its vaguely contemporary costumes, and the general tone of the dialogue. The author altered the maid's wicked character, showing her as basically a nice girl who is merely ambitious and tired of being everybody's flunky. The story continues essentially as in the Grimm version, except that before she weds the king the maid decides royalty isn't all it might be and she'd rather stay a maid and marry her true love, a common soldier. *The Goose Girl* has its roots deep in the Middle Ages. The story grew out of a feudal culture in which everyone was born into a stratum of society and occupied it for life. To attempt to move to a higher level was not only a crime, it was a sin against God, Who had placed one in one's niche. Therefore, when the wicked servant usurped the position of a sanctified princess, she deserved the hideous fate she decreed for herself.

When *The Goose Girl* is kept within the framework of such a feudal society, it all hangs together. Our sympathies lie with the abused princess, whose lofty standards of morality prevent her from breaking her oath and revealing the truth to free herself from degradation. But when *The Goose Girl* becomes the more or less contemporary, more or less American *Who Am I?*, what happens? The sympathies of today's children focus on the maid. Why shouldn't she want to improve herself? Why shouldn't she resent being ordered about? They like the princess and are happy to see her restored to glory at the end, but they feel somehow defeated when the maid they identified with settles for her old position.

What does this updated *Goose Girl* say to contemporary children? That they should appreciate who and what they are and be content; that it's stupid, if not actually wrong, to struggle to improve themselves. Appropriate to a rigidly stratified society of a millennium ago, this concept is antithetical to the values our own upwardly mobile culture has been imprinting on boys and girls since birth. It may be that other values are better—that's not the point. The point is that, inadvertently, this is the message the play delivers.

Americans, possibly due to a conflict among the values of the diverse elements that make up our population, have always been of two minds about intellectual accomplishment. We admire the work of inventors, scientists, professors, artists, writers, and such, but unless they make a lot of money or we are on familiar terms with them, we tend to think of them in somewhat contemptuous stereotypes as crazy inventors, mad scientists, absent-minded professors, bohemian artists, visionary writers, etc. We seem to have more confidence in the common sense and morality of the untutored horny-handed son of toil or the muscular athlete or brawny adventurer. The anti-egghead tradition goes back a long way in American literature and is reinforced over and over in popular entertainment— particularly entertainment for young people.

Though perhaps not the earliest example, one with which most of us are familiar is Washington Irving's *Legend of Sleepy Hollow*. The story is a triangle, with bold, hearty, uncomplicated Brom and scrawny, intellectual, superstitious Ichabod vying for the hand of beautiful, wealthy Katrina. The cards are stacked against Ichabod from the beginning. I've wondered why brains are so often equated with physical inferiority—or effeminacy—and emotional or intellectual idiosyncrasies. Poor Ichabod never has a chance.

Mark Twain's Tom Sawyer is among the more notable continuers of the tradition. Tom is portrayed as having all the charming independent (?) characteristics of a "real boy." These most prominently include dislike of school and study. Tom's contrast is supplied by his cousin Sid, a bookish tattletale, invariably depicted onstage and in films as a whining little creep. Huckleberry Finn is another of Twain's creations in whom masculinity is equated with lack of activity between the ears.

Horatio Alger's youthful heroes all made their way onward and upward in the world by doing and daring in the common-sensical paths of business. No intellectual curiosity or thought of truth or beauty distracted them from their goals. These protagonists exemplified what most of their actual contemporaries considered the best of young America.

Other popular literature and the theater of the day stressed the same values. *Our Country Cousin,* the play Lincoln was attending when he was shot at Ford's Theater, is of a genre that Americans have been particularly fond of since the Revolution. Stripped to its essentials, the theme has to do with native Yankee (or Western or Southern or hill country) shrewdness triumphing over effete European or city-slicker values, which include respect for the mind and the arts. In this the European (or city slicker) loses the hero/heroine to the honest, relatively uncouth American, or the American who has acquired a taint of European culture shakes it off to return to the relatively unsophisticated unintellectual society he/she should never have left.

When movies became the popular medium of entertainment, even more so when sound was added, this anti-egghead tradition came into its own. Although the Walt Disney Studios were not unique in their affection for it, they were—and still are— among its most ardent propagandists. Do you remember the animated *Silly Symphonies?* Among the most enduring of their themes was the conflict between the music of the "three B's" and other symphonic and chamber music or operatic composers and the then current forms of jazz. Invariably the enthusiasts for the former were depicted as long-haired, outdated, and irrelevant, and the latter as sharp, on the ball, with it. Either the jazz won hands down or there was a "compromise" —the other themes became the basis of a triumphant jazz production.

You'll note I've been careful not to refer to the "classical" music as "good," "serious," or "important," because to do so would imply that the jazz was not. As presented, the jazz was frequently superb, but again, this is not the point. The impression children would carry away was either/or. They were not given the option to enjoy each form for what it is, and by accepting both, to grow to their full potential. They were virtually lowbrowbeaten into choosing the popular, most easily comprehended forms and despising those that were less familiar or required effort to appreciate. In effect, the focus circumscribed the world of experiences children should be encouraged to explore. If a child investigates both and decides in the end he prefers to confine his listening to popular music only, that is his right, but it should be *his* decision, not the Disney Studios'.

The *Silly Symphonies'* heyday was in the thirties, but to this day the Disney Studios have been transmitting the same message. In 1974, for just one example, the live-action comedy *Herbie Rides Again,* featuring a "lovable Volkswagen," included a short scene—possibly not over ninety seconds long—in which a chase interrupts a garden party. Several men and women in formal attire are seated in stiff chairs on the obviously expensive grounds of a mansion. It's clear they are all rich, senile, and living in the past—the decaying remnants of an obsolete civilization which had never formed part of the mainstream of our culture. When they are disturbed briefly by the outside world, they blink and then continue to listen to the string quartet that has been playing for their pleasure. I can't remember the music—it was Vivaldi or Mozart, I think—but the anti-egghead point is made forcefully. In order to enjoy chamber music one must be in one's dotage or outside the popular culture, and the music itself is as ludicrously useless as those who listen to it.

This viewpoint has been echoed and reechoed in films and on stage, one way or another. The self-centered heiress or stodgy well-to-do young businessman eventually leaves the ivory tower and preoccupation with "serious" music, literature, and the other arts and comes down into the real world of popular culture. Seldom if ever do the ex-tower inhabitants bring anyone back into their rarefied atmosphere. In the long-running Broadway show *Grease,* touted as being for adults nostalgic about their high school days in the fifties, the same point is made. This was not my generation, but even so, I'm sure that there must have been *some* students concerned with grades, learning, and activities like the science club or the school newspaper. There is one in *Grease*—an object of ridicule until she abandons her highfalutin notions and joins the gang with its consuming interest in sex, cars, drinking, and rock. Agreed that the presentation is tongue-in-cheek and not meant to be taken seriously; the message remains.

Let's examine another facet of anti-intellectualism, in which new ideas and their adherents are made to appear obscenely ridiculous. In the Disney film *Superdad* (1974) we are given a man who creates nonobjective paintings and sculptures, working with found materials and unconventional forms and textures. He's portrayed as being unbalanced mentally, as well as fraudulent in his attempts to pass off this "garbage" as art to a gullible public. He is filthy, unkempt, and violent. He displays every unpleasant stereotype of the mad artist. The message? What could be clearer? All artists are suspect to some degree, modern artists certainly. If the child doesn't understand an object labeled as painting or sculpture, it must be a rip-off or a joke. Don't try to understand it—it has no purpose. Just laugh at it or smash it and go one's way. Neither the object nor its creator merits thought on the viewer's part. By extension, this attitude applies to other forms of creativity beyond the child's daily experience and comprehension. Without antidotes, a full dose of this indoctrination can result in an adult whose imagination and appreciation of beauty, new concepts, and differing viewpoints are so atrophied and rigid the individual never approaches his/her potential as a mature human being.

These—the ideas the updated *Goose Girl* puts forth and the

anti-intellectualist bias of so much other entertainment—are
only some of the possibly unintentional thoughts and prejudices
children's entertainment has communicated.

TV, that omnivorous consumer of amusement material,
would be happy to present even more old low-budget short and
feature-length films from Hollywood than it already does, but
the source has been pretty well mined out. An examination of
the old films TV has been compelled to reject reveals such
blatant racism they are embarrassing to watch. Has the earth
moved so far that we can look at films made within the lifetimes
of some of us as though they were from another planet? How
could we have been so insensitive as to be unaware of—or even
worse, to laugh at—gross insults to the dignity of individuals
and races? How can we still be so insensitive to old films that
have somehow found their way to the TV screen that we let
ourselves accept them without comment and let go undisturbed
our children's oblivion to their offensiveness? Which old films?
So many! Old Tarzan pictures, among them—the attitude of the
white hunters to their black bearers, who are regarded as less
than human. Or old spy or crime stories, with as villain a
heathen Chinee or some other dastardly member of venal Ori-
ental background. Take any old Western with Indians—not one
in a dozen pays more than lip service to the Indians' side of the
conflict. Almost invariably they are portrayed as bloodthirsty
barbarians, ready to go on a drunken rampage at the puff of a
smoke signal.

But most of these films were produced in the forties and
fifties, and no one makes movies that are so racistly stereotypical anymore, right? Wrong. In 1974 the Disney Studios released
The Castaway Cowboy, starring James Garner as a shanghaied
Texan who jumps ship and lands on a Hawaiian island. Vera
Miles is a pretty widow in desperate financial straits, and Robert Culp is the villainous author of her problems. Let me quote
from my review on radio stations WNYC AM and FM:

There is no doubt that children will enjoy this picture tremendously. It has a twelve-year-old hero for kids to identify with, splendid scenery, and lots of action with a minimum of romance. There are at least three major hand-to-hand combats involving exotic death-dealing techniques. There is a cattle stampede. And a strong uncomplicated story line that keeps the plot moving and clearly differentiates the good guys from the bad. Yes, children will certainly like it.

Will *you* like it? Well, if you look at it with the eyes and mind of an eight-year-old, yes indeed. But if you are conscious of attitudes and viewpoints shown on the screen, along with the story, you may be able to restrain your enthusiasm. What, for instance? . . . The economic and cultural colonialism the film implicitly supports. All the values are weighted in favor of the white man, nobly bearing the burden of the happy-go-lucky simple-minded natives, who see no reason why they should prefer onerous toil for someone else to the enjoyment of nature. No respect is shown for their way of life or inherent dignity, which are warped unconscionably to fit into an arbitrary pattern imposed on them. Our great white Texas father shows the same callous disregard for their lives and limbs he displays for their culture. . . .

The Castaway Cowboy was made for children, and made well. It's a pity the Disney people didn't take into consideration *everything* it says to its audiences.

American-made films for some years have been careful about overtly depicting minority individuals as unattractive caricatures. Yet as late as 1972, at the Tehran (Iran) Seventh International Festival of Films for Children and Young Adults, included among some excellent movies were a number of short animated films that outraged me. These were Balkan and East European concepts of American Westerns. There were a cowpoke, hosses, perhaps a sheriff, plus a saloon or a cactus or two to pinpoint the locale. The white cowboy was not drawn with any affection, but he was a charmer compared to the repulsive figures of the Indians and Mexicans. The Indians specialized in huge hooked noses that made them look like vultures; the Mexicans came complete with mustachios, sombreros, and serapes, together with a wall to doze against. I was informed that the producers had hopes to sell these cartoons to the American market and couldn't understand why there were no buyers.

In 1975 in Moscow I attended a show for children at the world-famous Obraztsov puppet theater. I was awe-struck at the number of puppeteers, the superlative manipulation, and the artistry which created some of the most beautiful stage effects I've ever seen. The story was a standard Russian fairy tale, *The Pike's Wishes,* about a peasant lad who competes against three foreign princes for the hand of a princess. All went well with the play until the entrance of the third prince. He was an African, as ugly a caricature as could be found since Reconstruction. To make sure the audience didn't miss anything, the orchestra switched from the folk music background it had been playing to a few bars of Stephen Foster—"Swanee River" or "Old Black Joe." I asked a fellow member of my party who had spent much time in Russia whether the hideous caricature was unique to the Obraztsov theater. No, he said. His admiration of Russian theater was second to none, but this kind of depiction of blacks seemed to be an inexplicable blind spot that he had come upon many times.

To deny any aspersions of racism, nearly all American TV shows for young people have, if it's at all possible to work them in, token blacks, Hispanics, Orientals, and an occasional Indian (U.S. type). Watching them, one grows overconscious of everyone's race and waits to see if everybody will play by the rules. (For example, the "token" can't be the bad guy, unless there's another token as a good guy to offset him, and a whitey at least as bad as the bad token.) Although the appearance of these minority representatives, both in animated cartoons and live-action films, is supposed to demonstrate open-mindedness, what it does more often than not is to reinforce stereotypes. Far too frequently the token individuals selected represent the least common denominator of their race. They offer children unworthy role models. Occasionally these minority representatives are permitted to speak an elaborately correct English, but this is usually done as an affectation or as evidence of their cultural and social distance from their fellows. The more "normal" speech patterns are those of the gutter, with four-letter verbs and adjectives eliminated or paraphrased, and emphasis on the ethnic aspects of their respective gutter. Ostensibly this is to provide identification with the children of that race. I'm insulted for them. Moreover, I question whether these ungrammatical speech patterns of limited vocabulary are doing children a service. If they want to enter the universal job market someday, they'll be handicapped by their difficulties in the use of standard English.

Other examples of racism come to mind. Several are in films that feature whites spreading American or European religions or culture to the benighted dark-skinned natives. This topic is usually handled with respect, even admiration, which extends to the white man and woman who resist all temptation to backslide and resolutely hold to the standards of their homeland. Some "dress for dinner" despite a climate that makes it absurd, and they never forget they must set an example of the better life for ignorant savages. But should a local culture win out and the protagonists "go native," this is generally treated as a humorous aberration or a tragic betrayal of one's own kind. These films may not have been made for young people, but children see them.

Such implications of racism or avowed espousals of it are tied in with sexism that's apparent to anyone who is alert to it. In American- and European-made films, the nubile white woman has been placed on a pedestal, epitomizing the ultimate desideratum of the (white male) film makers and the males of other human and nonhuman varieties. Then when the blacks or red men or yellow men—or, if this is science fiction, the green or purple men— snatch the beauteous white maiden, with rape or marriage (equally heinous) in mind, the courageous white men must recapture her and track down and destroy the despoilers of their race. Of course, in Japanese sci-fi films the kidnapped maiden is invariably Japanese, and I should venture the guess that if there are orange and blue striped men on Antares, their stolen maiden is orange and blue with stripes.

This is typical machismo, which projects its own desires and motivations onto lesser breeds as an excuse for wiping them out. In more grotesque forms this cuts across species lines, as when King Kong snatches Fay Wray. In the film Ms. Wray was a lovely lady, but I can't really believe a King Kong could be turned on by anyone but a Queen Kong.

This business of the white female captive is such a cliché very few adults think about it at all, and young children absorb the point of view like sponges. But reverse the situation and see what a shock it would be to white audiences. Imagine their emotional reaction should a black woman be ravished by white men, with the blacks coming to the rescue and shooting the whites to the last man. I remember a couple of films in which Indian maidens were kidnapped by brutish white men, and although justice was eventually meted out to them, it wasn't only for that. Over the years Gunsmoke, an adult TV Western popular with children, dramatized honestly and effectively some male/female situations with racial elements, but until recently only a handful of other television programs have made an honest attempt to conform to the single standard of racial sexual morality.

Just think: When a white man "goes native" and takes a native wife in a film or on a TV program, there may be some tut-tutting from the adults in the audience, but if he abandons his family to return to "civilization" he is accepted as having been somehow cleansed of his degraded past. When have you seen a story in which a white woman voluntarily adopts the customs of a more "primitive" society, even to taking a husband from it? I have never see one, but I have no difficulty in imagining the sequel to such a story should she desire to return to her home. I doubt whether she could ever be "purified" in the eyes of much of the TV audience. There have been several TV stories of a white woman forcibly married to a man of another race, but her efforts to regain her old status among other whites were depicted as hopeless—even when it was publicly acknowledged that she had been a helpless victim. In major cities, where interracial marriages are not uncommon, other adults and children may wonder what the excitement is all about. But in smaller communities throughout the United States, the situation doesn't seem appreciably more humane than in Bangladesh, where families cast out their wives and daughters who had been raped by enemy soldiers. This sort of racial stereotyping in the entertainment children watch goes a long way to nullify any counterpropaganda they get in school and on TV about equality and brotherhood.

Examples of sexist stereotyping abound in children's entertainment or adult entertainment children watch. When female contestants on game shows are asked who they are, there are still women who identify themselves as wives and mothers. These women define themselves not in terms of who they are, but what; not as individuals, but through their relationship to their husband and children. I've never once heard a male contestant reply that he was a husband and father. There are women who will describe themselves defensively as *only* housewives or homemakers—an honorable calling still. I can understand this defensiveness when I see how housewives are depicted in situation comedies (especially old reruns), films for children, and TV commercials. Happily for the human race, there aren't too many women who are genuinely guilt-stricken at ring-around-the-collar on their husbands' shirts or yellowing wax on their kitchen floors, and if they are, they deserve it.

Despite statistics spelling out the great numbers of married women who hold full- or part-time jobs outside their homes, most sit-com mothers are housebound, confining their interests to their families. They have only an occasional scout or PTA meeting to distract them (and these are family-related), with possibly a brief (one episode, one shot) stint as a crusader for political action (for a new traffic light, or to protect a tree—also somehow family-related).

For a long time, women who worked out of necessity were represented in service roles, as assembly-line hands, sales clerks, hairdressers, or waitresses, or they supported masculine domination: female secretary/male executive; female nurse/male doctor, etc. Teaching was an honorable career, but only if women abjured marriage to live almost like nuns. At the turn of the century and later, it was almost indecent for a teacher to be married, because women who taught the young should not have personal knowledge of sex. (But for some reason, widows could teach.) When men came into teaching in the public school systems, they took over the upper, more prestigious grades, leaving kindergarten and the lower grades as the province of women, except for a few men who confessed to liking to work with very young children.

Women who chose to work and succeeded in carving out impressive careers for themselves were suspect as not being "real" women, of wanting to compete with men rather than be "partners"—partners in terms defined by men, not women.

Popular entertainment has always reflected the times, and

the Disney films have been outstanding in emphasizing the stereotype of woman's place being in the home. If she labored outside, it was only until she could find a strong man to lean on who would take her out of the competitive world, to which she was unsuited, and enthrone her in front of a kitchen sink. There are too many such films by too many producers to list, and we've all seen them as children's entertainment and as family films. Heaven alone knows how many Hollywood films show Mama as housekeeper and nurse, with Dad taking care of the important stuff, like foiling thieves, catching outlaws, building bridges, drilling for oil, flying planes, going to the moon, conducting the world's business, and above all, bringing in money. Because women's salaries have traditionally been less than men's and we have a society that equates success with money, it follows that what men do is more important than what women do. In the career-girl film, where the smart, tough, successful woman has to decide whether to chuck her fabulous career to be an adjunct to a man (Rosalind Russell and Fred MacMurray in *Take a Letter, Darling,* typical of the genre), she must choose between two fates: she can become a wife and a real woman, glad to turn her verve and intelligence to helping him (provided a real man will let her); or rejecting his arms and protection, she can continue on her star-spangled path to glory, lonely, empty, and eventually embittered at having let happiness escape.

This refusal to take seriously women's goals beyond the home can be expressed in entertainment for young people in many ways, all of them an affront to women and girls and a disservice to both sexes. Derision can take the form of out-and-out mockery, as when it jeers at women suffragists, career women, and women active for principle's sake or humanity's in politics, service, etc. And derision can be subtle in slipping the knife between the ribs of women's self-esteem.

In the Disney *Mary Poppins* film, with Julie Andrews as the governess and Glynis Johns as the mother of a troubled household, Father is distant and worried about his job; the two children are a handful; and Mother is dedicated to suffrage for British women. She selflessly devotes her considerable energies to demonstrations and other activities to advance the cause and she enlists the support of her cook and housemaid as well. Her proudest insignia is a "Votes for Women" sash she wears across her chest. Mary Poppins, little Miss Fixit, comes into the ménage to straighten out the problems of her charges. She arranges for Father to get a better-paying position at the bank. She also has him realize he owes his family more of his time and love. As a move in this direction, Father helps his son build a kite, and he puts his arm around Mother's shoulders. Mother takes this to mean she will have an affectionate and supportive husband again, so when the kite needs a tail, what does she do? She whips off her "Votes for Women" ribbon and gives it to the kite. Her gesture to family solidarity. The scene couldn't have taken more than a few seconds, but it made its point: causes women involve themselves in are only something to keep busy with until the love of a good man fills their lives with a really important concern—him. That the film was unusually well made and enjoyed by millions of girls and boys makes this gratuitous denigration of women that much more reprehensible.

There are other ways in which girls and women are put down in the eyes of audiences. Long before the *Blondie* movies, now shown as films for children on many TV stations across the country, women have been shown as "delightful scatterbrains." Gracie Allen and Lucille Ball are among those who have continued the tradition. Allied to this stereotype is the idea that the more devastatingly attractive a woman is, the greater degree of imbecility she is allowed. (See Eva Gabor as a particularly beautiful moron in reruns of *Green Acres*.) She is not held to adult standards of behavior, ethics, or responsibility. No one expects it of her.

In *Herbie Rides Again,* the heroine, a lovely lass with a hair-trigger temper, hits the hero across the face with a lobster, preventing him from completing his explanation of a matter under discussion, and sending him from his pierside restaurant chair into the water below. Does he have her arrested for battery or do any of a number of other things logical in the circumstances—such as having her committed for observation? Of course not. She's pretty and female and therefore exempted from rationality.

The female scatterbrain was a staple of comedy in the thirties and forties (e.g., Katharine Hepburn and Cary Grant in *Bringing Up Baby*), and looking at these films on TV, where they are shown in late afternoons or early evenings for family viewing, adults may marvel that they seem so passé. But children are absorbing the message still that to be feminine is to be pretty and charming and an excuse for getting away with murder.

Akin to this stereotype is the one of the strong, competent, positive, achieving male and the fragile, helpless, indecisive, achieved-for female. She flounders around with her problems, getting in deeper and deeper until he comes along and straightens everything out—whether it's balancing her checkbook, saving her ranch, or beating off attacking Martians. In terms of children's entertainment, this is epitomized by Maeterlinck's *The Bluebird,* which I saw at the Moscow Art Theater (and which has since been made into an all-star film). The Moscow revival of the production Stanislavsky staged there in 1908 was something special. The hero and heroine were insufferable. The little brother was sickeningly manly and adventurous; his sister was correspondingly feminine and timid. Even in the first decade of this century, they must have been a lot to swallow and keep down. Today it's impossible to credit either little horror with life, but their ilk, with only minor modifications, are still to be found in dramatizations for children. In days of old when knights were bold, it was logical for a hero in shining armor to save the swooning damsel from a dragon, but Saint George and Lancelot have been away a long time.

Earlier we mentioned the racist implications of *The Castaway Cowboy*. Here is the same film's contribution to women's liberation, from the same review:

> The mother . . . [is] the typical Disney sexist stereotype of the sweet, helpless little woman who stands there wringing her hands, without an intelligent thought in her beautiful head, until a dweat big stwong man comes to the rescue.

But who hasn't seen variations by the hundreds on this theme?

Combine some of the stereotypes of women that children see over and over, and this is the image they develop: Women are scatterbrained and irresponsible and therefore not equipped to do the important work of the world, which should be reserved for men. They belong home, where they can be protected from a world they can't cope with and where they can create a comfortable environment for their husbands and children and relieve them of trivial but time-consuming tasks such as marketing, laundry, bed-making, etc. Only women who are not "real" women compete with men, and offered the love of a good man, they would be well advised to take it and go home.

It's interesting to note how stereotyping continues once the lovable dimwit becomes a wife. While she is still young and charming the image endures. But as she grows older, she falls into a very different category of female: the mature, experienced wife. Instead of the frivolous screwball, she is now utterly lacking in humor, sensitivity, and gaiety—everything that made her so lovable before. Now she walks through the house grimly in a butt-sprung bathrobe and flapping terry-cloth slippers, with cold cream on her face and curlers in her hair, sometimes armed with a rolling pin, lying in wait for her hapless husband, who has had the temerity to take an evening off to go bowling with the boys. The earlier stereotype is demeaning to women; the later one is demeaning to women and men both.

Perhaps the cruelest images children's entertainment projects—and adult comedy watched by boys and girls does too—are those of old age. Other cultures teach their children to respect their aged, if not for what they are, then for what they were. In the United States, contempt for the obsolete extends beyond machinery and hats to human beings. By the example their entertainment sets, our children are being taught to mock and discard as valueless what they themselves may someday become. We've mentioned the old people in *Herbie Rides Again*. This illustration, with minor variations, is widely disseminated in every medium. Palsied, deaf, querulous, unreasonable—old people exhibiting all the attributes of advanced senility are depicted as being typical and hilarious. Dick Van Dyke, Jonathan Winters, Arte Johnson, and Gene Rayburn are only a few of the TV personalities who repeatedly caricature old age in a way that is heartless and sadistic. Heartless because old people who are senile and helpless deserve compassion; sadistic because these portraits of trembling vacuity are not true of most old people. Most of us know men and women in their eighties and nineties who continue a broad spectrum of interests that include mental, physical, and social activities. They are in good health and as witty, sharp, and competent in many respects as ever. Propagating the falsehood of their utter decrepitude is tremendously damaging to the self-image of these able old people and harmful, as is any misconception, to those others who believe it. Portrayals of the elderly hardly ever show them capable of valuable contributions to society, where their wisdom, experience, and compassion are so greatly needed. Grandfather and Grandmother Walton are among the few positive portrayals of old age children see regularly in entertainment.

The scorn for old age that entertainment instills in children is pervasive. An old horse is an object of ridicule in cartoons and live-action films. There he stands with his ribs sharp under his skin, and his back swayed—the same steed who once was strong, tireless, and beautiful, who had been loyal, gentle, and loving. Why is this same animal grotesque merely because nature has continued its cycle? The strength and beauty are no longer obvious, but the loyalty, gentleness, and love remain, and the dignity. As he is depicted, these are worth nothing.

Back to *Herbie Rides Again.* There's a scene of an old Volkswagen that hears Herbie's call for help. The ancient car pulls itself together and limps off to do battle to the death for its friend. The audience is programmed to view all this as funny and laughs accordingly. What would be gallant in a young car (or man or horse) is shown as ludicrous in an old one. The makers of entertainment mean to say this, but I wonder whether they understand all the implications and how pernicious they can be to young people, who are being encouraged to overvalue youth and to dread what must be our common end, without being given to understand that old age has its wisdom and experience to compensate, sometimes very adequately, for what has been lost.

Children's entertainment can present thoughts that make a child more sensitive and humane or more callous and inhuman. Since we'll be discussing the subject in more detail later on, I want only to mention now how a story ostensibly about one thing can be filled with brutality and sadism that are either played for laughs or inserted almost subliminally, making for neither awareness of the suffering of others nor magnanimity of spirit.

Let's take the recent film of *The Three Musketeers* with its star-studded cast: Michael York as d'Artagnan, Charlton Heston as Richelieu, Geraldine Chaplin as the Queen of France. . . . In one of the opening scenes there's a shot of the Queen, a sympathetic character and one of Dumas's two heroines. She and her ladies are disporting themselves on a kind of merry-go-round operated by men pedaling vigorously. Her majesty parts her lovely lips and calls out imperiously, "Make them go faster! Whip them!" In a later scene, she and her attendants are seated on horseback watching two falcons fighting to the death overhead. She claps her hands prettily and says, as closely as I remember the exact words, "What fun! Hear them cry!" Then there is a brief glimpse of Cardinal Richelieu walking down a prison corridor along which hang iron cages holding men like captive birds. The wretches, in advanced stages of misery, mutely reach out their hands for mercy. The Cardinal and the camera pay no heed and proceed to a torture chamber, where Richelieu signs to the torturer that he is to release a prisoner whose thumbs are being mangled. The prisoner rubs his hands together and says, "That hurt." Torturer: "It was meant to." Big laugh from the audience. And there was much more of the same throughout.

This picture was rated as suitable for all audiences, with parental guidance suggested. I collected the reviews of all the major critics in New York City, and without exception they said it was "great family fare," "fun for everyone in the family," etc. I haven't been able to concur. This isn't what I want for children. When a "good" queen orders men flogged to provide her with a moment's pastime, how does this affect the way children consider brutality? Those two falcons, fighting for a sixty-second sequence in a make-believe story, were feeling actual agony and dying real deaths. How is this different except in degree from the slaughter of people and beasts that debased the Colosseum crowds in ancient Rome, who applauded the torment or yawned at it? When no comment is made on human beings tortured in cages, when such a sight is accepted as normal by protagonists, why should our children give their suffering any more thought? When the image of pain is treated as a joke, doesn't this encourage children to dismiss as inconsequential any pain but their own? I doubt whether the makers of *The Three Musketeers* wanted to do more than make a good profitable movie from this old swashbuckler. The little incidents I've mentioned, all together taking less than three or four minutes in this feature-length film, were no doubt inserted for a more colorful, richer portrait of an age. But if clear thinking had been applied to these episodes, keeping in mind the "PG" rating that was wanted, would they have been included?

If we train our eyes to take in everything a film or play states, we can find much to question, not only for our children but for ourselves. Some of what is done to animals for our amusement is so ugly it hardly bears talking about. There have been numerous articles in the press about how much more expensive it is to use a carefully trained horse that can fall on command than it is to set up a trip wire that will simply break a "cheap" horse's legs. This is not the worst that is done to animals for our "entertainment." At present there is discussion about the inclusion of a clause to precede any film with animals in it, to the effect that no animal has been hurt during production. This is not yet mandatory in the United States, and as far as I know, there is not even any thought of it in films made abroad. Children love animals, but if their entertainment inures them to such brutality, our boys and girls must grow to men and women lacking the compassion to make them truly human.

Entertainment can be guilty of presenting concepts of virtues in terms that render them unrecognizable. *The Giving Tree* has been dramatized from Shel Silverstein's book of that title and performed by the Little Theater of the Deaf, the National Theater of the Deaf's division for children. *The Giving Tree* has been widely acclaimed as a beautiful parable of love. It is the story of a tree and a little boy who love each other. He eats her fruit, plays in her branches and finds comfort in her shade, and the tree is happy. When he grows older he wants money to have fun with and the tree gives him her apples to sell. Later, he returns for help in building a home for his family and the tree contributes her branches. Years after, the boy—now mature and disillusioned—comes back. The tree gives him her trunk so that he can make a boat of her body and sail off into the sunset. Eventually, old and spent, he comes home to what is left of the tree. He wants nothing of life but to sit on her stump in the sun, and the tree is happy because she has her little boy again. My opinion is that she'd be better off with termites.

This story is sick-sick-sick. What kind of love is it when one party gives and gives and the other takes and takes? The "boy" doesn't even grant the tree respect—certainly not affection—once he's grown. This is a man with a neurotic need to be reassured over and over, insatiably, that he is truly loved, demanding as proof repeated willing sacrifice even to the death of the lover—mother, sweetheart, wife, friend, or whomever. If this sado-masochism is love, I'll take pistachio.

Any producers of children's entertainment would piously aver that nothing could be farther from their intention than to instill in young people a scorn of law and order. And yet, in the guise of drama and comedy, boys and girls are taught that the end justifies the means and that justice is what *they* say it is.

Among the large number of films and TV programs designed for adult viewing that are popular with children, the James Bond series and its imitators on various levels of literacy present a protagonist (I prefer not to call him a hero) who, armed with a collection of deadly, incredible weapons, sallies forth to do battle with evil. Because he's on "our side" and supported with unlimited wealth by a mysterious governmental department, his unawareness of the civil rights of those who stand in his way, and his heartlessness, are depicted as part of his dedication to the cause. He'll sacrifice his life and, if need be, he'll even more gladly sacrifice the lives of others, without thought of whether their contribution would be voluntary. Never is it even implied that when "our side" is so lawless and inhumane, "we" are no better than "they" are. According to the James Bond mentality, all that matters is which side.

Mission Impossible is a TV series about a group that also functions as an unofficial arm of a governmental or quasi-governmental authority on "our side." It uses all sorts of extralegal means (wiretapping, kidnapping, drugging) to combat evil and achieve its worthy ends. Psychological tricks are employed to trap its opponents or persuade them to betray or murder each other—such things as using their best, most humane instincts to destroy themselves. After the succession of actual political assassinations which shocked Americans, public opinion became hostile to this program and further production was discontinued. However, *Mission Impossible* is still popular on reruns at hours when it can be assumed there is a large young audience.

The James Bonds and the *Mission Impossible*s are both spy-adventures that make no bones about law breaking for a higher goal. If we want our children to respect the rights the Constitution secures to us all, these stories don't seem to be the most effective way of going about it.

Herbie doesn't even have the excuse of acting on behalf of any government. The "lovable Volkswagen" commits comic mayhem for its own ends or for those it designates as its friends. It takes upon itself a course of action that ignores the rights and feelings of anyone and everyone standing in its way. It careens into inoffensive citizens and demolishes property (either the "enemy" 's or that of third parties who couldn't possibly matter), ignoring rules, traffic lights, signs, and other evidences of restraint.

Over and over in entertainment for young people we come across protagonists who believe that rules were made for others, not for them. As a corollary, the opponents of the protagonists are represented as being evil, harmful to the cause, unpatriotic, or whatever else the protagonist happens to be against. Children identify with James Bonds, the *Mission Impossible* crew, Herbie, and the multitudes who are indifferent to society's codes—those dashing, colorful figures who are above all the petty restrictions children are fenced in with. Young people are not encouraged to identify with those on "our side" who support the causes of the protagonist in more pedestrian fashion and who have no reason for being in the story except one—as stodgy, dull, unimaginative, or cowardly contrasts to the prime character.

In another area, some parents may not care about ideas their children may pick up about smoking or drinking, but others have firm notions on the subject. If you watch TV sit-coms or films and keep score, it may amaze you how many smokes or drinks per hour are consumed on the air. Cigarettes and liquor exemplify sophistication, maturity, and glamor to young people, who want to pretend to these qualities before they can possess them. There is preaching today in films and plays on the dangers of smoking, and in public-service messages repeated from time to time on the air, but the counterpropaganda isn't commensurate with the examples children see the rest of the time.

The Bad News Bears, a "PG"-rated film starring Walter Matthau, takes a remarkable position on drinking. Most of the hilarity not evoked by shock language springs from the genuinely funny images of drinking and drunkenness supplied by

Mr. Matthau. The end of the film shows him, as coach of the team, treating all the eleven-and twelve-year-olds to beer in recognition of their metaphorical coming of age. The attitude of the audience about the beer was: Why not? Which is just why I question the morality of equating alcohol with maturity, particularly in times when drinking is a more serious problem among schoolchildren than pot, speed, and hard drugs. When boys and girls as young as third-graders come to class in various degrees of inebriation, or sneak muscatel from their lunch boxes at noon, I question whether humor based on drinking is valid in a children's picture.

As parents, teachers, or other guardians of children, we must be concerned with what they eat and with what they wear. We don't feed strawberries to a child they give hives to, or provide rabbit-lined mittens to a child allergic to fur. When we know there is a problem, we read labels carefully, because even a small amount of an allergenic substance can trigger a reaction that seems out of all proportion to the irritant. The irritants in entertainment are the implicit messages, and they can be blatant or subtle. They aren't labeled because even the producer isn't always aware they exist. Even though they may take a long time before they show effects on the lives of our children, we must be alert to counteract influences of which we disapprove.

Anti-intellectualism, sexism, racism, brutality, and other ideas that we profess to abominate can be fed to our children as entertainment. We can't always prevent the messages from getting through. We can discuss with our girls and boys how the messages have been conveyed and how the children have been given a one-sided and fallacious argument. We can arm our children to protect themselves by helping them to recognize these ideas and to know the facts that will render the ideas harmless.

7. Humor

As everyone knows and surveys confirm, what children want above all else in entertainment is humor. Those who purvey theater in its several media supply humor, or what passes for it, copiously.

Humor is one component of a production. Like any other, its function is to contribute to the whole, to be an integral constituent that strengthens the other parts by its presence. It can even be the major constituent, which the other parts serve to support. Regardless of what element is stressed—humor, suspense, action, mystery—the end product of any carefully crafted work should be an indissoluble unit.

When the humor is subordinated and used intelligently, it can make action more dramatic, suspense more acute, characterizations sharper, and so forth. Where the humor is dominant and used intelligently, the young audience will enjoy a production in which action, suspense, characterizations, etc., create solidly hilarious situations, intrinsically funny, with verbal and physical jokes garnishing it all.

In Shakespeare's *Twelfth Night,* the Duke opens the play by saying:

If music be the food of love, play on;
Give me excess of it, that, surfeiting,
The appetite may sicken, and so die.

There's an analogy here. In entertainment for children, the humor may laugh itself to death.

Before we go into why the humor works in some shows and not in others, we ought to examine what children think is funny, and we must remember they *are* children.

Children like physical, nonverbal humor. When an actor slips on a banana peel and takes a pratfall, when he trips over his own feet and pitches onto his face, when he catches his hand in a door, or drops a cannon ball on his foot, or gets his head stuck in a fence, this is terribly funny. When one Stooge thrusts his finger into the eyes of another of the Three Stooges, or knocks him over with a board, or drops a load of bricks on him, this is funny too. It's funny when pies hit faces, when Popeye the Sailor is smashed flat by a steam roller, when a load of gravel buries Fred Flintstone, or when Mr. Jetson's spacesuit lets him drop a mile to earth. It's funny when Tom and Jerry or Tweety and Sylvester or Heckle and Jeckle mangle or dismember each other. When a policeman steps into a bucket of paint, or the mayor's top hat blows off, or a Marx Brother's pants fall down, this is funny too. It's funny when two frightened pirates back into each other or when one scared character leaps for safety into another's arms. A Keystone Kops chase is funny, or a frantic car chase from any number of Disney films. And double takes, explosions, etc., etc., etc.

Is all this funny to adults? That depends. It depends on how well all this mayhem, these assorted mime tricks, are committed—the surprise, the precision of the maneuver, the reactions of the other performers. . . . But since we are adults, something else is important to us: whether the pain inflicted is genuine and whether the loss of dignity is truly wounding. Take a pompous, portly gentleman in his prime, whose hat is knocked off by a snowball, who falls on his backside, and who then picks himself up, dusts himself off, and proceeds on his way little the worse for wear. Now take a sweet, grandmotherly old woman who is hit on the head by a stone, falls on *her* backside, and is hospitalized with severe concussion and a fractured hip. Adults may find the first quite funny indeed—if it's done on stage or on film, and they know it's all an act. They may even find it amusing if they see it actually happening in the street. In the second case, I doubt whether many adults would find anything to laugh at even if it were an animated cartoon and they knew no real person was involved. The mere thought of an old woman with a broken hip is disturbing. In no circumstances would they laugh at a real elderly woman's suffering.

The difference between adult reactions and children's is experience. Adults will first see if there is genuine hurt, and then laugh, partly in relief, if there is not. Adults have lived through enough to be more concerned with eliminating pain than enjoying it—except for certain practitioners of pain as an art, who are not germane to this discussion. Children have all had some experience of pain, but it requires a degree of maturity to be able to realize that a kick in the shins hurts someone else as much as it would hurt them. It takes children a long time to associate the cause with the effect, the comical action with the resulting discomfort, embarrassment, or disaster. In the old silents, Harold Lloyd and Buster Keaton were masters at this sort of thing, as Dick Van Dyke is today, convincing us that the actions that occasion the catastrophes, and the catastrophes themselves, caused no permanent damage to the persons or psyches of the victims. Adults need this reassurance to laugh comfortably. Children don't.

Destruction can be funny too. The more extravagant the

destruction, the funnier. Some of the old Laurel and Hardy films are without peer in the way they build from trivial damage to a climax in which the entire set and props are demolished. Ten cars in a pileup can be ten times funnier than one car hitting a tree. A truckload of smashed eggs can be funnier than one broken box. Adults can laugh as heartily as young people at these comic disasters. For one thing, both know they are supposed to be amusing. Both know no one is really imperiled. They are familiar enough with the stock characters to recognize that, no matter what, they'll all be back unharmed in another episode. Popeye will find a can of spinach, ingest the contents, and become just as three-dimensional as he was before he ran afoul of the steam roller. Messrs Flintstone and Jetson will stagger to their feet, shrug, and be as good as new. Tom and Jerry and all the rest will recover instantaneously from the havoc that has been wreaked on them.

Boys and girls have a curious capacity to believe completely in the cartoon characters they are watching, while at the same time keeping in a corner of their mind the knowledge that what they are looking at is only animated drawing. I've talked with nursery school children of three and four about this. They watch cartoons with relish, but many refuse to look at live-action Westerns. "Because," a four-year-old informed me, "when Porky Pig gets shot he's not really hurt because he's not really real, so it's funny. But when a cowboy shoots another cowboy, that's real and that's not funny."

I have considered how this agrees with what I said earlier—that it takes young people a while to feel someone else's pain. This is not a contradiction. Children recognize the intent of a scene. Porky Pig is programmed to be comedy, and in the context of comedy, in this make-believe world, no one really hurts or dies permanently. Westerns are not filmed with the same intent; here the idea is to create a semblance of actuality. Even if children don't feel the cowboy's hurt, they know he's supposed to be damaged, and if he's shot through the heart he doesn't get up again.

Children can translate physical action into humor, and manufacturers of entertainment use this for all it's worth, and more. This isn't new. Presumably the first tree-dwelling human beings laughed their heads off when one of their number fell out of a tree, and nonverbal physical humor has had a long and honorable career ever since. Mimes and clowns have been making the world laugh for centuries and they are as popular today as ever. There isn't so much of it on the air today as when Sid Caesar, Red Skelton, Danny Kaye, and other inspired clowns were the favorites of children and adults alike, but a new generation of comics is learning the body language of comedy. The Punch and Judy puppet show is a direct inheritor of the ancient slapstick tradition, traceable to the commedia dell'arte of the sixteenth-century Italian streets, which, in turn, can follow its origins back to the Roman comic theater and its Greek progenitors.

But to return to our original point, this humor must be part of a show, not the whole thing. Unless the program merely consists of vaudeville routines strung together formlessly, humor needs a structure. It needs a plot to give it an excuse for being, a frame to support it. It needs characters to express it. And, as we mentioned earlier, a believable environment.

So let's look at some of the ways physical humor works and some of the ways it doesn't. When Geppetto is carving his puppet Pinocchio and one of its wooden legs flies up and kicks Geppetto in the rump, children roar. It works because the action is plausible within its context. When a fairy tale king turns his back on a gardener, who kicks his majesty in the rump, children roar the same way, but it doesn't work because the action is *im*plausible within its context.

If Cinderella's sisters are gauche and clumsy at the ball and fall on their faces into pies, this can be hilarious. They are unsympathetic characters and children laugh at them willingly, enjoying their discomfiture as a form of revenge for their cruelty. If Cinderella is as gauche and clumsy, the "humor" will destroy the story. The children love Cinderella and identify with her. Her shame or embarrassment is theirs, and the ball should be a time of glory for Cinderella and children alike. The boys and girls will howl gleefully should she stumble into a pie because, with good timing, stumbling and pies are sure-fire laugh programmers. But the audience will lose its identification with her and consequent involvement with the plot.

If a wicked fairy tale cook drops a load of crockery in circumstances that seem to serve him right, the children will laugh. If the disguised princess serving him drops crockery she'll be punished for breaking, the children won't laugh unless the scene is played for comedy. They will laugh then, but at the cost of the play.

What it all comes to is whether the physical humor is part and parcel of the production, or whether everything in the play is distorted for the sake of the laughs.

The same problems arise with verbal humor, which children also love. What kind of word humor? Anything and everything. Puns. Riddles. Jokes. Games. Alliteration. Repartee. Stammering. One-liners. Accents. Name-calling. The opportunities for laughs are seemingly unlimited. However, physical humor or sight gags have advantages over verbal humor. Sight humor cuts across age lines and language barriers. Unless sexual overtones color a mimed routine, anyone of any age will comprehend and react. No explanation is necessary for a clown tripping over his own enormous shoes. With words, problems are created. Not everyone understands verbal as readily as nonverbal humor.

Comprehension of words can be difficult at times with an audience of middle-class youngsters with standard speech patterns and middle-class school education or better. But not all boys and girls have standard speech patterns and such education. Audiences are composed also of children who speak English as a second language and who have not yet attained proficiency in it. Many homes and schools don't familiarize their children with the "standard" stories and poetry the majority take for granted. It may not be easy for boys and girls to understand even the most crystal-clear articulation onstage, and articulation isn't always as clear as it could be. Plays on words and other word fun that can have some children holding their stomachs with laughter can leave others irritable at being on the outside of jokes they don't understand.

And of course, there's another problem peculiar to entertainment for children. What's a funny word game to a twelve-year-old can be meaningless to a child of six. Combine this with a vocabulary beyond the comprehension of very young children plus differences of cultural orientation, and you can come up with something like this tea party scene from Lewis Carroll's *Alice in Wonderland,* frequently taken verbatim in dramatizations:

DORMOUSE: Once upon a time there were three little sisters, and their names were Elsie, Lacie, and Tillie; and they lived at the bottom of a well—

ALICE: What did they live on?

DORMOUSE: They lived on treacle.

ALICE: They couldn't have done that, you know; they'd have been ill.

DORMOUSE: So they were; *very* ill.

ALICE: But why did they live at the bottom of a well?

DORMOUSE: It was a treacle-well. . . . And so these three little sisters—they were learning to draw, you know—

ALICE: What did they draw?

DORMOUSE: Treacle.

ALICE: But I don't understand. Where did they draw the treacle from?

HATTER: You can draw water out of a water-well, so I should think you could draw treacle out of a treacle-well—eh, stupid?

ALICE: But they were *in* the well.

DORMOUSE: Of course they were—well in.

I've watched audiences while this delicious nonsense was going on, but I've never seen an audience that understood it. Oh, individual children comprehended the dialogue, particularly if the book was a favorite and they had had all the passages explained. But most American children don't know what a dormouse is, and that treacle is molasses, and the meaning of *draw* in the sense of *extract.* And so many city children don't know how a well functions. Most if not all of the point of this conversation escapes them.

Another example from Alice, this time from the Lobster-Quadrille:

What matters it how far we go? his scaly friend replied . . .
The further off from England the nearer is to France.

This is probably comprehensible to British children, but it means nothing to young children here, who scarcely know what and where Europe is, let alone the relationship of the two countries facing each other across the Channel.

Alice in Wonderland is chock full of bits like this, and if we want our children to understand the fun in the word games, we may have to give them some preparation. Or take the children to a version that has been Americanized or otherwise clarified so that what is genuinely humorous survives in a way that makes sense to an audience other than the little English girls to whom it was first told.

There is some vocabulary that is universally understood by children. The adult theater has extended the limits of language to include as a matter of course expletives, adjectives, and verbs which only a few years ago would have shocked audiences out of their seats. Something of this has at last reached entertainment for children. *The Bad News Bears,* the film we referred to earlier, uses gutter language for humor to achieve contemporaneity and identification. In this film, a group of shiningly scrubbed middle-class WASPs forms the nucleus of a Little League type of ball team, with tokens from other elements of the population. The joke is the contrast of the angelic faces of the children on the team with the obscenities and profanities that flow freely from them. References to "Jews, niggers, and spics" are also good for hilarity, but shock value is all they contribute. I couldn't find that character or plot development justified the usage. The laughs came thick and fast, and I haven't met one boy or girl who has seen the picture who didn't love it. I resent that the audience was being manipulated by the device of the shock language, but when I discussed the scurrilous speech with children, they all, even first-graders, said it was mild compared to what they hear every day in their schoolyards. They were without exception amused by it and couldn't understand my lack of enthusiasm.

The language in *The Bad News Bears* had the dubious virtue of being understood by its audiences. There are all too many productions for children that aim their verbal humor over the heads of the young audience and at the accompanying adults. It is surely desirable to keep the grownups as happy as the children, and there's no reason why humor for the younger set can't be clever enough to keep their elders equally amused. But in a production for children, the prime audience must not be baffled, as in this scene from the Off-Center Theater's *Noah's Ark:*

Scene: *A town in Biblical days. Enter a man in a loose, tacky robe carrying a shoeshine kit and a whisk broom, which he puts down.*

NARRATOR: And here we have a typical beggar of the times.

BEGGAR: Hello. I'm a typical beggar of the times.

(Enter another man, dressed similarly but not quite so tacky, carrying an attaché case.)

NARRATOR: And here we have a typical businessman of the times.

BUSINESSMAN: Hello, my name is Hoffman. I'm a typical businessman of the times.

(Beggar approaches businessman and begins to brush him down vigorously with whisk broom.)

BUSINESSMAN: Stop that! What are you doing?

BEGGAR: I'm dustin' Hoffman.

For this performance, most of the children were four to seven. The name Dustin Hoffman meant nothing to them and they were confused by the guffaws from their accompanying fathers. This is analogous to inviting a guest for dinner and then serving everyone but him; or, as did the Fox and the Stork in Aesop's fable, serving your guest food in such a way that he cannot reach it.

In productions for children, I have seen and heard all kinds of subjects mentioned that could have no interest for young people: political references, in jokes about the actors' working conditions and labor union, puns and other gags built around the names of persons the children could have known nothing about, or jokes built on events that were relevant only to those much over ten years old. Over and over I've sat through entertainments at which the adults howled and the children were mum or laughed politely when their parents did. This sort of thing could make a good supper club act or a routine for a TV comic, but it's an insult to a child.

One more example: The Pixie Judy Troupe put on a *Rumpel-stiltskin* containing a scene I still remember with painful clarity. The little man has just finished spinning a heap of straw into gold and it lies piled in a shining mound. He plunges his arms into it and holds aloft fistfuls of the gleaming stuff. "Eat your heart out, Harry Winston," he gloats.

I can recall one campy TV series that at first glance could be considered an exception. *Bullwinkle,* an animated cartoon series, was full of puns boys and girls didn't always comprehend and allusions to matters beyond their frame of reference. I suspect it was made for adults originally, but it was successful with a wide age range of children. They didn't necessarily recognize the satire that underlay the situations and characters of the episodes: the spy with the heavy Slavic accent, the honest-and-true Canadian Mountie, the mustache-twirling, mortgage-foreclosing villain. . . . These characters and their lines were amusing enough in their own right so that it wasn't essential to grasp the underlying meanings as well. These meanings became evident to boys and girls as they grew older and saw the episodes repeated in reruns. Several children have told me they particularly enjoyed *Bullwinkle* because it was funnier to them each time, and the additional comprehension was a bonus to top their pleasure in an already diverting program. I said it would appear to be an exception at first glance. But it's not an exception. In *Bullwinkle* the children weren't being cheated. They laughed at the jokes adults laughed at, but on their own level of appreciation.

The usual campy show is willing to sacrifice all credibility in its environment for a gag that's too tempting to resist. Earlier I mentioned the City Center *Merry Widow* and the BMT subway. In the same scene an actor stamped his foot on the stage, which had been scheduled for renovation. The floor creaked noisily under his foot, at which the actor ad-libbed, "Good thing this is our last show here." The audience, mostly adults who knew about the plans for the theater, applauded him, but the line destroyed whatever illusion had been sustained that the story was being enacted anywhere else than on West Fifty-fifth Street.

The wrong kind of laugh is very good at shattering whatever illusion of magic has been created—including real fairy tale magic, with which a fairy tale play should be suffused.

Example: *Cinderella,* a musical by Elliott Taubenslag Productions.

> Scene: *The foot of the staircase down which Cinderella has just fled at midnight. The prince looks about disconsolately for his lost love. Enter the king with a shoe in his hand.*
>
> KING: Don't feel bad, son. See, here's a clue. She left her name in her slipper: A. S. Beck.

At that time the Beck stores were as familiar to children as Woolworth's, so all but the youngest recognized the gag. And when Cinderella's slipper comes from the corner shoe store instead of from the fairy godmother's wand, what becomes of the enchantment? It's gone as if it had never been.

Those employing humor must exercise discretion as to the objects of their laughter. Some things just aren't funny, and encouraging young people to find them amusing can help turn our children into adults we don't like very well.

In the area of nonverbal humor, misery isn't funny. A child being tormented, a dog or a cat with a can tied to its tail, a starving beggar, a waiter with sore feet, a drug addict in withdrawal—these are some of the things children have been encouraged to laugh at in TV, movies, or stage productions. A long list of physical infirmities is also considered risible: deafness, blindness, palsy, wooden legs, twisted backs, limping, the weaknesses of old age, limbs in traction. . . . The list goes on.

Where words are concerned, we should be just as careful,

perhaps more so. It isn't true that sticks and stones may break my bones but names will never hurt me. Words can be deeply wounding. A joke with a sting that will be felt by members of a minority in the audience can kill those members' pleasure in the performance; they came to enjoy themselves, not to be insulted. Likewise accents—they can be funny and charming or they can be funny and vicious, a distinction not made frequently enough. Cruel jokes and accents can be as bad for the rest of the audience, training it away from sensitivity and concern toward bigotry and callousness. Stammering and stuttering can also be good for laughs, but to children with speech problems, such "humor" can be agonizing, particularly when it sets patterns for classmates to adopt on their own when the show is over.

Players should be careful in the use of names. I remember one performance in which an actor reeled off a number of girls' names that were supposed to be ugly or funny. When he came to "Agnes," a little girl in front of me burst into tears. Her name was Agnes, and she had always thought it pretty. After the performance, when her grandmother tried to make light of the incident to quiet her, the child grew hysterical and forbade anyone to call her again by the "horrible" name.

One of the surest laugh-getters is to have two characters engage in a name-calling bout. Whether they insult each other in contemporary terms (jerk, dope, dummy, fathead) or in more archaic ones (nincompoop, ass, dolt, blockhead), the children roar. As the characters grow more intense, so does audience reaction, until the boys and girls are almost literally rolling in the aisles. Parents and teachers (and I) don't care for this sort of thing, but it does have one point in its favor. It enlarges the children's vocabulary and offers substitutes for some of the more limited and unquotable invective they hurl at each other in more informal circumstances.

Situations can also be supported or devastated by the humor. Nor is this anything new. In *Long, Long Ago,* a volume of reminiscences, Alexander Woollcott says:

> The first time I ever went to the theater it was Rose Field who took me. This was a matinee at the Coates Opera House, and the play was Sinbad the Sailor. . . . Although at the time it could have been said of me that I should never see six again, I had not yet become fastidious. When many years later it would be my role to write sternly on such matters, I would be careful to deplore as heavy-handed such antic moments as the one when Sinbad (with what struck me at the time as great presence of mind) threw a cake of soap to a man overboard so that he could wash himself ashore. But in 1893 this had me in stitches.

Today's children would still be in stitches. But see what it did to the story. Instead of remaining involved in the storm that was raging over the ocean, the audience felt its belief in Sinbad's peril vanish, as did the tension and suspense on which the story was built. Dramatically, the author might have wanted to lighten the serious moment briefly, but in that case, the joke was ill-chosen. A gag that maintained the illusion of the tempest's terror and Sinbad's helplessness would have added to the audience's excitement and conviction in the story, and it could have got just as big a laugh.

I've asked myself again and again whether writers are afraid of children's audiences, whether they fear that if boys and girls aren't laughing noisily they are indifferent to the production. So much humor, like the kind ground out weekly for the Saturday-morning kiddie shows, seems to have an almost desperate quality to it. The audience *must* laugh, no matter how or at what. The audience responses are programmed to come like machine gun bullets, and plot, characterizations, and logic are all subverted to that end. But the Saturday shows aren't the only offenders, as anyone knows who goes to entertainment for children with any frequency.

Examples of destructive humor have been given throughout this book. What is evident is that if respect for the audience and the material had been present in these examples, this in itself would have changed the viewpoint of the writer and director so that negating situations and gags could never have occurred. But it goes deeper.

It has seemed to me, as I've sat through hundreds, perhaps thousands, of productions shattered by inept humor, that this kind of writing is an admission of incompetence. Writers who are masters of their craft should be able to devise humor to support characterizations and mood and to advance the story line. Only a lack of understanding of and a limited ability in children's playwriting can make playwrights settle for the cheap joke that can set at naught the rest of their efforts.

What can you do about this? Not much about the already produced play or TV show or whatever else asks your children to accept an easy laugh instead of comedy of intelligence and substance. You can complain after the fact to the theater or TV station. You can also take up with your boys and girls how funny they thought the laughs were, how much they believed in the people and the story, and whether they imagined that the people could really have said and done the things in circumstances the play arranged for them. The children may tell you the best part was the jokes and that the rest didn't matter. But once *you* develop the habit of looking with an appraising eye at entertainment for your children, you'll be able to help them understand the difference between laughter with and laughter at, and between humor that enriches a production and humor that devastates it.

8. Sex

One of the areas in which children's entertainment varies from entertainment for adults is the treatment of sex. Adults can enjoy the way sex is handled for young people, but boys and girls are not ready for some of the ways sex is depicted in adults' entertainment. All of us, children and adults alike, are bombarded by messages with sexual implications in advertising, in news programs, on magazine covers, in popular songs, and so much else. We should be concerned that children's entertainment contribute to neither a salacious picture of sex nor one that adds to a child's store of misinformation. It's important that a wholesome, nonthreatening concept be presented.

Vive la différence may be what a great many adult productions are built on, but for children up to twelve or so most parents—and the boys and girls themselves—prefer a story that emphasizes other relationships.

Either it's difficult for the producers of children's entertainment to look at sex from a child's viewpoint or they can do so but feel that inserting a hot little number into the production will do something for the tired businessman who might be watching. *The Island at the Top of the World,* a Disney film, for instance, is to all intents and purposes an all-male adventure film until about halfway through, when a beautiful Viking maiden is introduced, who helps the hero and his friends escape from her oasis in the frozen North and accompanies him to his own England. Love between them is as pure and innocent as her scrubbed fresh face. The face goes with an ample bosom straining to burst its bodice. If the Disney people had wanted the audience to be genuinely uninterested in her physical endowments, they could have substituted a less spectacularly structured young woman or, keeping her, they could have dressed her in a blouse two sizes looser and two inches higher at the neckline. This girl costumed in this manner was an attempt to eat one's cake and have it too—profess a lack of interest in the female sex while making sure it's in evidence. This treatment is all too typical of an uncounted number of films for young people, and it offends me.

I'm deeply offended, too, at the way sex is represented or referred to in films and on the stage. In *The Bad News Bears,* already mentioned, young Tatum O'Neal is introduced as the identification figure for the girls in the audience. Walter Matthau tries to enlist her as a pitcher for his otherwise all-boy ball team. Tatum protests that she's too old for boyish games; she's ready for a training bra. Big laugh. In a later sequence, having given her loyalty to the team, Tatum goes off to recruit a reluctant boy hitter. She challenges him to a game of pool or some such. If she wins, he will join the team. "And if I win?" he asks. "What do I get?" "Anything you want," says she. Another big laugh. I was revolted.

When puppetry figures of girls or women are shown, it seems to me that they more often reflect the puppeteers' sexual fantasies than the images a normal little girl of six or eight or ten would identify with. Almost invariably when Bil Baird creates a marionette of a human female over the age of five, unless she's a comic virago, she has a wasp waist, breasts like circus balloons, and hips like a roller coaster. This stereotyped sex object has little meaning to a girl child, who would prefer a puppet like herself, or one she feels she might grow to be like. For boy children, it introduces the impossible dream.

We've already discussed at some length sexist stereotypes in Chapter 6, Implications. We've grown so inured to these stereotypes and our thinking has been so conditioned by them, we don't always appreciate how inexcusably gross they are. If people mentally transpose every humorous or degrading reference to (usually in euphemism) or depiction of a woman's anatomy to its masculine equivalent, they would be up in arms. The very men who are most hearty in expressing their amusement about female bodies are those who would be most shocked if the derision were directed at theirs.

I have witnessed any number of scenes in which an actor shapes an hourglass in the air with his hands and then juggles two invisible heavy melons, to the hilarity of the audience. Unusual entertainment for children? Not at all. I've wondered how hilarious it would be if an actress described the hero's sexual attributes in as explicit mimed detail, including what she would like to do with them.

And speaking of sexual attributes, the standard cartoons for young people are remarkable in this regard. Some masculine indications are unmistakable: men have beards, mustaches, or bald heads; stags have antlers; bull elephants have tusks; lions have manes, and that's about as far as it goes. Women may or may not have a swelling between the collarbones and the waist, but cows have udders and female seals have a daintiness the males lack.

Similar to the convention in animated films of drawing people with four fingers instead of five, there are the conventional sexual taboos and stereotypes—initiated, I'm sure, by masculine animators. In animation, the primary sex organs are the eyelashes, which are to be found only on the female, regardless of the species: girl, doe, mare, goldfish, or snake. All have long, furry, fluttery lashes covering soft, melting eyes, lashes that could give one pneumonia if one stood long enough in their breeze. Without hair, antlers, tusks, and mane, a male is recognizable as such by his lack of eyelashes.

Fortunately, none of these cartoon characters has ever to eliminate solid or liquid body wastes, because the organs to perform these functions, as well as the function of reproduction, are conspicuously absent. Ogden Nash wrote:

The turtle lives 'twixt plated decks
Which practically conceal its sex.
I think it clever of the turtle
In such a fix to be so fertile.

That fix is nothing to what the animated figures are in. I think it terribly clever of all concerned that the lack of a reproductive system doesn't inhibit them from providing whatever offspring the play scripts demand.

There is still hypocrisy about sex in entertainment for children. Much of this can be traced back to the policies established for the Hollywood industry when Will H. Hays was chosen movie czar in 1922 in an attempt to provide self-censorship for films. Mr. Hays set up rules for American films which attempted to keep sex to an irreducible minimum. Married couples, regardless of the length of their marriage or the number of their children, could never be shown in bed together; twin beds were *de rigueur.* If the husband sat on the edge of his wife's bed, at least one of his feet had to remain on the floor. A kiss could not be held for more than a prescribed number of seconds. Pregnant women had to be as flat as boards, even in their ninth month; the baby just "appeared" at the hospital.

The false impressions of family life and the relationships between the sexes created by these old films are still being perpetuated on television. Because producers couldn't be forthright about sex and family relationships, they had to resort to subterfuge to express sexuality. The results are a prurience that is substituted for honesty. Although the Hays Office is a thing of the past, its heritage is still apparent, not only in old reruns but in the newer films of organizations that put down their roots under its administration.

The United Artists film *Mixed Company,* with Joseph Bologna and Barbara Harris, is a case in point. The wife has been badgering her husband to make her pregnant with their fourth child. He is reluctant, but she knows what to do about that. After a spate of ear nibblings and nuzzlings, the lights go out. The audience is then regaled by a darkened screen filled with the sound of connubial giggling that lets us know she has demolished his will power. When the movie was released for TV, the giggles were cut from the sound track.

Mixed Company handles another sexual subject "humorously." When the wife fails to become pregnant, the presumption is made that the problem is hers. Then it develops that Father had come down with mumps while on the road recently; sterility resulted. Father indignantly denies its possibility, being proud of his sexual prowess. The implication is clear that sterility in the woman is either a tragedy or a misfortune, depending on whether she has already borne children. Sterility in the man is comical, even grotesque. Although the film includes more on male sterility than a young audience needs to know, there is no further explanation of the part mumps played in it. This could raise fears in the mind of any boy or girl who ever had the disease or who comes down with it subsequently. It's a case of too much and too little sex information for children.

A film like *Mixed Company* doesn't seem to be able to by-pass any sexual stereotypes, so of course Mother is portrayed as always being able to get her way with Father by shedding a tear or by being devious and manipulative. Also, while she does occasional volunteer work for an adoption agency, she is a model housewife and mother. I found the depiction of this role interesting: mother and the children were busy in the kitchen and did some cleaning up after meals, but no one lifted a finger at any time to clean or tidy the upper-middle-class house the family lived in. There was never evidence of a maid, yet the floor was always dust-free and gleaming, the rugs and furniture always immaculate and in good repair, the woodwork spotless. Inasmuch as there were six healthy children occupying every inch, I envied the mother her secret of success.

Actually, this was a dream family in a dream house mas-querading as reality, all as phony as a three-dollar bill. The film presents to the audience only selected aspects of situations which will develop the film's premise. Every dramatic work does this. Selectivity is a writer's basic tool. But work of merit uses believable selections from believable situations: the selec-tions give in microcosm a sample of a larger reality. When the selections are false to the larger reality, as in *Mixed Company,* we get an elaborate make-believe in which the artificial relations between husband and wife and the fairy tale home run by the mother are typical of the shoddiness of the whole movie.

Equally phony and far from the fake sentiment of such Hol-lywood marriages and affairs are the relationships which make no pretense of including love. Physical passion without emotion is enough for the James Bonds, Matt Helms, and Superfly types who embody the male wet dream in which one supremely desir-able woman after another flings herself into their automatically receptive arms. In these fantasies the protagonists—and those members of the audience who identify with them—are able to perform sexually with never diminishing prowess. In the process James Bond et al. may be somewhat brutal and sadistic. No matter; it all adds to the lady's pleasure. If it becomes "necessary" to kill the woman when our hero discovers she is exercising her charms on him for her own nefarious ends—to extract his secrets or even to lure him to destruction—then he kills her, his only qualm being the elimination of so lovely an animal. The moment of her death can come at a climax of ecstasy in his embrace. Her death is triumphant for her, for how can such happiness as he has given her ever again be equalled, let alone surpassed? What higher fate can woman aspire to than to die in her moment of glory?

To see these situation for what they are, reverse the roles. How many male dreamers can accept being knifed or shot in a climax of perfect rapture as the ideal way to depart this world? Instead of finding the same positive values as when the woman dies in their arms, the picture seems out of focus when they contemplate dying in hers. They're more likely to think of the female insect who begins to devour her mate's head at the instant of fertilization.

Loving—or caring, affection, or whatever you call it—is frequently absent in many relationships between men and women young people see in films and on TV. Sex is limited to copulation. This portrayal is as damaging as that of the Hays Office, and perhaps more hurtful to children whose lives it influences by establishing false expectations of adult behavior.

Honesty and dignity in the presentation of sex to young audiences are of outstanding importance. Much of children's attitudes about sex is formed by absorption from their families and their peers, but much of what children choose to emulate in this area of behavior comes from their entertainment. In Chapter 6, Implications, we discussed stereotypical male/female images and roles, and so on. A relatively few programs for young audiences, regardless of the medium, deal with a mutually respectful, loving relationship between a man and a woman that is free of sexist overtones. If you who want this for your young people fail to make your voice heard, we'll continue to get films with mucho macho heroes and others like *The Bad News Bears* and *Mixed Company*. They've done very well indeed at the box office, and producers will need to be convinced that you are not content with their point of view before they will change it.

9. Violence

————————⟨∞⟩————————

Violence above all troubles those who are solicitous about the emotional and mental health of young people. Studies of violence have been made in the United States and abroad by pediatricians, psychologists, sociologists, educators, governmental bureaus, journalists, and research arms of the film and television industries. The results are often contradictory. A psychiatric thesis on violence doesn't necessarily draw the same conclusions from the same evidence as one funded by the media.

The body of evidence by nonindustry-connected evaluators is that we live in violent times and young people are exposed to violence in many aspects of their lives—news telecasts about murder, rape, political terrorism, skyjackings, riots, and crime in the streets; comic books, newspaper cartoon strips, lurid magazine covers; disorders in the classrooms and schoolyards, and, possibly, family disagreements settled by physical means. Among these specialists there is universal agreement that violence in their entertainment compounds the effects of the other forms of violence, and is not good for young people. There is lack of unanimity as to how much damage is being done to children, but only as to the degree. Disturbed sleep patterns, increased hostility, and fearful behavior are only some of the harmful effects that have been traced to entertainment violence. Since our subject is Understanding Your Child's Entertainment, let's think about what children want. After humor, what they like is action. This is the problem for dramatists and for other adults concerned about boys and girls. Our concept of what action is will to a degree control our thinking. Is action of necessity "violence"?

In a production for a young audience, the writer and director are aware the emphasis must be on action instead of talk. Children want to see what is happening, not be told about it. There must be a certain amount of physical movement on stage or on camera to hold the attention of the spectator. This is true for adult theater; it's even more essential for boys and girls. But what many theater people don't seem to understand is the difference between action and activity. The essence of drama is conflict. Action is the development of this conflict through movement in plot, mood, and characterizations. If a player jumps on a table and sings, if two actors scuffle, if one chases another up an aisle—all this must be germane to the story. If it's not germane, if it contributes nothing to advance the *play*, then it's merely artificial activity with no purpose but to keep attention focused on the scene or to "pad" the production by having the business extend its running time. As we said in another context, better writing, direction, and acting should hold the audience without this activity. No matter how frenetic the busyness is, it's still activity, not action.

Activity can be anything: someone walking up and down, bouncing a ball, carrying a candle from one side of the room to another. . . . So can action. The test is whether what is being done advances the production in any significant way. Violence can be either activity or action, subject to the same criterion.

If violence is activity, there is no more reason for its inclusion than for keeping any other kind of activity. Indeed, there is less reason. If the violence is action, what does it contribute? Can the contribution be made through other means? Does the play present values that put the violence in perspective?

So now we come to the heart of the problem: When is action violence and when is violence justified dramatically?

A Webster definition of violence includes: "Strength or energy actively displayed or exerted; vehement, forcible, or destructive action; force. . . . Vehemence in feeling; passion; ardor; fury; fervor."

Some forms of forceful physical energy are not considered violence: an all-out tennis match, men laying railroad track, racing horses. . . . But change the circumstances somewhat: a hockey game in which a difference of opinion is debated by fists and hockey sticks; bandits shooting at the railroad men; one jockey trying to force another off the track. . . . These are violent.

Take another instance. A teen-ager fears his neighbor is ill in a darkened house and breaks down his door to go to the rescue. The same teen-ager breaks down the same door in the same darkened house to loot and vandalize it. Clearly, only the second is violence. But since the acts are identical, it is the intent that is the determinant. Or take two individuals. Suddenly one picks up a nearby object and hits the other over the head. Suppose one is a man with a full wallet and the other a mugger. Now suppose that the two are year-old babies and the object is a rattle. In the latter case the circumstances and the intent change violence to the most innocuous of occurrences.

Dr. George Gerbner and Dr. Larry Gross, professors of communications at the University of Pennsylvania, make annual studies of TV violence, published as the "Violence Profile." For the purposes of these surveys, violence is defined as "the overt expression of physical force." This force may be intentional or accidental. It includes catastrophes and acts of nature, as well as acts by persons. It gives equal statistical weight to incidents whether their context is humorous or serious.

These studies, among others, tabulate instances of violent acts in programs and in commercials. The preponderant evidence indicates that the hours in which young people may reasonably be presumed to be watching TV are filled with violence. I agree wholeheartedly that there is far too much of it, but I feel that sometimes these surveys lack the moderating influence of common sense, which even young children possess.

Although Gerbner and Gross define violence their way for their purposes, for ours we must make distinctions they don't. In our concern for what displays of insensitivity, brutality, sadism, and the like are doing to our children, we needn't consider that the violence of a volcanic eruption, an earthquake, or a hurricane is within our purview, as long as the violence is confined to nature's fury. When the camera relishes bloody corpses of human being and animals—in glorious Technicolor or its equivalent—then it is our concern.

A survey may record it as a violent occurrence if a schoolboy takes a playful swing at his friend. I should not. As before, the intent is what would govern my decision as to whether or not an activity is "violent." Intent, and whether hurt or damage results. A pie in the face is certainly violence of a kind, but it's not our concern here.

Further, accepting that an action is violent if the intent is destructive and nonhumorous, and if it results in hurt or damage, there are degrees of violence. The pie in the face is not to be equated with napalm that burns one's head off. Kicking a bridge partner's shins is not the equivalent in violence of deliberately running down a man with a car.

Even allowing that some of the surveys on violence are lacking in perspective, the amount and degree of serious violence young people see on TV and in films is genuinely appalling. Over the span of a week, children can be presented with demonstrations of how to kill or maim other human beings and animals that range from the prosaic (guns, knives, bludgeons, poisons, electricity, gas, garrotes, hatchets, drownings) to the more exotic (bee venom, boomerangs, spears, maces, spike heels). They are shown from time to time how to make and handle firearms, Molotov cocktails, and other grisly weapons, and often given justification for their use.

Violence can be entertainment of a high order to young people who are hooked on it. I speak in terms of addiction because violence *is* addictive. When boys and girls are bombarded by the violence spewed from TV and films, they can lose interest in dramatizations that posit problems resolved through thoughtful, sometimes laborious efforts of a peaceful nature. It's easier to identify with the action figure than the thinker—not that I imply action and thought are antithetical. But violent action can be the result of thought insufficient to develop other solutions. The image of Alexander cutting the Gordian knot with one slash of his sword is more appealing than that of an aspirant patiently trying to undo the knot by the rules. Violence can be a glamorous form of escapism to children fenced in by regulations in every aspect of their lives.

Boys and girls have, in most cases, concepts of good and evil. Justice may be an abstract term that means little to them, but I've yet to meet a child who didn't know what was "fair" and what wasn't. They rejoice to see "fairness" or good or right triumph over "unfairness" or evil or wrong, but the depiction of violence can betray and confuse them. It can betray children by persuading them violence is the only appropriate or possible solution—whereas, if instead a less inflammatory, more critical analysis of the situation were made, any number of peaceful alternatives might be discovered. It confuses them by presenting the violent figures of the bad guys as more dashing, more desirable to emulate.

Take Robert Louis Stevenson's *Treasure Island.* The plot is sure-fire, particularly with older boys and girls who daydream swashbuckling adventures on magical isles.

The protagonist is young Jim Hawkins, into whose widowed mother's inn comes a mysterious seafaring man, who dies leaving a map to buried treasure. Jim turns to influential members of the community, who unite into a small band to charter a ship and take the treasure. Their ship is manned by pirates led by Long John Silver, and action follows thick and fast until Jim and his friends are safe with the treasure in England. Long John, who had protected Jim from his fellow ruffians, has escaped, and the pirates are marooned on Treasure Island.

Involvement is dependent on how admirable Jim is, so that he can embody the audience's ideal selves. When the story is done as a musical, there are opportunities for rousing songs to stir the blood. But dramatizations of *Treasure Island* fail, even with a strong Jim and credible situations, when the pirates come off as being far more exciting than the good guys. The squire, the doctor, and the captain, and whoever else represents the side we are meant to cheer for, can't compete with the lusty, swaggering, roistering pirates. When the pirates invite Jim to join them, the audience thinks he's lost his mind for standing by the anemic, colorless, downright dull friends he started with. The audience forgets what has been insufficiently stressed: the pirates are scum who want to murder them all.

Making good more attractive than evil is a problem many dramatists don't work out, and nowhere is it more essential of solution than in *Treasure Island*. It's Long John Silver's character that embodies whatever ambiguities the story holds. He must be repellent to the audience, who must comprehend his and Jim's mutual ambivalent attraction. (The old black-and-white film with Jackie Cooper and Wallace Berry captured this as none of its successors has been able to do.) The story shouldn't center around Jim's decision whether to join the more magnetic bad guys, but around the continuing struggle of right against wrong, developed in terms of strong action from first to last. As long as this action doesn't result in visual or imagined horrors, the "violence" is justified dramatically.

The *Treasure Island* dilemma plagues productions that portray the outlaw/gangster/mercenary soldier of fortune as more gallant, more free-spirited than the sheriff/policeman/law-abiding businessman/laborer, whose life is restricted by laws and consideration for others. When the good guys wear white hats and the bad guys wear black and characterizations are equally direct, there's no difficulty in choosing up sides. However, when complexities of characterization and plot contrive to encourage less stereotyped roles and stories, there's always the danger that the violent bad guy will win out over the not-so-violent good guy in the sympathies of the children. Where the good guy is just as violent, this is an unhappy alternative, because it shows the sympathetic side, the one to emulate, using violence to settle any questions. The film *Death Wish* is an example. As the hero, Charles Bronson forms a one-man vigilante committee to destroy the criminals who prey upon innocent citizens. He is judge, juror, and executioner. Despite his horrendous conception of justice, his personality is so forceful that even adults are seduced into accepting his values and his murderous career as admirable. The audience of which I was a part cheered wildly each time he shot a malefactor. They yelled at the screen to egg him on: "Kill the bastard! Get the rats!"

Violence betrays and confuses children in other ways as well. The underworld used to call a revolver an "equalizer." It meant that with a loaded gun in his hand, a small, weak man was the equal of anyone else, no matter how tall or strong. Intelligence didn't matter, or courage, or integrity—only the gun. Likewise, violence levels all causes, all reasons for being, all solutions. An average TV drama of an hour, an average film of 90 to 120 minutes—neither has time to deliver a history, sociology, or anthropology lecture before the story begins, to set the scene and establish an understanding of the events to be depicted. An adequate explanation of the reasons out of which the dramatized situation grows, with conflicting issues and complexities of personality, economics, and ethnic, religious, or patriotic loyalties, is not possible. Nor can this information, necessary to comprehend *why* we start from where the play opens, be easily incorporated into the production within the time limit.

Adults can be presumed to have lived long enough to recall from their own experiences what some depicted events are about. Many adults took active part in the Vietnamese conflict, the Korean "police action," World War II, or the Spanish Civil War. Many can remember from first hand the Great Depression, some the Roaring Twenties, even World War I and earlier. They have heard their elders speak of the Spanish-American War. The American Civil War was lived through by our grandparents' grandparents. Where information about the past is not personal, adults acquire it through study or general reading. When they view an "action" drama of the past, recent or distant, they can supply from their own background the details to fill out the whys and wherefores, or to correct historical errors. Adults understand the larger scene of which the film or TV drama is only one part, and the actual consequences of the events on history and individual lives.

Boys and girls can't do this. Few children can remember clearly anything that occurred before they were three, and then their memories are personal. Children five to seven years old, as we mentioned when discussing nostalgia, have only the haziest notions of the world before they were born. They are nine or ten before they get a beginning grasp of historical events.

In the educational system of New York City, the one with which I'm most familiar, boys and girls begin to acquire a superficial knowledge of the past when they enter kindergarten at five. Here they learn little anecdotes of patriotic figures, usually tied in with school holidays. They cut out paper turkeys for Thanksgiving and hatchets for Washington's Birthday, and in assembly they may see a playlet performed by older children for Columbus Day. Because this is the first experience away from home for most children, concerns of the kindergarten class are more with adjusting a child to the school system and to other children than with formal study.

In the first three grades, in an expanding fashion, children learn what goes on in the school and the neighborhood, and the function of "community helpers"—police, firemen, letter carriers, etc. Not until the third and fourth grades, at eight and nine years of age, do pupils learn the past of their city, the original Indian tribes, the coming of the Dutch, the sale of Manhattan Island. . . . In the fourth grade, pupils take up the explorers. The Revolutionary and Civil Wars are studied by fifth-graders (ten years old). In the fifth grade, too, first studies are made of Europe and the rest of the world. These programs shift from year to year as the Board of Education reconsiders the curriculum in the light of current pressures. For example, a black history program, supplementing social studies, was recently instituted. Its inclusion meant adjusting other subjects.

School systems throughout the United States vary in details, but there is no important difference among them in subjects covered, except in local history.

The implications for entertainment are clear. A seven- or

eight-year-old knows little if anything about Elizabethan sea battles, invasions by Mongol hordes, Colosseum spectacles, scalpings in the French and Indian War, the French Terror, Vietnamese fire bombings, Pharaoh's army in the Red Sea, the rum runners of Prohibition, or even the attack on Pearl Harbor. When such events are dramatized, the big climactic scene, and often scenes leading up to it, always shows the gory siege of the castle, the armada in flames, the enemy dying in the trenches, the massacre of the rival mob, the decapitation or maiming of a few characters, or the shoot-out at the O.K. Corral.

Violence designed for adults but frequently seen by children is displayed, often proudly, under the spurious guise of patriotism, religion, or education. As "patriotism is the last refuge of the scoundrel," so the purveyors of violence present themselves as supporters of causes the general public considers laudable. Whatever value much of this "action" has for adults, it has none for children, to whom all that matters is which side they are encouraged to identify with. Cain's murder of Abel and David's slaying of Goliath aren't "religion" to a small child; except that the players are wearing loincloths and sandals instead of chaps and boots, there's no difference between them and a confrontation with six-shooters at high noon in front of the Last Chance Saloon. The rebels storming Bunker Hill, the Battle of Gettysburg, the Siege of the Alamo, or the Battle of Corregidor—these teach a child little of patriotism. It's just our side versus theirs, with a change of costume and armament.

Crusaders' battles in *Ivanhoe,* the harrying of the British by the Indians in *The Last of the Mohicans,* the wars of El Cid— these teach neither history nor literature. Aside from the dramatizations' distorting the facts more often than otherwise, children don't have, nor are they given, a frame of reference which differentiates one cause from another. Without understanding better what's involved, young audiences make little distinction between the hanging of Nathan Hale and the hanging of a horse thief; between fighting the British in the name of freedom and fighting the police opposed to bootlegging. A chase is a chase. Simon Legree and Eliza, the townspeople and Frankenstein's monster, the Indians and the wagon train— fiction or reality, young children don't distinguish.

In the name of patriotism, religion, or education, the selective use of violent episodes creates false notions not easily dislodged from the mind. Boys and girls are "educated" by the media to look at the past as a jumble of one meaningless bloody incident after another. Long peaceful years are seldom depicted, and even when they are, they don't compete in the memory with violent ones. Taken out of the context of their time, facts as presented can be little more than lies by implication. When causes and motivations are presented only as an excuse for violence, then violence is the equalizer, and it equalizes on the most debased level. Ethical and moral judgments, respect for life, property, and the civilized arts, even common humanity, are "equalized" by violence with corruption of spirit, cruelty, and sensationalism. Violence can topple a citadel of learning as easily as it demolishes an assassin's stronghold. Only "we" and "they" matter, whichever. As humor that is irrelevant or inappropriate can take over a production to its detriment, so can violence, with the added factor that presentation of violence is, according to most specialists, harmful to the child.

There's more. As violence ignores causes, it ignores effects. When a castle is besieged, we may or may not be shown a man screaming as he is hurled from the battlements. We almost never recognize and identify with minor characters before they disappear in agony. This one is not depicted as a man but as an object, or, if an enemy, as one of "them" and therefore expendable. But he's not an object. He had a mother and a father who loved him, perhaps brothers and sisters, and other relatives to whom he was dear. He might have a wife and children of his own. He might have loved cats, fishing, and roasted chestnuts, and detested bedbugs, skittles, and turnips. In short, he was a human being, and if he is to be killed for our amusement, we should appreciate him as such. This isn't irrelevant. We saw him being wounded. If the victory—or the defeat—has any meaning, we should be aware of its cost. What happens to him next, this nameless "thing"? Is he left a mangled heap of bones and flesh for the crows to peck at? Do his friends drag him away, so that the shreds of his life are saved by his having both legs amputated? Does he eventually return home on stumps, a helpless embittered beggar, to be a drain on his family? Do his children sink into poverty when he can no longer support them?

Let's come up to date. So many films show a holdup in which the gas station owner or the proprietor of a little papa-mama candy store is killed. Once he's dead, the attention of the audience follows the "important" character, the teen-ager who has shot him. The sympathies of the audience are directed to *his* problems. The shopowner has ceased to exist, as if he was never more than an excuse for the "protagonist's" troubles to center on briefly. Indeed, it's frequently implied that if the shopowner hadn't been so obnoxious as to provoke our protagonist by resisting the holdup, the "hero" wouldn't have been forced to kill him. Therefore, it's his own fault and no one else's that he's dead. This is the same kind of logic that called the Jews and not Hitler responsible for their slaughter. This fictional proprietor, who may be on screen only for the few moments it takes to rob and kill him, is every bit as real as his fictional murder. He may have a wife who is hospitalized with a heart attack after she falls over his body. His thriving little business must be boarded up until it falls apart under the weight of continuing expenses and loss of income. The mother the proprietor was supporting goes on welfare and his children are placed in foster homes. They become emotionally disturbed, in constant trouble, and with a prospective bleak future. Unrealistic? Not at all. This kind of chain of events is not uncommon when senseless, violent disaster strikes at a family unprepared to deal with unreason and terror.

To a boy or girl, a mugging, a beating, or a killing is presented as a one-two-three moment of exhilarating action. The "kicks" they get are warranted by the inconsequential damage to inconsequential victims. But children should know that these victims are people, and they and their families may suffer lifelong pain, grief, and ruinous expense, not in any way commensurate with the momentary thrill the perpetrator enjoys.

Sometimes, as in *The Godfather,* which many children have told me they have seen, the violence is sickeningly, sadistically personal—we meet the victims before they die so graphically. But most violence in films and TV, and in life—unless it happens to us or to someone we know—is as impersonal as a computer print-out. When a submarine sinks a liner, neither the commander of the U-boat nor the seaman who releases the torpedo knows one passenger or crew member. When the Germans sent the V-1 and V-2 rockets into England, they could have no knowledge of which individual lives would be snuffed out. Neither could the men on Allied heavy bombers in their forays over Dresden, nor in the American planes that dropped the atom bombs on Hiroshima and Nagasaki. Someone aboard merely pushed a button at a prescribed moment, and death visited thousands of anonymous men, women, and children. I doubt that the button-pushers could have carried out their assignments face to face with the victims or if they could have permitted themselves to think of the men as their fathers and brothers, the women as their mothers and sisters, and the children as their own. This impersonality was their defense against guilt in time of war, when the end, many of us believed, justified the means. This refusal to recognize victims as human carries over to much entertainment for adults, which children see as films in movie houses or later on TV.

This kind of violence, too, is an equalizer. Unless children can rid themselves of the impersonality, the lack of interest that converts victims to things or "them," we are bringing up people with deadened perceptions and diminished humanity.

Children have told me their parents have taken them to *The Exorcist* and *Jaws,* two of the most terrifying, suspenseful films produced in years. The boys and girls thought the pictures were great, super, wow! Yes, after seeing them they wouldn't sleep without a light in their room. Yes, they had bad dreams afterward. Yes, they were afraid to go swimming. And yes, they would like to see both movies again. I've asked parents why they take children to these films, *Death Wish,* and similar ones, and I've been told:

- "We couldn't get a baby-sitter."
- "The children are too young to understand what's going on."
- "The children are too mature to be upset."
- "The children are so used to things like this, a little more won't hurt."

Pediatricians and psychologists don't agree that films like these cause no personality, psychical, or physical damage. But parents are no different from anyone else, and we all rationalize.

To go back to our question: When is violence justified dramatically? It's impossible to justify on any ground entertainment violence of the nature we've been discussing. The lack of sensitivity about pain or death, the absence of a context setting forth the full history leading to the violence, the distortion in thinking violence creates, the misconceptions violence perpetuates, the lack of alternatives to violence, and the immunity to the results of violence—these cannot but be contributing agents to the increase in real violence in our culture.

The *New York Times* of August 25, 1976, on its op-ed page, printed the views of William Serrin on "The Decline and Fall of Detroit." Mr. Serrin, a journalist who has been writing about that city for eleven years, accuses a long list of those who are responsible for the "destruction" of Detroit, including:

> Black people like Fred Williamson and Jim Brown [who] found they could make a bundle making violent, sex-filled movies. And the young blacks started acting in the fashion of the Hollywood actors, and it was no longer acting. It was violence and death on the Detroit East Side.

Of course, it doesn't follow that all violence in entertainment leads inevitably to violent action; other factors in a violent climate must share the onus. But there are those qualified to judge who feel entertainment is not blameless, and I go along with them.

Teachers have told me that at one time they dreaded Fridays. This was because on Thursday nights ABC-TV aired a program called *Kung Fu,* starring David Carradine. Although the premise of the program was that violence is abhorrent to a sentient being, all its problems were eventually solved by the hero's (reluctantly) hurling his opponent into unconsciousness, breaking his bones, or performing some similar little act to point out the error of his ways. All the next day in school the children, boys and girls alike, were difficult to control. Not only in the corridors and yard but even in the classroom, scraps erupted at every turn. The children kicked out at each other, mostly in play, but not always. Discipline was exhausting to maintain. The familiar expression "Thank God it's Friday" had ironic implications for teachers as long as *Kung Fu* kept its Thursday time slot.

Children's play reflects their interests, and play deals more and more with imitating favorite TV shows. When puppies and kittens romp with each other they are developing skills nature intended them to use as hunters. I don't think it too far-fetched to draw an analogy with the games TV is teaching our young children to play.

Earlier we referred to Alexander's cutting of the Gordian knot, but there was another point to be made which the same example illustrates, and which violence stresses: immediate results, immediate satisfactions. Violence, the equalizer, makes no distinction between a protracted court trial and a vigilante committee's arbitrary judgment and execution. It doesn't distinguish between riches acquired in a lifetime's laborious honorable efforts and a five-minute bank holdup; between success in a career based on solid preparation and craftsmanship and a flash-in-the-pan lucky break to stardom. Only results count.

So much for the violence we've been discussing, for which we can find scant justification. Is all violence in children's entertainment equally reprehensible? Speaking as a critic of the dramatic values of a production, as well as with a concern for the audience, I say No. Emphatically. To deprive an audience— including an audience of young people—of violence in all circumstances is absurd and unfair.

We must remember that many children like to be frightened, as long as they know the danger is pretend. At amusement parks the House of Horrors, with its skeletons, ghosts, and monsters leaping out of the darkness, is one of the "attractions" many children make a beeline for. Roller coasters carry screaming boys and girls, who plead to go around again on another heart-stopping ride.

If a child is to relish this titilating fear, to indulge it must be a voluntary decision. If he enters the Horror House or rides the roller coaster pressured by his peers or by threat of the stigma of cowardice from a parent, then his fear is genuine and there's nothing enjoyable about it, including a possible aftermath of nightmares or tension. Fear can be fun only while it is make-believe.

We must also remember that most children are as insatiably curious as cats. They want to see and to know all kinds of things their elders already know about and don't care to contemplate further. At a magic show in the Felt Forum at Madison Square Garden, a magician purported to cut a girl almost in half with a rotating electric saw. The illusion was perfect, with the white surgical sheets and medical uniforms of the "attendants" spattered with clotted gore. The audience was invited onstage to examine the "body" more closely, with the saw half-buried in it. I couldn't bring myself to look, nor could some other adults, but a long line of grownups and children filed across the stage. Near me one boy of six cried bitterly when his older brother came back with a report full of gruesome details. At the close of the performance, I followed him from the theater to find out why. Because, he explained, he hadn't been allowed to see for himself.

As adults, we have to come to a reasonable appraisal of how much of this kind of experience our own children can take safely. Do you want yours to see *Jaws* or *The Exorcist* or *Death Wish?* Do you want them to ride the roller coaster on a full stomach or at all? Do you want them to see the woman half cut through? You know your boys and girls, and what they want. You also know what *you* want for them. Where you disagree, you should know why.

What is involved in permissible violence for children?

The violence must be necessary. It must be more than logical—it must be inevitable. The audience must understand there is no alternative when Jack cuts the beanstalk and the giant falls to his death, or when Gretel pushes the witch into the oven.

It must satisfy the children's sense of justice and convince them the protagonists are permanently safe from the evil that has threatened them.

The age of the child is a factor. What could be thrilling to a ten-year-old could overwhelm a child of five, who has neither the relative emotional maturity nor the experience of the older child to protect him.

The distance from the source of the violence is to be considered. In *Jack and the Beanstalk,* the threat comes from the giant. In arena staging, where the giant is almost in touching range of many of the children, or in a conventional theater where he runs up the aisle seeking Jack, brushing past the seats, he can be a figure of genuine terror to small children. He is *alive* and he is *right there.* He is removed from this intimacy by a proscenium arch, curtains, and the height of the stage. Dramatically he's just as effective. Physically he's less disturbing. A film in a movie house can be as threatening as a live play. The large-screen close-ups can bring violence overpoweringly near to a child. The small TV tube reduces the size of the giant, but it brings him directly into the home, the sanctuary.

A child's reaction to fear may be modified by other circumstances: whether he is in a theater with other children mostly, or whether parents are there with a reassuring arm, or whether he is alone in an empty house with the TV set.

The kind and degree of violence are to be considered in the question of permissibility. A fistfight between two pirates could highlight a scene. The fight could be be played for blood and guts, straight drama, or laughs. Obviously the audience would react differently in each instance. The fight could take some moments, building to a climax, with the excitement of the audience also building. If neither fighter is seriously hurt, the children would be involved in the action and also diverted by seeing adults doing on a larger scale what they themselves do sometimes. On the other hand, if the pirates are using cutlasses and seriously intending to sever limbs or kill, then the fight should be brief, and be over before the audience can be worked up into participation. It should not be graphically realistic for a young audience, and the results should be clean and swift, with a minimum of gore and overt pain, and unless the story demands it inevitably, no death or dismemberment. The suspense created must not cause fear in the audience; it must be relieved before it continues too long or is too intense for the age group. Most pirate films seem to dispose of pirates neatly and efficiently by having them fall from masts or be hurled over guardrails into the sea. Shooting violence for young people is frequently of the bang-bang-you're-dead type, where the victim clutches his heart and drops. It's usually over almost as soon as it starts. We've spoken about the unrealistic lack of suffering earlier. Now we're dealing with unreality as a protective device, rather than as a dramatic cop-out.

The object of the violence must deserve his fate. Children's sympathies can be readily enlisted on the side of fair play by intelligent writing and characterizations. Their sense of justice demands that the good guys be rewarded and the bad guys get what's coming to them. A deep sense of outrage is stirred when this isn't so. When the witch goes into the oven, this is violence they applaud. Not only is she a danger to Hansel and Gretel while she lives, but she represents life's evil to the audience. When she burns, the audience is freed of its dangers as well. If the witch pushed Gretel, with whom the audience identifies, into the oven, it would be unutterably hideous. When Jack kills the giant, the children rejoice; if the giant slew Jack and his mother and took back the treasure, the audience would go into shock.

The audience must have all the facts where violence is concerned. We have discussed the fact that children watching battles or other violent scenes from adult dramas know little of events leading up to those scenes, and perhaps even less of their consequences. In dramatized folk fairy tales, the audience knows everything that is relevant. There is no past. The story just happens. The characters are types more than individuals, and attributes are delineated clearly and without complexity. There is no future but happily ever after. The references are not to a time and place, but to the story's meaning to children. In the chapter on Relevance we mentioned a few of those meanings. Now it's time to consider the violence in these stories, which so many parents are afraid of.

Jack, we've said, must kill the giant. The alternatives to this act of violence are unsatisfactory. Not only is the only safe giant a dead one, but we mustn't diminish Jack's heroism by giving him a hollow enemy or a reformed one. The end of the story is foreordained, and rightfully so.

Let's consider now one of the most violent of all fairy tales for children: *Hop o' My Thumb.* There are a great number of stories like this, in which the hero is called upon to perform acts that are bloody by any standards. As in *Hop o' My Thumb,* his enemies are shown to be wicked, so evil that the audience acquiesces enthusiastically in their demise. But audiences also cheer Charles Bronson on his assumption of the role of vengeful justice in *Death Wish.* What's the difference? Plenty. Bronson roams through the film like the Angel of Death; he entraps other men into attacking him so that he can with a clear conscience destroy them. Although they are the scum of the earth, they are still human beings with civil and moral rights, which he violates as if he had every law of God and man behind him. In *Hop o' My Thumb,* the violence centers around the ogre. An ogre is an eater of human flesh. In folklore he's the embodiment of all the nameless fears people possess. No actual figure, including his, can be as terrifying as what we are capable of imagining. He attempts to kill Hop and his brothers and, killing his own children instead, brings justice upon himself. When Hop destroys the ogre, there is no doubt he is saving himself and his brothers from being "harvested" like cattle. Hop by this deed not only demonstrates his superiority to his larger, stronger brothers, he puts to rest permanently the terrors we dread in the night. The audience grasps without explanation that the ogre is not human—not even something that could exist—but is the personification of a mythical concept; more, the issue of good and evil is unambiguous. With this as with other fairy tales containing typical characters, children old enough for school know that the stories are allegories (of course not in that term) and not realistic; they know this is a "pretend" story that could never be. The audience for *Death Wish* knows each victim in the film has his real counterpart walking the streets; members of the audience are manipulated to abet the protagonist in taking the law into his own hands, action contrary to the principle of any civilized society, which action they abhor in more rational hours. The emphasis in *Death Wish* and other films with basically similar points of view is always on convincing simulation of the real world. Therefore, for children in the right age range, the violence of *Hop o' My Thumb* is justifiable; that of *Death Wish* is not.

In *The Table, the Ass, and the Stick,* there is no question of law, even corrupt or inefficient law, to mete out justice. Law does not exist. Accordingly, when the thieving innkeeper is beaten by the magic stick he has stolen until he makes restitution of other stolen property, he calls his punishment down on himself. This is satisfying to a child's sense of fair play. No one is permanently injured and justice has been done in the only way possible.

The witch-queen in *Snow White and the Seven Dwarfs* is analogous to *Hop*'s ogre. She is as wicked as he, and as determined to destroy the protagonist. As a figure of magic, she has no more actuality, and the children in their own way recognize her as a symbol of evil. She has to go, and—like the innkeeper, but to a much greater degree—she brings her fate upon herself. It is important that no stigma for her death attach to Snow White or her friends, so the queen is shown to expire in an excess of rage. Interestingly, Rumpelstiltskin, who has been foiled in his attempts to steal the child of the miller's daughter, meets his doom the same way. In both instances, dramatists have been ingenious in devising ways to kill off the queen and Rumpelstiltskin without having any messy bodies lying around the stage. One of the most popular is to have them disappear in a blinding flash.

I remember a *Puss in Boots* enacted by puppets for a young audience. The playwright was afraid the four- and five-year-olds would be frightened by the ogre, so she wrote him out of the story. The result was that Puss, the true hero of the play, missed his big scene. He had no one to contend against worthy of his mettle and he was lessened by the lack. So was the production. Unforgivable. If boys and girls are old enough to know the tale of *Puss in Boots,* they're old enough to see the whole thing. Instead of being frightened, if the director is sufficiently skillful to keep the ogre remote from the audience, the children are amused and delighted that Puss is able to trick him into becoming a mouse. They appreciate, even so young, the ludicrous aspects of the situation, and they cheer Puss's cleverness and courage in using brains where brute force won't work.

In *Ali Baba and the Forty Thieves,* the slave girl Morgiana kills the thieves hidden in the oil jars to protect her household. She's neat and tidy about it and there are no shrieks or groans or other evidences of agony; the robbers die quietly. Later, in her dance to honor a guest, she knifes the disguised robber chieftain—again, neatly. The children, who all know the story, wait for both episodes to occur, and they sigh with pleasure or applaud vociferously when they come off. Several dramatizations of *Ali Baba* try to get out of killing the chieftain. They have Morgiana and Ali Baba's son capture him, or do any number of other things of which young audiences disapprove. They know the chieftain has committed all sorts of murderous acts and the boys and girls feel he is literally getting away with murder if he escapes. I agree.

As I said in the Introduction, this is a personal comment, and a subjective one. Over twenty years of looking at entertainment for children and at the children themselves, the whole question of violence has been deeply troubling to me. More than any other phase of theater for children, I have discussed this with specialists who deal with young people. I've read what I could about violence, and thought about it, and developed the opinions set forth here. Whether these will be my opinions some years hence, I don't know. For now, I make a clear but not always intelligible distinction in my own mind about the kinds of violence I should make taboo and the kinds that safely give children pleasure. I can lay down no rules. All I can give are the ways I have come to my conclusions. If these are valid where your children are concerned, or if they help to clarify your thinking in other directions, I'm glad. What is permissible violence may be a subjective matter, and the final arbiter may have to be the taste with which violence is presented and your own judgment of each situation.

10. Death

————·⋙·⋘··————

Some years ago in a book—I wish I could remember who wrote it—I came across the idea that children don't interpret death the way adults do. Yet it seems to me that how children react to death has much to do with the attitude of the adults around them. It still amazes me that there are parents who will shield their children from any contact with real death, but will allow them to look at death in its most gory aspects pictured as entertainment. Though these parents won't let their children attend a funeral or touch their own dead puppy, they will permit them to view scenes of carnage on TV and in films without a second thought.

The treatment of death leaves much to be desired. In films, it is frequently the most savage, the most unhappy aspects that are shown. By far the largest number of deaths occurring in films and on TV are violent. The fact that the majority of real persons die of natural causes or accidents is barely indicated.

When it's reported on the news that forty men were swept away in a disaster at sea, we know this is a major tragedy. Forty human beings have died—sons, husbands, fathers, brothers, friends—no one knows whether quickly or slowly and painfully, and how much grief their dying has left behind. In the story of Sinbad the Sailor the seamen are swept away; not drowned or killed—"swept away" and out of the story. Children dismiss them from their minds and concentrate on the adventures of the leading character. In a fairy story or other tale of enchantment, there are a host of characters who have no real existence; they perform their function and then disappear. Not so with a pirate in *Treasure Island*. If *he* is "swept away," he has more reality and his being swept away has more serious implications. Sensitive direction can rid the story of subordinate characters in such a way that the audience is unaware real death has struck.

In a different way but with the same results Shakespeare handles his minor characters in *Macbeth*. To cover the murder of Duncan, Lady Macbeth smears the sleeping guards with his blood. The guards are then killed off quickly, and no further heed is paid them. In a story about royalty, nonroyal persons are, in effect, nonpersons and as disposable as facial tissue.

The ancient Greeks considered it unspeakably vulgar to have anyone die onstage, and all violence occurred elsewhere. A horror-stricken messenger would bring in a full report to the audience.

All these treatments are satisfactory within the intent of the *Arabian Nights,* the Elizabethan drama, or the Greek theater. All beg the question of death so far as young audiences are concerned.

Pediatricians and psychologists have said a reason children are so fond of games with mock slaughter—the bang-bang-you're-dead we referred to—is that by acting out their make-believe adventures of cops and robbers, cowboys and Indians, Terrans and creatures from the moons of Jupiter, they are able to express their fears of death and defeat it. Children can "die" simply and matter-of-factly: clutch their "wound" and drop like a stone. A real artist can make a Metropolitan Opera production out of it: he will grab at his belly, double over, groan, fling up his hands, stagger in a circle, drop to his knees, gasp, grip his belly once again, fall over on the ground, straighten out, convulse two or three times, twitch feebly, roll his eyes, and with a long sigh breathe his last. Children understand the rules of the game and they know no one is hurt, let alone dead. This is perhaps why children love a Punch and Judy show, and the more slapstick there is, the more dramatic the deaths, the better. Adults who are upset by the "violence" miss the point. Boys and girls understand Punch and Judy. They comprehend it's a puppet game of death, like the one they play, and it's hilarious to them.

But this is still begging the question.

Plays and films such as *On Borrowed Time, Death Takes a Holiday,* and *Outward Bound* are popular with older boys and girls. These fantasies comfort them with the idea that the great unknown is friendly. These beg the question too.

In the first examples, death is ignored. In the second, death is defeated. In the third, death is denied. None of these treatments confronts a young audience with a realistic, nonfrightening view of death.

Seldom is death treated as a nonviolent fact of life to which we must adjust if we are to survive as healthy persons. Euphemisms, evasions, and fantasies have their place, but so has truth. Harm lies in scarcely ever presenting to children through entertainment the truth of death. Entertainment usually gives half-truths or impressions so contrary to truth that they are falsehoods. The truth is simple: death is final. Whatever religious convictions parents instill in their children regarding an afterlife, the fact remains that in this one, once one dies it's finished. Permanently. Sometimes a child may grope toward this knowledge, but entertainment can all unwittingly interpose a veil between him and reality.

I'm not referring to instances where the good fairy waves a magic wand and everyone who has died is restored to life, or to *Sleeping Beauty,* in which death is transformed to a sleep of a hundred years. Or to a Dracula who revives when the stake is pulled from his heart. I mean something more subtle. In the theater, the "dead" actor rises to take a bow. In films and TV, children recognize the same actors in many programs. If a character dies in one show, the child will come across the actor in another. The distinction between the player and the role sometimes blurs in a child's mind—as in the minds of adults on occasion—and the finality of death is blunted. It can be confusing to a young child particularly to hear his elders mention that a certain actor has died, while that actor's image is very much alive on the TV or movie screen.

It can be difficult to explain *finality, finished, over, all gone.* A TV program is over, but it will return as a rerun eventually. The cookies are all gone, but a day or so later the crock will be full again. Leaves fall, but spring comes around and life bursts out again. But what is *dead* stays *dead.* If it is a person, what made that person someone unique has gone, and what remains is buried in the earth or burned. And neither the inert husk nor the spirit which animated it will ever return, at least —according to your religious convictions—in recognizable form during our tenure in this world. No matter how dearly we love what has died, we cannot mourn to the point where we ourselves die. Life is for the living. Those who remain must accept that the end of life is as natural as its beginning.

Life is tenacious, which is also a truth. Although we face death as inevitable, we cling to the idea of personal immortality.

Truth can be expressed in more than one way. In allegorical form it can say what a children's audience cannot accept or comprehend in more direct terms. According to Dr. Bruno Bettelheim:

> Fairy tales recognize the dilemma of wishing to live eternally by occasionally concluding, "If they have not died, they are living still." As for the ending "And they lived happily ever after," it does not for a moment fool the child into believing that eternal life is possible. Instead, it indicates that which alone can take the sting out of recognition of the narrow limits of our time on this earth: forming a truly satisfying bond to another. The tales teach that when one has done this, one has reached the ultimate in emotional security and permanency of relation available to man, and that this alone can dissipate the fear of death. If one has found true adult love, the fairy tale makes plain, one doesn't need to wish for eternal life.

Fairy tales dramatizations that understand this can allay children's fear of death without their being aware the topic has arisen.

Truth about death can also be told more realistically, but since it's not disguised as in a fairy tale or other allegory, it must be handled with a sensitivity most entertainment lacks.

A beautiful film for young people that deals openly and honestly with death and the emotions it evokes is *Where the Lilies Bloom,* based on the book by Vera and Bill Cleaver:

> The mother is dead and the father is dying. He turns over to a girl not yet in her teens the responsibility for holding the family together. She has to manage an older but incompetent sister and a younger brother and sister, earn enough to feed and clothe them, and see that the younger children continue with school. The children bury the father secretly, fearing separation should the outside world know no responsible adult is in charge. The girl manages for a time against staggering odds. Eventually she is forced

to admit the task requires adult strength. She comes to forgive her father for dying and being mistaken in much of the burden he placed on her. She realizes that although she has a duty to the other children, she also has legitimate needs of her own, which she will someday fill.

Far from being the desperately grim film it could have been, this story of Appalachia is funny, warm, and life-affirming, while at the same time accepting of death. In addition to its other intrinsic shining merits, it has a further point in its favor: most of the players are unknown, or relatively so. Because they are not associated with other parts they have played, the children in the audience are free to identify completely with the actors in their roles without having the impact weakened by memories. I should like each boy and girl to see this film at the right psychological moment.

Death as part of the inner workings of a story, as in *Where the Lilies Bloom,* is different from the death of a leading figure which makes for an unhappy ending. Parents and librarians have told me children love Hans Christian Andersen's *The Little Match Girl* and *The Little Mermaid.* When I was a child I loathed both. It seemed to me then, and it still does, that the death of the Match Girl was avoidable and gratuitously cruel. The first time I read the story I cried. After that, it infuriated me. I've seen *The Little Match Girl* as a film with the prescribed ending and I resented it. I've also seen it as a puppet play, which was flawed in several areas, but had a wealthy family find the child half frozen in the snow, take her home, and adopt her. Without insisting on a saccharine ending for the sake of sweetness and light, I consider this version to make at least as much sense to children, as well as to me. Unless one is an advocate of the Life Is Hell school of thought, there's no compulsion to let the child die.

As for *The Little Mermaid*, if ever there was a dirty deal that violated every canon of fair play, this is it. To have the Mermaid go through such suffering to obtain feet, and then for her to dance with those bleeding feet at the wedding to someone else of the man she loved—come, now! She's cheated of the reward of her sacrifice and the object of her adoration never learns that she has lived and died for him. I've never seen a dramatization that justified this situation to me. I've thought the tale bears too strong a resemblance to *The Story of O* to present to boys and girls, but forgive a personal observation that may conflict with your own possible fondness for *The Little Mermaid*.

Many parents are afraid their children "can't take" an unhappy ending. They feel boys and girls will come away frightened and depressed, and that's not what entertainment should be about. I don't agree on either point. If the unhappy ending is justified by the internal logic of the story, and if the unhappiness resolves the premise so that there has been some positive accomplishment, the net effect on the children can be one of thoughtful pleasure. And limiting entertainment to merry antics cheats boys and girls of the stimulation to their minds and hearts that more serious theater can encourage.

Joanna Halpert Kraus is the author of an unusual play, called *The Ice Wolf,* about a tribe of Innuit of the far North.

A fair child is born into the tribe. Because her eyes are blue and her hair yellow, the dark-eyed, black-haired, dark-skinned people want to destroy her. Her parents manage to prevent this, but not the mockery and abuse that are heaped on her whenever anything goes wrong. She is the scapegoat for all trouble, including the death of her mother and father. Up to this time she has had one friend only, a boy her own age, but with her parents gone, she is cast out to starve or freeze. She prays to the Great Spirit to make her a wolf so that she may survive, and in that guise she ravens among the tribe. The wolf finds the boy who was her one friend caught in a trap set for her, and in staying to help him, she is killed by the hunters. As she dies she regains her human form and is recognized. The question is asked: when was she really killed—then or long ago by their cruelty?

I've seen performances of this play by several companies. Though productions varied, the play never failed to move the audiences and to cause them to think. Children have told me that they "wished the wolf hadn't of died," but if she "hadn't of" it wouldn't have taught the people a lesson. For third-graders up, this is an exceptionally intelligent piece of work.

The old Jack Benny radio shows used to have a running gag that would start in October and continue until December every year. The joke concerned a shrewd old turkey which had managed to avoid being the guest of honor at many Thanksgiving dinners and wanted to continue his record. This spot was a favorite, and the audience would roar when each week it had a new trick to escape being beheaded. As a child, I remember, I didn't think that any creature's fear of death, including a turkey's, was all that funny. Sometimes the dialogue was so clever that in spite of myself I laughed as heartily as the studio audiences. Making mock of the fear of dying of a steer, a lamb, or a pig strikes me as an excellent way to desensitize an audience to the emotional and physical pain of these animals and to inculcate a consequent disregard of the lack of humanity with which they are treated, in their life as well as in their death. Now that I'm older and presumably wiser, I can realize all this is true; but it's only part of a larger whole. What we were really laughing at was our own fear of death, projected onto the hapless bird. By laughing at death, we made ourselves for a time superior to it and safe. But I still question whether there isn't a better way than through use of a scapegoat, which dehumanizes us.

It's never easy for children to accept the death of a loved one, whether a grandparent or a cat. It's more difficult when the one who dies is struck down by violence before his time. I have seen several moving television dramas for children that dealt with the death of elderly persons, and occasionally with the death of a parent through illness. They were provocative to children who had never come in contact with death and, I trust, helpful to those who had some experience with it. I have never seen a play for children that confronted realistically the death of a close family member by violence.

The Yearling deals with another facet of the problem of death, which, by extension, has many analogies. A young boy has to come to realize that it is necessary to kill his beloved pet, a young deer, which has been ravaging the crops on which his family subsists. His acceptance of the inevitably of the yearling's death brings the boy closer to maturity.

We all are closer to maturity when we can come to terms with death, and a healthy, sensitive approach to death through the medium of entertainment can help children on their way.

11. Anthropomorphism

Over the centuries, for the sake of a good story, it's been customary to endow with human life all sorts of inanimate objects or to project human patterns of thought onto other kinds of beings. This is done in stories dramatized for children, sometimes quite successfully. An outstanding example of this genre is *The Tale of Peter Rabbit* by Beatrix Potter. Peter has been made into a human creature, complete with blue jacket and other attributes that in effect convert him from a rabbit into a little person in rabbit form. Young children identify with Peter and the simple mischief he gets into and they are glad as can be when he escapes his perils to return safely to mother to be cuddled and dosed.

This is a far cry from *The Gingerbread Man*, which I've also seen dramatized on several occasions.

> An old woman makes a gingerbread man. He jumps out of the oven and runs away. Everyone tries to catch him in a story that builds by accumulating episodes. After each escape he utters a chant, adding details:

Run! Run! Run!
Catch me if you can!
You can't get me!
I'm the Gingerbread Man,
I am! I am!
I've run away from a little old woman, I've run away
from a little old man, I've run away from a cow, I've
run away from a horse, I've run away from a barn full
of threshers, I've run away from a field full of mowers,
and I can run away from you,
I can! I can!

He meets a fox, who tricks the Gingerbread Man into crossing a river with him, and snip, snip, snap, the Gingerbread Man is devoured.

In this case, a cookie is invested with the attributes of a child running away from danger (or the fate for which he was created, depending on whether the viewpoint is his or yours). Boys and girls are invited to sympathize with him and to identify more and more closely with his bravado, episode by episode. When the fox eats him in the end, if the dramatization follows the folk tale, the children are shocked, as they are when they hear the story for the first time. They have a right to be shocked. Their sympathies were solicited and betrayed.

This is one of the troubles with anthropomorphism in children's entertainment. If an object—a gingerbread man or a Volkswagen—is given personhood, then it must be respected. You just can't create a person, make him a protagonist, and then abandon and destroy him, without establishing a situation pointless at best, even heart-wrenching to a young audience. I've heard parents and librarians trying to explain to small children the ending of *The Gingerbread Man,* but they were no more successful with their children than I was with mine. What it comes down to is that once a person is created, like Franken-stein's monster, the creator owes him responsibility.

Hans Christian Andersen wrote a number of stories about inanimate objects to which he gave human thoughts and human feelings—a needle, a toy soldier, a fir tree. . . . We become interested in their thinking, we follow their adventures, we hope at every moment something will intervene to avert final obliv-ion, but it doesn't. The Fir Tree is hacked down, made a Christ-mas ornament, forgotten, chopped into firewood, and burned. What of it? It happens to Christmas trees all the time. But *this* tree was given human emotions, and when it burned it *died.* The Steadfast Tin Soldier was only a toy destroyed by a child on impulse. But he had been given courage and the ability to love a paper dancer. Therefore, when the child threw him into the flames he was murdered senselessly.

There are any number of dramatizations in every medium about toys that come to life at midnight or some other specified time for a jolly fling and then return to inanimacy again. These usually happen without involving the audience emotionally and they work well enough if the boys and girls haven't seen too many such jolly flings. I think this whole idea of a doll or jack-in-the-box coming to life is more an adult conception of what a child likes than one children care for.

Throughout all literature for children there are friendly ani-mals who come into the scene when the protagonist is in trou-ble. Puss in Boots has a name, but there is no reckoning the number of anonymous doves, ducks, eagles, horses, foxes, wolves, bears, fish, ants, bees, etc., which understand the prob-lems of the hero or heroine and keep a promise to come to the rescue in gratitude for earlier assistance, or perform other brave and intelligent "human" acts. These are comforting figures to children, letting them know that no matter how desperate their plight, someone or something will come to their aid. These humanized creatures may merely put in a brief appearance in a crisis, but whether they are onstage for a moment or are major characters, they must be dealt with fairly. The forest creatures in Disney's *Bambi,* for example, and the talking horse Falada in *The Goose Girl* are treated fairly. If they must die, their deaths advance the story and are important to it. We aren't seduced into cheering them on to disaster. If there's no reason for them to die, they don't (e.g., Cleo the goldfish and Jiminy Cricket in the Disney *Pinocchio*). To a degree they all participate in the victory of their respective protagonists.

Another problem plagues reverse anthropomorphism in children's entertainment. There are, unfortunately, writers and directors who feel that when they convert people into animals for the sake of telling a story, they are free to abandon common sense. When George Orwell wrote *Animal Farm,* in order to make his comment as a parable he turned all his primary characters into animals in a way that was logical, consistent, and effective, as no other treatment could have been. Not so with the Disney *Robin Hood.* Here Robin and Maid Marian are a pair of foxes. So far so good. But Marian's nurse and chaperone is a hen. Robin's dear friend in the forest is a rabbit. Does it make sense to you that a hen and a rabbit would be the nearest and dearest of a vixen and a fox? Not to me. Any more sense than that King John's army in England's Sherwood would be a herd of rhinoceroses.

There's a distinction between fantasy and idiocy. Fantasy, to be convincing, must be rooted in reality, and there's not much reality where foxes must be compelled by circumstances to be vegetarians. Fantasy, especially, must have consistency, and there's not much of that either in this *Robin Hood.* I've never seen any of the delightful Thornton Burgess animal stories dramatized, but I'd like to. Part of their great charm is that while each little animal is given the ability to speak and be a tiny person, each stays within its role of skunk, chipmunk, fox, etc., and never does anything within that role that would violate its nature.

Turning fictional creatures and objects into people works better than projecting human attributes onto real animals. When my son was small he came into my room one day with his favorite cat draped around his neck, purring into his ear. "Wouldn't it be wonderful if cats could talk?" he asked. "Wouldn't you be glad if they did?" I thought about that. Wonderful, yes. Desirable, no. The best thing about animals is that they *are* animals. They are to be valued for what they are, not to be sentimentalized into imitation cutesy little people inside furry skins. People who make animals into their own image are missing the point of what being an animal is all about. "No," I said. "I'm glad animals are the way they are. I'm glad cats can't talk and bark and I'm glad dogs can't talk and climb."

In *The Living Desert* (made by Disney in 1953 and on the whole deservedly a classic) there's a scene audiences of all ages laugh at. Two scorpions are fighting and the music on the sound track is that of a country square dance. The music, in mood and tempo, alters the life-and-death struggle into the appearance of a comical charade. If two boxers were hamming it up in the ring, such music might be appropriate; if they are hurting each other and their futures depend on the outcome, the music would be an insult to their desperation and would destroy the audience's conviction in its seriousness. In the scorpion sequence, the music cheats the audience of the sense of what the camera saw.

Like any other facet of entertainment for your child, the use of anthropomorphism must be honest and responsible. It is an important device because young people can often project fantasy and emotion onto animals and animated objects, or persons so disguised, more easily than onto real persons. It can be a stepping stone to genuine appreciation of animals, or it can be a block encouraging misunderstanding through false, sentimental notions of what animals are.

12. Pandering

———⚮———

I have come to believe that much of what is wrong with entertainment for your child is due to sheer ineptitude on the part of the producers. But not all. There's entertainment that, focusing on a particular segment of the population as its market, flatters it outrageously, saying what its public wants to hear. This may consist of ego-building lies or a rationale justifying otherwise indefensible behavior.

For the Disney film *Superdad* the market is the young teen set and below. The action throughout is based on assumptions that parents are blundering idiots of dubious probity and that young people have a monopoly on intelligence, sensitivity, and integrity. These virtues are interpreted by the teen-agers according to their own definitions.

Superdad also makes the point that ambitious youths with "square," responsible jobs are stuffy prigs. It represents bad manners as being terribly amusing. The film goes on to denigrate art and artists by telling teen-agers more of what they'd supposedly like to hear: that art, and by implication other subjects requiring the investment of time and study to understand, are not worth the effort.

The fact that *Superdad*'s premises are false seems to be beside the point. Generally parents do have more sense than their young children, their concern for their well-being is genuine, and their sense of right and wrong may be at least as acute. Many ambitious, responsible young people are more imaginative and engaging than the so-called free spirits who refuse to conform to any rules but their own. Kindness, as expressed through courtesy, isn't yet outdated. And there are many subjects that repay long years of arduous attention for those with sufficient maturity to cling to long-term goals.

Superdad is a frothy bubble of a picture with no serious intentions except to earn a bundle. But armed with the moral support the film furnishes, teen-agers are more comfortable about any inclinations to irresponsibility, disobedience, disrespect, and discourtesy, as well as intellectual and physical inertia.

The Cavern of the Jewels, the play discussed earlier, makes many of the same points, but without the froth of *Superdad.* Ambition is represented by a father no child could want to emulate; institutions, by a corrupt archbishop. More than disrespect and disobedience is justified here—flight or rebellion is the only alternative to the standards imposed by all the adults.

This pandering to young people is by no means limited to these expressions of wishful thinking. There are "black" films of an exploitive nature which also have no purpose except to make money and which assure young people that black is not only beautiful, it's more beautiful than any other color. These movies are explicit in their depictions of blacks' superiority in physical prowess and native shrewdness. They encourage young people to take back "their own," which centuries of persecution have deprived them of. If these means to recovery entail robbery, burglary, looting, and vandalism, even rape and murder and other personal violence, what of it? These are crimes according to white law only, to which blacks are not subject. Conclusive indications that it is other blacks who suffer most from these crimes don't seem to figure in the thinking.

These exploitation films build up the ideal of the swaggering, foul-mouthed young man and woman who are masters of their fists, their guns, and their knives. They have a black belt in karate and maraud among whites and Uncle Tom blacks. (Definition of Uncle Tom in this context: anyone who doesn't hold with the same philosophy.) They take what they want, whether sex, property, or pleasure in physical abuse, as their right—to the stomping, cheering approval of audiences whose enthusiasm reaches its height when the objects of their prowess are white.

In these exploitation films, the route to the protagonist's success is immaterial to the audiences—they seem indifferent to whether he achieves his Cadillac and his expensive clothes and apartment as a result of outlaw violence or smart, brutal pimping. Legal means to success are seldom suggested as possibilities. These films are as flagrantly, stupidly racist as those that go the other way, and as dangerous to those who accept their message as truth. This "truth" encourages its exponents to fall afoul of the law or of a tougher exponent of the same "truth" who is in conflict with them.

There's another kind of pandering to the public at large in film and TV programs that children see, although children are not the prime audience. These are the "patriotic" films that wrap the flag around incidents in American history so as to conceal or distort facts that disagree with romanticized versions we should prefer to believe. These "historical" dramas seldom portray objectively "our" relations with Indians, Mexicans, and other peoples whose territory is included within our fifty states, with blacks before and after the Civil War, with the internment of Japanese citizens during World War II, or any number of other conditions over which an idealized haze has descended.

Most films show us pictures of our past the way we'd like it to be. Instead of being truly patriotic by letting us understand facts as they are, they feed us illusions, and these illusions contribute to mistakes of individual and collective action by those they influence.

Pandering to special-interest organizations also gives our young people false notions of the workings of the world. Except for occasional depictions of a quack carefully identified as such, audiences are given to understand that medicine is practiced entirely by saints. These holy men and women see into the human heart and, godlike, rearrange the lives of their patients, for the patients' own good. Many, but not all, live high on the hog, though nothing as crass as money touches their hands. Some of the saintliest, to demonstrate their sanctity, go to opposite extremes. If any mention of payment arises, money is passed unobtrusively to a nurse or secretary. No doctor ever refuses a patient who can't pay, no hospital ever turns away anyone in need, no nurse is other than selfless and sacrificing. Of course there are in real life doctors and nurses who give concerned, competent care to their patients, but I wonder at the proportion of Dr. Welbys and Florence Nightingales among them.

In one respect, dramatized lawyers aren't so lucky in their image. Since every lawyer in a courtroom battle is in an adversary position, chances are that some protagonists will come up against other lawyers whose skill, courage, and saintliness are not their equal. But members of the bar have an advantage over members of the American Medical Association: they have, along with an unerring instinct to distinguish between right and wrong, an ability to solve crime that any police department envies. Only the more venal members of the profession argue with their clients about fees, because all these heroic figures are interested in is Justice.

TV particularly knuckles under to professional associations like the medical and legal to give audiences an idealized, unrealistic picture. The relatively small number of exposé documentaries are usually not aired in children's viewing time, and the balance is on the side of the angels. Young people who hold to these pretty illusions may have difficulty in locating a sanctified personification of Big Daddy when they need professional help as adults.

13. Age

————⟡————

Throughout *Understanding Your Child's Entertainment* we've mentioned that how old your child is should be a determining factor in many areas of what he or she views. It bears repeating that the age and emotional maturity of children should affect virtually every aspect of a production: the complexity of the story, the subject matter, the amount of tension and violence and the nature of the violence, type of humor, etc.

The TV market, according to Action for Children's Television, lumps all children together in the two-to-eleven-year-old age range. We are concerned here with children not as a market but as individual maturing human beings. It is obvious that two-year-olds, no matter how intelligent, cannot comprehend on the level of an eleven-year-old. Likewise, it's an affront to the eleven-year-olds to give them the kind of production enjoyed by twos, or fours, or even sixes. For whatever reasons, commercial or otherwise, the television industry considers this agglomeration necessary, the results of such thinking have been the "wasteland" so much of children's television is. Movement and activity will hold the eye of any child, even a two-year-old, so action is a staple ingredient in programming. Older children want a story, but the plot must not be too complex for a five-year-old. All children like to laugh, so sight humor—pratfalls, crashes, and other "humorous" catastrophes of a physical nature—figures importantly; canned laughter on the sound track cues the child who might not readily appreciate the "comical" situations. Characterizations have no time to develop and no use for the subtlety a four-year-old might not comprehend, so roles tend to be unshaded black and white. Rock music can be depended on to attract a wide following.

In the attempt to reach all children, the commercial networks end by reaching few of them with programming of worth. Only when they design for a limited age span—as for the sixes up with the CBS *Children's Film Festival*—do they fill their time with anything of substance. Most programming for this two-to-eleven-year catchall is little more than a baby-sitting service in which the "babies" are receiving minimal opportunities for emotional and intellectual growth.

A few seasons back, parents and organizations fed up with the inordinate violence shown on these children's programs persuaded the networks to eschew violence of all kinds on Saturday mornings. Eliminating violence—and with it much genuine dramatic conflict—and putting no appreciable effort into developing stories based on themes of relevance, either in reality or fantasy, the networks have increased their reliance on rock, slapstick, and activity requiring no intelligence for its comprehension.

Some small progress in breaking up the two-to-eleven monolith has been made by local commercial stations, cable, and public TV, especially the last. *Sesame Street* is successful with preschoolers; *Mister Rogers' Neighborhood* is loved by those too young even for *Sesame Street; The Electric Company* and *Zoom* are popular with older boys and girls—and all with good cause.

Local and public television stations don't find it necessary to appeal to children across the board. Non-network and cable shows with smaller budgets need not bring in the income only nationwide exposure can furnish. And many public-TV children's shows, if not all, are subsidized one way or another.

In the area of cinema, a frequent assumption made by producers and parents alike is that a film "for the family" or for children means for any family and any children. This isn't always the case. The Disney film based on Jules Verne's *Twenty Thousand Leagues Under the Sea* is an example. In the audience I observed, the older children were attentive from beginning to end. Those about eight to ten were interested most of the time, but were turned off by any sign of romance between characters. Younger children were enthusiastic about the fistfights and the attack of the giant squid, but in between these scenes, they gave the film no attention whatever. When they felt that talk without action had gone on too long, several had to be restrained physically by their group leader from leaving the theater. The rest rooms and the candy counter did a thriving trade. This was not the fault of the film, which engrossed those of the proper age for it.

This kind of mistaken attendance is the fault of advertising that doesn't spell out honestly and clearly whom the film is for, and of those adults who send children to it without full inquiry as to its suitability. Few advertisers will want to limit their market by indicating that a film is inappropriate for certain segments of it. Now that rating codes have been instituted, advertisers consider that whatever responsibility they might have had in this area no longer exists.

The "G" rating, as many parents know, often means little. It carries no indication of whether a film contains unsavory violence or subject matter that could horrify or bore young people; no indication other than that no nudity is displayed.

Parents are at the mercy of those who give or withhold information about a film. Frequently the theater manager has never seen the film he has booked and couldn't answer questions even if he wanted to cooperate. Few critics review from the standpoint of young people. However, a few national "women's" magazines are making constructive efforts in this direction and may be helpful as a guide to films you wish to learn more about for your boys and girls. Barring this, it's hard to know what to do when a ten-year-old wants to see a film suitable for his age, and his five-year-old sister wants to go along, and you are unsure whether it is right for her. Particularly if you have something else to do, the temptation is to send all the kids to the movies; and if you know no specific objection to it beforehand, why not? It's only afterward that the children tell you what you should have known before you let them go.

As parents' guides, the "PG" and "R" ratings can be as meaningless as the "G." I've seen "R" pictures, containing nudity, that I thought were honest and nonprurient—virtues I haven't always been able to credit "G"s with—and would have presented to children without a qualm. Generally, the subject matter is what would make me say No flatly to a "G" or a "PG." A crime film, a psychological thriller, a Western with lots of shoot-'em-ups—in these instances I should want to know why I *should* send a child, rather than why not. Also, but for different reasons, I should not want to take a child to see a romantic talky film with little action of the robust kind young people prefer. Boys and girls like no more talk than necessary to explain action, and it's an old but true cliché that they'd rather see the hero kiss his horse than a woman. Boring children at the theater is in its own way as heinous as frightening them—possibly worse, in their opinion.

Something else bores children, and that's subtitles on foreign films. Even when the story is something that holds them, few boys and girls younger than third-graders can read well enough to understand all the words or quickly enough to keep up with the titles. Although the film you'd like your boys and girls to see might be an award-winning fairy tale in French or Swedish, I'd recommend you hold off unless you're prepared to whisper a running translation. You'll also have to brave the displeasure of adults in surrounding seats who may express annoyance at repeatedly hearing: "What did he say, Mommy[Daddy]? Tell me what he said!"

Movies whose theme and action center around a philosophical concept are another type to stay away from unless it is developed through images your child can understand. These films are likely to be talky, and if the talk isn't humorous, and the humor a sort the child appreciates, you're going to have considerable squirming to deal with before it's time to go. The older the girls and boys, the wider the range of their intellectual curiosity, the greater their interest in ideas, but in ideas demonstrated actively.

A so-called family film doesn't necessarily mean that five-year-olds will have any comprehension of what's going on. A "children" 's film doesn't necessarily mean every child from the age of three will enjoy it. While very young children may find pleasure in such pictures, until you learn otherwise about individual movies, you'd be safe in assuming that eight up is a better age for them. It's a pity there aren't more good family films. Unfortunately, a large number of adults are suspicious that films without violence and nudity could only be tiresome and fit for little old ladies in Dubuque. This is a misunderstanding of the enormous scope of subjects and treatments that are possible, as well as of little old ladies. Perhaps one day good family fare will be turned out in quantity, but until then, my thought is that children don't *have* to go to the movies or see on television pictures that are unsuitable for their age because of violence, sex, and inappropriate subject matter, humor, and talk. They *could* play ball or take a walk in the park instead. They could even listen to good programs on radio. They tend to forget this.

The lack of age distinction has all but ruined much live theater for children in the United States. Because the immediacy of live theater can be so strong, small children who wouldn't be upset by a TV giant can be panic-stricken by a giant six inches away. Parents protest that a story is too frightening if a four-year-old wails aloud when the giant brushes his seat or looms behind the footlights. The older children may be having a grand time, but the four-year-old is inconsolable, and his parents are irate. So what do the sponsors (bookers) of entertainment do? Instead of setting a minimum age limit, they require that the giant be toned down. The giant must be less threatening, to the audience as well as to Jack; or he must be a friendly giant who loves little boys and girls, or he must be given some other characteristic that will strip from him any quality that could make even the smallest member of the audience uncomfortable. The result? What could be expected. The excitement that older children have a right to look forward to never develops. Theater for children has got younger and younger, until there's virtually nothing left for the child of ten, eleven, or twelve—perhaps the age when theater should mean most to boys and girls. Children can be let down by plays when they expected to see a story the way they know it, and all the "good parts" were cut out or soft-pedaled: Ali Baba's robber chieftain is merely tied up and arrested instead of being slain by the slave girl; Beauty's beast looks more like a large house cat than a lion; Puss in Boots's ogre never appears. . . . Disappointed at having the conflict reduced and the purpose blunted, with no triumph to share with a strong protagonist, these older children are reluctant to return to a theater that holds little for them. They look around them and see small boys and girls, even toddlers on occasion, and they resent having themselves in their relative maturity equated with these babies. It becomes a point of pride to outgrow theater for children, just as young people are proud to see that the growing mark on the wall is an inch higher than last year's, or that their new shoes are a size larger.

So many parents are so eager to have their children experience all kinds of events to stimulate intellectual growth that they lose normal perspective. About ten years ago I was being interviewed on a radio program by a well-known commentator on the passing scene. It was one of those open-ended sessions and I was told we could discuss entertainment for children up to an hour, as long as it was interesting for the public. I anticipated no problems in keeping the conversation going for the full time. After about ten minutes, my host said it was a great pity theaters for children weren't made so that boys and girls could be allowed more freedom of movement. He had taken his three-year-old daughter to a play recently, and she had loved it. But an usher had made her go back to her seat and refused to let her wander up and down the aisles. He had been quite insistent and had brought her back to her seat several times, and Father didn't think that was right. His little girl understood everything that was happening, and confining her limited her pleasure. What did I think about that? So I said, keeping a straight face, that it was too bad his little genius was restricted, and wasn't it a shame that other three-year-olds weren't as bright as his? My host responded like an insulted father and huffily cut our discussion short two or three minutes later at the first commercial break.

It would seem to anyone with any objectivity that if a child is too young to sit still, she is too young for a communal entertainment experience. I should go further. Except for simple plays or revues designed for very young children, I would bar boys and girls from the theater until they are old enough for school. If they're not old enough for one, they're not old enough for the other. If the very young are restricted to plays for their own age, older children would have a source of embarrassment removed; they would feel that shows they go to are for them, not babies. Theater would then be something children would be proud to grow into, not out of. This feeling would be enhanced if the third or fourth grade were an additional dividing line for audiences as is the situation in some European countries.

Several years ago I had an enlightening conversation with a children's librarian while we were waiting for the curtain to rise on a children's play. Looking about, I could see youngsters from four up seated among older ones. "I'm sorry," I commented innocently, "to see preschoolers at a production meant for much older boys and girls. They don't belong here. Why couldn't they have something for their age that would be better —like a story hour?" The librarian's wrath was immense. *She* was fed up with little children being brought to story hours meant for children of eight. People were always presuming that their children were old enough to understand what other people's children the same age were too immature for. Parents *would* bring their kindergartners to fairy tales and adventure stories that were for second-and third-graders, and if she turned them away they were indignant. She felt that preschoolers should have little puppet plays or some such and keep away from her until they were ready.

There seems to be no limit to some parents' confidence in their children's comprehension. It's not unusual to see two- and three-year-olds at the theater, but I confess I was truly startled at a fund-raising marionette performance to see propped against a woman's bosom a child who couldn't have been ten months old. His feet were planted in her lap, and she aimed his head at the stage. When he slipped down or dozed, she pulled him up against her and pushed the nipple of a milk bottle between his lips. She maintained a running commentary throughout: "See, look what the doggy is doing! Look at the man walking on the wire. It's very hard to walk on a wire. If you're not careful you could fall off the wire. The doggy is walking on the wire. He's a smart doggy. What do doggies say? Doggies say bow-wow." She fascinated me as much as the production did.

Parents who are more realistic about their children's capacities sometimes want to take youngsters to an adult show. Older boys and girls can be charmed by musicals like *The Sound of Music* or *Naughty Marietta,* or a play like *Harvey.* The trouble is that these days you don't always know what you're getting. About fifteen years ago I went to a Broadway production and thoroughly enjoyed it, so that when it was presented in revival a couple of seasons ago, I looked forward to seeing it again. The first time, I saw it for my own pleasure. I was not reviewing it. Thinking about it subsequently, I realized it was a delightful play for young people. But not the way it was produced the second time around. The intervening years had brought a different outlook to many directors, and this time, although not one word of dialogue had been changed, it was another play. In several instances, while the protagonist was acting out his prescribed role, in the background of the restaurant, bar, and other locations, couples were pawing each other and grappling in what used to be considered intimate positions. All this was by way of "updating" the play, but it was no longer anything I could recommend to girls and boys.

When critics review adult plays for an adult audience, they are not concerned with suitability for children at all, let alone age ranges. Nor should they be. Their concerns are in other areas. However, unless the plot makes the play impossible or some comment of the critics gives a clue, parents are in the dark as to whether they should take their boys and girls. The best way to decide if you have any question is to try to find someone who has already seen the production, someone whose opinion you respect, and ask about it. Is there any dialogue or song lyric you would prefer your children not to hear? Any suggestive movement or situation you think they aren't mature enough for? Some aspects of a production a six-year-old might not notice at all could be upsetting to a twelve-year-old who is conscious of his changing body and emotions. Or, contrariwise, a situation that could be traumatic to the six-year-old could mean nothing to the older one. Adult theater being what it is today, check before you buy the tickets.

Speaking of tickets, a few seasons ago I was covering the Ringling Bros. and Barnum & Bailey Circus at Madison Square Garden. I sat directly in front of a father and his son, who couldn't have been much over two. The boy had one of those red flashlights on a string, and for the entire first act he ignored the events in the three rings and played with it, opening and closing the little cap and swinging the flashlight in circles. Intermission came after an hour and a half, and the child was tired and cranky. I doubt whether he had ever been up so late before. He became aware of all the people around him and the size of the Garden, and it was all too much for him. He whined to go home, but his father refused to leave. He put the boy on his lap and shook him whenever he nodded. "Listen," he told the child. "These tickets cost eight and a half dollars apiece, and you're going to stay awake and have a good time!"

Circuses advertise that they are for children of all ages. I don't agree. Certainly that two-year-old wasn't ready for even a one-ring circus, and Madison Square Garden's three rings would have taxed the stamina of a much older child. I have seen boys and girls grow frustrated and fatigued from the effort of trying to watch all three rings simultaneously. They fear that if their attention strays from one area, that's the very one where the important action will occur. They become tense with strain, and the noise of the huge crowd and the lights bombard their senses. Older children, particularly those used to crowds, can take all this in stride and have a wonderful time. Younger children—how young in the case of yours, you will have to decide—just can't. For younger children, the smaller, more intimate one-ring circus is a happier experience. There's only one thing happening at a time. The excitement is lower-keyed. The demands on a child's nervous system are less intense, and there is more pleasure and less exhaustion. I don't mean to limit one-ring circuses to small children only; older children and adults may also be more comfortable when concentration is easier. But definitely, very small children will find their first circus experiences less strenuous in the one-ring arena.

Clowns are an integral part of all circuses, and the assumption is that all children love all clowns. They don't. Many small children are terrified of these strange creatures with the odd clothing and painted faces. I've seen parents shove shrinking youngsters at a clown, insisting that they shake hands with the funny man. Sometimes the clown tries to reassure the little one, but this can make things worse. A sensitive clown, or an experienced one, will move back and give his attention to more welcoming children.

As all children are supposed to love clowns, so they are supposed to be thrilled by magicians. This is true in most instances, but again, not in the case of very young children. And why aren't they also dazzled and bewildered? Because they are too inexperienced to know what is possible and what is impossible. Until boys and girls are mature enough to appreciate the difference, they accept whatever the magician does as almost routine. Very young children can believe anything. If the magician says he will make a lady float in the air and does it, a very young audience will clap politely, but without excitement. He said he would do it and he did. So what? If he swallows fire, or grows pigeons at his fingertips, why not? As children learn the distinction between what can be done and what can't, their enthusiasm for such illusions can be boundless. Almost every child at one time or another wants to be a magician and saves up to buy a trick or two. So if your little one is unmoved by a spectacle that leaves you breathless, just wait a year or so.

A word of warning regarding magicians and difficult or impossible stunts a child may see: A magician holds his hand in a flame or a torch against his body. A yogi eats broken glass or drives a spike through his tongue. An acrobat walks a tight rope between two high points. Peter Pan flies out the window. Children are tempted to imitate these exploits, and the younger the child, the less restraint in emulating the hero. They must be cautioned that they have neither the skill nor the magic to make these feats possible and that the consequences will be disastrous.

14. Audience Participation

A local periodical used to supply questionnaires to its reviewers of children's plays. The first question was: "Is there audience participation?" If the answer was No, credit was automatically deducted from the production's total score, regardless of whether the production was satisfactory without it.

Audience participation is highly regarded by many specialists in children's theater and in education. The audience is invited to involve itself in a play by supplying information to the actors on request, instructing the characters which course of action to follow, if asked, or performing some act that enables the play to proceed. On occasion, children from the audience can be invited to participate in the action onstage. The experts point out that young people enjoy feeling part of a play through physical involvement; the quality of their attention is better when they participate actively; they remember details of the production more clearly in those circumstances; and "letting off steam" through participation enables them to be comfortable in their seats for longer than otherwise. This viewpoint has been discussed, praised, and taught.

I've seen hundreds of productions calling for audience participation. I detest it in plays.

I see no reason children need shriek information and advice to a player in order to feel they are "participating." The most active and intense participation, I firmly believe, comes from emotional and intellectual involvement—kinesthetic too, if the players are employing physical skills audiences can feel in their own bodies. This involvement demands only that a spectator give full attention and be persuaded that what is happening onstage is important to the characters and to the audience. A child giving this attention and succumbing to this persuasion is participating actively. The superficial participation of yelling and jumping are necessary only if the play is too weak to involve the audience on a deeper level.

Often the kind of participation many plays call for gets out of hand. The audience becomes more interested in opportunities to make a racket than in the play. The children watch the play only for cues to shout advice, or merely just to explode into noise or other activity. They may be having a good time, but not through theater. They can be stimulated to this kind of disorder by any situation that presents them with a socially acceptable way to release energies ordinary circumstances would require them to hold in check. It's easy to work boys and girls up to cooperate in participation. It isn't always as easy to turn them off when the actors want a demonstration to end, or when they require a dead hush for the next scene. In extreme cases, I've seen customarily well-mannered audiences ignore the play altogether, except to abuse it, and carry on in their seats until the players left the stage. There are less striking effects of unruly participation that are nonetheless damaging. If audience responses take too long to control, the actors must wait until they can be heard above the din and the tempo of the play falls off. Its dramatic impact is vitiated. So is the sense of the play if the audience is "participating" too loudly to listen to it.

I think, too, that it's often a mistake to invite children up and enlist their help in performance. If the actors call for volunteers, children swarm from the woodwork in larger numbers than are required, and many must be turned away, to feel rejection. If the actors insist that the children remain seated until selected, this is equally rejecting to those who have not been chosen. Moreover, as far as the play goes, the results are unpredictable. The most vociferous and demanding child, when actually on-stage, can become tongue-tied, stiff, and uncomprehending. Or the ham in every child comes out and takes over, seizing the spotlight at the expense of what the actors had in mind. I recall a Pixie Judy Troupe production about a circus. The climax was to come in the last scene, when a child from the audience was called up to be the littlest clown, the star of the circus. A willing small girl was picked, who lost all her enthusiasm when she discovered she was to be made up onstage as a white-face clown. She protested adamantly and the play dribbled to an end in utter futility.

There's another clinker in onstage audience participation. Even when the children are having a marvelous time being pages or bunnies or assistants to the magicians or whatever else, the show usually stops dead in its tracks while the participants are being selected, brought to the stage, and instructed in their roles. While all this is going on, the rest of the children sit in their seats with nothing but these preparations to look at. They may be frustrated at not having been selected themselves; they are certainly bored and restless while they are waiting, and it's not right to put them in this condition for the sake of a gimmick.

But this is the least I have against audience participation. My major complaint is that the way most productions use it, it is unethical or inconsistent, or both. And frequently destructive.

How unethical? Because the production solicits from the audience advice or assistance, giving the children to understand it will be acted on in determining the course of the play. This is downright dishonest, because no matter what the boys and girls provide in instructions and other help, the characters will follow a predetermined course of action. If the king asks the audience, "Shall I let this villain live?" whether the children shout Yes or No, the king will hear only what he wants to, and his question was a fake. It couldn't be more contemptuous of the children.

There has been at least one play for children that prepared two endings, so that whichever way the audience decided, the players would go. The children were respected and listened to. Perhaps there have been others equally honest, but I haven't come across them. Even time-honored Peter Pan is a phony: when he asks boys and girls to demonstrate that they believe in fairies so that Tinker Bell will live, there is generally an outburst. I'm living for the day the audience shouts No. I'm sure Peter will go on as if he had received unanimous support, and Tink will be as good as new again.

How inconsistent? Because the director uses the audience only when he wants it and ignores its presence the rest of the time. The prince asks the audience for directions to the witch's house. He gets them from hundreds of treble voices. He acknowledges the children and follows their instructions. Then he runs into trouble and needs someone to lend a hand. Does he turn to the young people, who are no farther away now than when he asked for advice? Now they've ceased to exist. He'll call on them when he wants them to make enough noise to frighten the witch, or to clap for magic to make him invisible, but when it doesn't suit the convenience of the playwright or director to remember, the audience is dismissed. Audience treatment in *Peter Pan* is similar. Throughout most of the play there's no indication that the performers know there is anyone on the other side of the curtain. Suddenly, when Peter asks for help for Tinker Bell, there the children are. Then where were they when Peter and the boys could have used their assistance against the pirates? This kind of audience participation is gadgety, slick, and empty.

How destructive? Because the role of the audience is frequently conflicting, confusing, and best ignored. Children seem to have no loyalties where audience participation is concerned. In *Jack and the Beanstalk,* for example, the boys and girls clearly identify with and support Jack. They cheer to the rafters when Jack absconds with the hen. He tiptoes across the stage and asks the children not to tell the giant which way he's going. He exits stage left. A few seconds later the giant lumbers onto the scene. "Which way did Jack go?" he demands, and almost to a child the audience points to stage left and shouts instructions. The giant says, "Thank you, boys and girls. If you see Jack don't tell him I'm chasing him," and off he goes stage left. Almost immediately Jack reappears with the hen under his arm. The audience is almost hysterical in its haste to tell Jack the giant is in pursuit. "What did you say?" asks Jack. "The giant is chasing you!" the children roar. "What?" Jack repeats. The children are in a frenzy. "The giant is chasing you! The giant is chasing you!" "Oh," says Jack in astonishment. "The giant is chasing me? Which way did he go?" "That way," scream the kids. "He went that way!" "Thanks," says Jack. "Be sure you don't tell him where I'm going," and he jumps from the stage and runs up an aisle and out the back of the auditorium. At once the giant returns. "Jack went there," the children volunteer, before the giant can ask. The giant is bewildered. "There?" he asks, pointing in the wrong direction. "No, no," the children howl. "That way. *That* way. He went *that* way!"

The giant gets it, and follows Jack's route through the house and out.

This makes clear several facts. No matter how strongly the children are involved with Jack, the desire to yell and cut up is stronger. The play has lost its best asset: the children's concern for Jack. The giant has ceased to become the dread figure on whom the conflict of the drama depends; he has become someone the children are willing to assist. The audience has forgotten its concern with the ethical values involved, as Jack tries to regain his father's property. On every count, the play has suffered through this audience participation, and what the children have gained is self-defeating.

I used to say jokingly that one reason I dislike audience participation is that it gives children bad theater habits they may carry over to adult theater in due course. I could visualize these same shrieking children years later at a performance of *Hamlet.* He goes into one of his big moments: "To be, or not to be . . ." The audience rises as one, shouting Yes or No, each participant defending his position by the loudest possible volume of sound. I was assured my worries were groundless. Children, I was informed, know where conduct of this nature is appropriate and where it isn't.

I don't know whether I'm joking when I say it today. A producer of children's plays told me just recently he's been running up against a problem new in his years of experience. Whenever a musical number starts in one of his productions, the children pick up the beat and after a couple of bars clap along spontaneously. I shrugged this off as the woes of an individual producer which were not common to other companies. Possibly he needed more expertise in handling children. A few evenings later I went to see Alvin Ailey's great dance suite *Revelations.* I was stunned when a number of young adults began to clap to the rhythm of one of the spirituals, until half the house joined in. It was living through a nightmare.

So far as I'm concerned, all this kind of audience participation is worse than useless. Unless and until the playwright and cast are willing to be consistent in their approach, to consider the audience as a constant, logical part of the production from opening curtain to closing, audience participation is witless. Unless and until the production is ready to abide by the advice and information it requests, audience participation is fraudulent. Unless and until members of the production have the skill to direct the children's exuberance and control its effects, audience participation is ruinous.

Audience participation in nondramatic productions is something else again. Here it may be justified by its purpose and the way it is used, and by the skill of the performers.

In learning situations, audience participation may be not only justified but necessary. Many programs for young people are lecture-demonstrations, in whole or in part. A Sioux or Blackfoot may teach the audience sign language or a little song. The children repeat the movements that are shown and echo the syllables and the musical line. A dancer from Hawaii or India may explain the finger movements that tell a story, and the audience imitates them as closely as possible. The audience mimics the gesture language of the Little Theater of the Deaf. In each instance, there is an honest reason to ask the children to participate physically. If children are invited onstage to learn an Iroquois social dance or a game Catawba children used to play, this is interesting to the rest of the audience. The instructions are meant for those boys and girls as well. Participation works even better if the children to go onstage are selected beforehand and ready to go up on signal.

In folk song or sing-along programs, where it is intended that the audience join in, participation of this sort is natural and unforced. Most folk singers I know have a larger repertory than the young people in the audience, so that when the performers ask for request numbers they listen to the song titles the children call out and are able to sing them. If the artists don't know a song they usually say so—a far different matter than ignoring the child who requests it.

Magicians, clowns, and other "variety" performers who play directly to the audience and not to other characters onstage may have reason to call for audience participation. They do their tricks and tell their jokes to the children they are conscious of at all times. If they request help from the audience, and treat the boys and girls courteously, this is honest and justified.

15. Dance

Dance is a medium about which many adults have mixed emotions. There are its passionate adherents, who look upon it as the oldest and greatest of the arts, the one that communicates most universally and directly from one person to another, body to body. At the opposite extreme are those who refuse to grant dance dignity as an art form and consider it a harmless, entertaining, but essentially trivial way of releasing physical energy. Or regard it suspiciously as a medium through which "degenerates" express themselves. Or, bound by the old ethic that sees it as a temptation of the devil, fear that the display of bodies will arouse unholy passions in the spectators. And of course, there are those who have never thought seriously about dance and who, if they are aware of it at all, have a vague confusion of impressions rather than ideas in the back of their minds.

Even among dance enthusiasts there are those who regard only the romantic ballet of the nineteenth century as beautiful, and the movements developed by Martha Graham, Doris Humphrey, Merce Cunningham, and other great innovators of modern dance as meaningless and ugly. There are others who can enjoy the familiar folk dance of, say, Ireland or Yugoslavia, but are hostile to more exotic forms, such as the ethnic dance of Khmer or Japan. Some are convinced that while they might enjoy the Radio City Music Hall Rockettes, they would be bored by anything in dance that might have pretensions to being more than diversion.

The attitudes children bring to a performance are strongly influenced by the adults around them and by comments made on TV and other media. I've watched hundreds—literally—of children's dance audiences and it's been obvious that the younger the children and the less affected by adults beforehand, the more open they are to accept new impressions without prejudice and the more they respond with understanding to what they see. If no one has told them modern dance is ugly, they react spontaneously, being stirred where emotional response is called for, finding funny what was meant to be humorous, discovering pleasure in the rhythms and patterns of movement, and appreciating the physical skills of the performers. Watching an audience of children, one can feel their kinesthetic reaction to the tensions of the dancers.

Young children can accept other dance forms as readily, though they often can have more difficulty with the conventions of ballet than with those of modern movement. But even if their eyes are untrained in the artificialities of balletic styles, they can and do grasp the athleticism all dance demands of its practitioners. A child who hasn't been "informed" that ballet is effeminate in both its artists and its devotees finds thrilling the strength, balance, and precision necessary to go on point, leap, turn, or support a partner in the air. A child who hasn't been told that male dancers are less than totally masculine would be astounded by the concept after seeing the display of machismo by the men who perform the dances of Spain, black Africa, the Ukraine, and other parts of the world where people dance as unself-consciously as they walk.

I've talked with many children about dance, and most of them seem to have more difficulty in comprehending religious strictures against it than in visualizing David dancing before the ark, or other Biblical passages which indicate that dancing is pleasing in the sight of God. They have little trouble with the idea that dance is an integral part of the religion of many peoples.

Older children, who are not necessarily aware of the changes in their bodies as they grow toward puberty, can react very differently to dance performances. Depending on their level of sophistication—or lack of it—they may explode into laughter when dancers come into physical contact with each other. This reaction is not always obvious where there are as many adults in an audience as there are children, as when boys and girls are accompanied to the theater by their parents. It is unmistakable where young people predominate in an audience, as for a school assembly program with, perhaps, one teacher to thirty students, or more strongly, in out-of-school-time performances where the only adults are an occasional usher. When a man and a woman dancer come into contact, as for a lift or other support, the children's nervously raucous response indicates an intense awareness of the sexual potential—much more awareness than the choreographer or the performers may possess. This hysterical laughter can be as great when two men dancers come into contact. Whether the children read into this contact homosexual implications or preparation for violence, the uproar can take some moments to subside. For some reason, two or more women putting their arms around each other is acceptable without tension.

This laughter can spell disaster to a performance, particularly for a company unused to young audiences. It demoralizes the dancers, who fail to understand the reaction and fear they are being somehow unwittingly ridiculous. Not only does it indicate that the audience is deriving an unintended meaning from the dance, but the true meaning is being lost and the emphasis displaced onto factors that destroy the timing and the balance of the dance as a work of art.

In a program designed for children, it's so easy to eliminate this unfortunate response with a brief discussion from the stage before the performance begins, when the school principal announces the program, or a narrator attached to the company speaks about the dances. This preparation could include an explanation that dance is an art, the way music is. Just as musicians have their instruments, so dancers have theirs, but the instruments of dancers are their own bodies. Just as musicians make patterns in sound and time, dancers make designs in space and time. Just as a clarinet may perform alone or be backed by a piano and drums, so a dancer may be a soloist or be supported by other bodies. The musician achieves mastery of his instrument by long years of practice so that he is able to communicate his musical ideas with it. So dancers must train their bodies through years of arduous exercise to create the forms in space that will convey the desired meaning to the audience—and the costumes must not in any way limit their ability to move freely. As in music, the dancer's design need not have a literal, narrative meaning. It can, of course, tell a story, but it may convey a state of mind or a mood instead, or merely be a combination of movements just for fun. In a program not necessarily for young audiences, where it would be inappropriate to have this little message delivered from the stage, you can prepare your children yourself.

Laughter in a dance program should come at the point where the choreographer wants it, but there is something else that can trigger it at the wrong time. In the trade this is known as the "crotch problem" and it has at its heart the children's same nervous preoccupation, conscious or otherwise, with their own developing sexuality. When a male dancer clad only in a fig-leaf equivalent or leotard appears before a mature audience, the adults are likely to regard his anatomical structure as a unit and concern themselves with what his entire body is doing. With a children's audience, the focus of attention is frequently more circumscribed, particularly when the dancer wears a codpiece that exaggerates his natural endowments. Sometimes this is *all* a young audience notices. No matter how vainglorious the dancer may be in displaying his masculine attributes, this is not his primary purpose in being onstage. The male dancer has no need to make himself appear sexless for a young audience, but he should keep in mind the immaturity of these spectators and present himself as a whole being. This is very easy to do where the costume is the typical doublet and hose of the classical ballet. Simply lengthen the tunic a few inches so that it covers the full torso.

The crotch problem has its counterpart with female dancers, but its expression is different. A woman can appear onstage in a skin-tight leotard without evoking a titter, but let her wear a skirt and perform a movement that reveals a white undergarment—that's it. The children are convinced they've seen something they shouldn't, and they seize the opportunity to consider it salacious. It's so easy to eliminate the sniggering by (1) letting the children know that if they see something, they're entitled to see it, or (2) having the costume designer realize that petticoats or panties or whatever can be made to look like part of the costume, in color, texture, trimming, etc. These days many dancers don't wear bras, and and the children will pay no particular attention to the bosom if movement of the breasts during a dance is minimal; otherwise they will concentrate on it. In any event, the performer would be well advised to have enough fabric between herself and the audience so that every contour is not explicitly defined, or the audience's concentration will be on her chest to the detriment of her dancing.

If you want your children to enjoy dance as an art capable of enriching them through life, then what they see must be *good* dance. You can't take them to a tenth-rate student ballet company whose standards appall you and expect your children to be enthralled merely because they're children. They have as much right as you to become bored and fidgety with incompetent technique, tacky sets and costumes, badly played music, and whatever else may make the ballet of less than top professional quality. Just because *The Nutcracker* is "for kids" doesn't excuse it from adhering to the highest adult standards. Let's face it—*The Nutcracker* is a pretty dopey story that requires great dancing and superb staging to lift it into the realm of bearable entertainment, let alone art. A bad *Nutcracker* can make a child hate ballet forever.

The same top quality is requisite in modern or ethnic or folk dance, or however forms other than ballet are categorized. If what children see isn't performed well, they won't respond kinesthetically, that is, they won't feel the tensions of the dancers' bodies in their own muscles, and much of what the dance can offer them will be lost.

A successful program of dances for children may consist solely of virtuosic displays. Jazz dance, or tap, or anything else backed up by popular music in the contemporary idiom is something most boys and girls respond to with immediate enthusiasm. They identify first with the music they're familiar with and then enjoy the movement that kind of sound evokes. If these are the kinds of "fun" dances children do themselves, their response is virtually automatic.

A group of fine Spanish dancers can hold a young audience without difficulty. The obvious skill required, the tensions inherent in this kind of dance, the varieties of movement—classical court, flamenco, and peasant dances—theatrically effective costumes, guitars, and castanets, even without explanatory comment can rivet attention on the stage for the hour or so many programs for young people run. Dances of Africa, too, have enough exuberant vitality to thrill boys and girls when the movement is backed up by insistent drumming and exotic percussion or reed instruments. American Indian, Balkan, and other cultures employ dance movement that is sufficiently forceful and inherently exciting for children to get caught up in it even without understanding whatever social, dramatic, or religious content it embodies. But although young people can appreciate the movement for its own sake, it has more meaning for them if they are given some understanding of what the dance signifies to the dancers. If the children know this dance is one of welcome and that a harvesting ceremony, or this a courtship rite, another a preparation for battle, and yet another a social get-together—all this helps a child differentiate the dances, particularly in retrospect, and puts his comprehension on a deeper level.

Sometimes the commentary is conveyed in program notes, as is generally the case with a recital for adults. However, since many young children can't read easily, if at all, and even older boys and girls may have difficulty with some of the technical language that may be used, a verbal explanation of the dance's meaning is frequently helpful. For children's programs, a narrator will sometimes discuss some of the more important features the audience should comprehend. This works well if a brief explanation immediately precedes the number it describes, but it can be worse than useless if the narrator comments on the entire program in one summation at the beginning. The children may be able to remember what applies to the first dance, and perhaps, though not likely, to the second, but from that point on, the rest of the explanation will be a blur of confusion in their minds. If you're taking children to a performance for adults where you suspect you may have to rely on printed notes, it might be a good idea to take a tiny shielded flashlight to the theater so that you can read them to your young guests between numbers, if the houselights don't come up full—but never during the performance.

Some forms of ethnic dance *demand* an explanation if the audience is to obtain more than an inchoate impression of bizarre movement and swirling, glittering garments. Among those forms are dances of India, Indonesia, and other parts of the world where the gestures are inherently small. The dance may be essentially a storytelling medium at times, with the hands telling the tale, the face indicating the emotions, and the feet establishing the rhythms. The dances of Hawaii and other islands of the Pacific also have storytelling forms. If these dances are to have any meaning at all to an inexperienced audience, the children must know what the hands are saying in their exquisite, formal patterns. The explanation, when one is given, should immediately precede its dance, and can frequently include—logically and effectively—audience participation. If the narrator demonstrates the hand gestures to the boys and girls and encourages them to learn some of the movements, the children will not only remember them more clearly when they see them performed subsequently, but the gestures can provide unexpected flashes of poetry that illumine their lives permanently. A gesture that means elephant, or unfolding flower, or butterfly can bring sudden insights to a boy or girl who has never really thought about these things before. In addition to the preliminary explanation, but only if it doesn't interfere with the music, a commentary running simultaneously with the dance, repeating the story, can be most helpful to a young audience. The repetition adds a sense of security to the children, who are then free to watch the dance without the fear that they are losing the meaning of the tale. The stories, not incidentally, are usually from the folklore or great epics of the people, and along with their music and costumes serve as an introduction in a most sympathetic way to the grace and culture of their civilizations.

Where modern dance or ballet is presented in a program for children, there is frequently an introduction consisting of a demonstration of classroom exercises to give a glimpse of the rigorous training a dancer must undergo and of basic techniques. This demonstration is welcomed by the audience as a rule, particularly if each dancer demonstrates a different movement. When the dances that follow show how these exercises become part of a performance, the children's comprehension can be exhilarating to audience and performers alike.

Though children can respond to jazz dance and other abstract forms, they love stories as much when told in dance as in other media. Accordingly, when you're choosing for your children, it's wise to select a program that has at least one story whose subject matter is of interest to them. Generally speaking, a story will hold a child's attention for a longer period than a dance without a story, so abstract dances are best when they are shorter and more and varied than when they are longer and fewer. Boys and girls don't understand or like dances based on intangibles, such as hope, remorse, suffering, justice, and such unless it's made clear to them what the dancers are being hopeful, remorseful, suffering, or just about. Dance movement for the sake of movement alone they can enjoy, but if there's a hint of literary meaning in any of it, they'll leap to the conclusion that there are other implications they don't understand and will worry at the dance, looking for a story that isn't there. A story dance must be completely comprehensible, and abstract dance completely abstract, or the audience will come to a conclusion about the dance's intentions which neither the choreographer nor the performers will recognize.

Among dances to which children don't respond well generally (of course there can be exceptions) are those without accompanying sound—music, percussive beats, electronic score, whatever. Adults will accept a dance in which the only sounds are the dancers' breathing and the fall of their feet. Children won't.

Other factors can prevent children from enjoying a dance program to their utmost. A lack of understanding, on the part of those putting it together, of the capacities and limitations of the age of the audience can be disastrous to the degree that they are in error. This can go two ways. The material and its presentation can be so cutesy and condescending that every child above kindergarten squirms in embarrassment and resentment and closes his mind against whatever genuine values the dance may contain. Or in an effort *not* to condescend to the children, the company can present an adult or high school program way over their heads, which includes material outside a young audience's comprehension or interests; either no explanation is offered or it is too advanced in its ideas or vocabulary for the audience to understand what is being talked about.

In order to find subject matter that will interest a wide age span, dance companies have resorted to a variety of devices, some of which work and some don't. A fairly common one is to build a number around nursery rhymes, and this appeals only to sentimental adults or to children young enough to have affection for these little verses. Older children are frequently insecure at having left that part of their childhood so recently behind; they want to look forward to more mature ideas and not be reminded of their late comparative vulnerability. Some dances are games built on the alphabet, and these work better with older boys and girls; younger ones may be just learning to read and may be struggling with mastering the letters on the printed page. The same letters, exaggerated and distorted as they are created by human bodies, may be meaningless to first- and second-graders.

Dancers new to children's audiences sometimes make another mistake. An adult audience will sit quietly after a number has been concluded, or will move around if the break is long enough, and then return to the seats ready to continue as before. But with children, if something isn't happening onstage to hold their attention in the breaks, the quality of that attention is shattered and seldom returns at its best. If a narrator or a musician appears before the curtain to keep the audience occupied during necessary costume changes or rest for the performers, the children will maintain their interest at the same high level afterward. But this in-between entertainment can go too far: one dance company, still surviving on the shreds of a once-great reputation, used a merry-go-round as its signature, and involved the audience in the carousel's breakdown and repair not only as curtain raisers and closers but between dances as transitions and to hold the attention of the audience. The merry-go-round was too successful. The children were more concerned with it than they were with the dances, which became something to sit through until the merry-go-round returned.

When parents consider taking a child to the ballet, they usually think of *The Nutcracker,* performed at holiday seasons by ballet companies around the country. As currently presented by the New York City Ballet, this is an overwhelmingly opulent full-length program set to Tchaikovsky's delightful music, with magnificent costumes, stunning sets, and, it goes without saying, glorious dancing. All the story action is in the first act, while the second is a succession of charming divertissements. A child who already loves dance will be enraptured from start to finish. Even one who doesn't will be impressed by the sumptuousness, the glamor, of this all-out presentation.

But there are other ballets for young people besides *The Nutcracker. Coppelia,* in the repertory of many major ballet companies, has a story that makes more sense than *The Nutcracker*'s. The music by Delibes is as memorable to children as

Tchaikovsky's, and although *Coppelia* is not so lavish as *The Nutcracker*—what could be?—its sets are dramatically picturesque, and varieties of costumes and dance keep the visual aspects consistently entertaining. Many boys and girls prefer this story of the village maiden whose boyfriend falls in love with Dr. Coppelius's magic doll. The girl daringly enters the mysterious workshop to discover the truth and win his favor again. If your children are reluctant to see a story about magic dolls, tell them it's about a mad inventor and his robots, and they'll love it.

Swan Lake is another old tale children will like, provided they're prepared for a much slower pace, greater length, a full load of divertissements during which the story comes to a dead stop, and an unhappy ending. Tchaikovsky's score is one of his loveliest, and a variety of choreographers have staged their own concepts of the ballet. The same composer's *Sleeping Beauty,* another full-length spectacular ballet, has much the same advantages and disadvantages, except for a happy ending. In a first-class company, the sets and special effects for both can be striking: splendid ballroom and forest scenery; mists rising from the waters; and, in *Sleeping Beauty,* the great tangle of thorns overgrowing the castle. . . . Breathtaking!

La Fille Mal Gardée is a jolly tale, merrily making the most of how a young girl and her beau outwit their elders. *Graduation Ball* is light-hearted too, and there are other story ballets equally successful. But not all dance for children need come from this romantic period. Agnes de Mille's *Rodeo* delights today's children, who find that her picture of the rip-roaring West speaks their own language. The same is true of Jerome Robbins's *Fancy Free,* a romp about three sailors on shore leave. And of his *Interplay,* a kind of a competition between two groups. Alvin Ailey's *Revelations* is exciting to young people, whether or not they understand all its implications. And of course there are other adult dance programs children will enjoy.

Programs for young audiences to stay away from—again, there are exceptions—are those dealing with stories or emotions beyond their stage of emotional development or outside the scope of their concerns. Or individual nonsubject dances that are too long for their attention span. Or dances based on allegorical, abstract ideas. Or any of the other types referred to earlier to which children respond negatively.

Billy the Kid, choreographed by Eugene Loring, is often assumed to be ideal entertainment for boys and girls by nature of its subject matter. But if I had to select a list of ballets unsuitable for children, *Billy the Kid* would be near the top. As the title implies, this is the story of the outlaw. He has been traumatized as a boy by seeing his mother shot down. When he grows older he kills one man after another, symbolically destroying over and over the man who killed her. He completes through his girl the interrupted relationship with his mother and is eventually shot himself. However one feels about the story, the way in which it is presented is pure chaos to children. Billy's long-dead mother and his very much alive sweetheart are portrayed by the same dancer, indicative of their identification to Billy, but confusing to children, who don't understand that two different women are being depicted—not one, risen from her grave. His mother's killer and all the men Billy murders, one after the other, are played by a single dancer, who wears a green hat throughout. Boys and girls don't understand how the man whom they saw dead at Billy's feet can come to life in another costume to be shot again. As if that weren't more than enough, there are a flashback and a dream sequence that complete the disorientation in time and muddle events still further in a child's mind. Only very young children, too young even to try to follow the story, enjoy *Billy.* All that interests them is the bang-bang-you're-dead played by grownups the way they themselves play. Older children are frustrated and irritated in their largely futile attempt to make sense out of the ballet.

Sometimes dances children like and the meaning they extract from them can be startling to an adult. Jerome Robbins's *The Cage* is the story of a community of female insects who mate with their males and then destroy them. Two males wander into the community and a young female is reluctant to slay one when he has fulfilled his function. Eventually tribal pressure compels her to abide by the tradition and she is then accepted as a mature member of her society. The man/woman relationship and the sexual commentary are savagely explicit. After a matinee by the New York City Ballet, which included two other ballets on the bill, I interviewed some dozen youngsters, from eight years old to fourteen, to learn their reactions. Without exception, each chose *The Cage* as the one enjoyed most. They liked the set, overlaid with a large web that covered spooky shadows in the corners; they liked the costumes; but most of all they liked the story. One child told me it was about a couple of strangers who tried to invade a village; they were killed and they got what was coming to them. Another said it was about a girl who had considered betraying her people with an enemy but had finally done the right thing. The others came to some variant of these conclusions. Not one seemed aware of the venomous sexual implications so obvious to their elders. And after considerable contemplation of the interviews, I've decided that from the viewpoint of most children, this is satisfactory material. For the exceptional child capable of understanding the real meaning, or one who has a parent who feels compelled to explain it, I'd suggest waiting a few years until the child's emotional and social development catches up with his intellect.

Can children see adequate dance on television? Unfortunately, no. Dance is one performing art that seldom translates well into film or tape. The sense of space, basic to dance on a stage, is destroyed by the camera. Stripped from the movement is any feeling of traversing of distance or urgency. The moving camera distorts the viewer's perspective, the angle from which he views the dance, and his power of seeing the entire stage at one time, along with his ability to concentrate on a specific part of the onstage activity. And of course, the perception of scale is diminished to the vanishing point on the small screen. All this contributes to a lack of the immediacy that can make dance such an intensely personal experience in a theater. The communication, body to body, between artist and spectator, which is dance's unique province, ceases to exist.

The only way your children can appreciate dance fully is to be taken to the theater or to have dance brought to them.

There are many small professional dance groups that are successful in bringing dance into schools, Y's, settlement houses, parks, and other places where they can find audiences of young people. If you want dance for your children, these groups should be considered as supplements to, not substitutes for, the major companies. These smaller dance groups are willing to tour off the beaten track, while the huge organizations usually limit their activities to the larger cities and perform primarily for adults. If you are connected with a school, community center, etc., as a member of the PTA or in some other capacity, you may want to bring one or more of these small dance groups in to perform for your children. Here are some thoughts to hold if you do:

Some solo performers with magnetic personalities can keep an audience entranced for a full hour, but in many instances two or more dancers onstage at one time can capture the children's attention more easily. Also, if there are costume changes, what means will the soloist use to occupy the audience when he is offstage?

If you want a group, be sure your stage area is large enough for the number of dancers. The average elementary school auditorium, for instance, can't accommodate more than six on its stage, and fewer might be better.

Dancers of India and others whose movement stays low to the ground can perform where the stage ceiling is low, but performers of most other types of dance, which include jumping and leaping vertically, need ceilings high enough not to interfere with them.

Dancers require a good floor. Wood is best. Cement is murder on their feet, legs, and backs. There should be no splinters or protruding nails and the floor should not be waxed or varnished except with special stage varnishes, and it should be washed with water, not oil. Slippery floors are the dancer's nightmare.

Wing space and the crossover (the passage at the rear of the stage behind the cyclorama or the back curtain) should be cleared so that a dancer can leap offstage without crashing into anything and can move from one side of the stage to the other in safety behind the scenes.

Many children, after attending a performance, want to become dancers, and parents, wanting to gratify them, think ballet lessons. Ballet lessons are fine, but don't forget there are many kinds of dance, and possibly your child might be more emotionally attuned to another form. So before making a final decision, let your child see various kinds of ethnic dance, and modern, jazz, and even dance of the school of Isadora Duncan. If you do determine it is ballet you want for your little girl, be sure she is not allowed to go on point until she is physically ready. Most great dancers and teachers feel that to go on point before a girl is ten years old can irreparably damage her feet and legs. If it is your son who will be studying dance, this is no problem. Males do not go on point.

Whether children are dance students or just intelligent members of the audience, dance can give them in terms of movement what they're most fond of—superbly controlled physical action, humor, even a story. . . . They can soar or drop or spin with the dancers, feel the pull and strain of their muscles and echo the movement in their own thighs or backs or stomachs. Dance can give them an appreciation of their own bodies and can open to boys and girls vistas of the possibilities of beauty their bodies are capable of. The delight that children find in dance is one that can be increased by your sharing it with them.

16. Opera
and Other Matters

MIME

Akin to dance, but a theatrical form in its own right, is mime. Unlike dance, which may be an abstract composition of forms and movement, mime seeks to create illusions of reality. The movements of mime are stylized, but they must clearly define whatever they are describing.

A narration may be helpful in starting the audience off, setting the scene, so to speak, and sometimes placards announce the subject. But if the mime is so unclear and fuzzy that the audience is confused about what is happening, then it's not seeing good mime.

Classical mime uses a minimum of props, sets, and costume alterations to create an enchanted world. Some modern mimes mix pure mime movements with dance and even with speech. While these are occasionally effective, I can't escape the suspicion that dance and acting are substituted for a technique that more rigorous training in a demanding art form would have supplied. Superb performers like Moni and Mina Yakim and

Tony Montanaro need little but their own bodies to build a magical environment.

Children are puzzled by mime movements and try to imitate them. They are fascinated by the way a mime can appear to walk and run great distances, or climb stairs, while remaining in one spot. They try to use their own hands and bodies to describe an invisible wall, or box, or piano.

Mime can tell a brief anecdote or a joke with one performer, or a program-long story with many performers.

Aside from its being on a par with other great theatrical forms, mime is good for children. It gives them an awareness of their bodies and the space in which they move. It heightens observation and perception, and develops insights into character and the quality of movement. First-class performances of mime should be part of any child's theatrical education.

OPERA

Possibly the most difficult theatrical form to present to children is opera. Opera is like dance in many respects—one must accept its conventions if one is to enjoy it; and the main instrument is the human voice, part of the body. Like the dance, too, opera can—indeed must—employ other theatrical ingredients: costumes, sets, and lights, as well as a story line, acting, etc., which dance doesn't alway require.

"Introductions to opera" for children have the best of intentions. More often than not, instead of charming boys and girls into loving opera, the effects are as opposite as if hating opera had been the goal.

Few operas have been written for children. Gian Carlo Menotti's contemporary *Help, Help, the Globolinks!* and *Amahl and the Night Visitors* are conspicuous as being not only of this rare genre, but successful with their audiences. Humperdinck's *Hansel and Gretel* has beautiful music and is often staged superlatively, but I've met as many children who disliked it as who adored it. Massenet and Rossini each composed a *Cinderella* that has its adherents, and there are a handful of other operas either specifically for children or with stories young children find intelligible or of concern to them.

Several mistakes are made only too often by those who present opera to young audiences. The first is in using less than good voices. Since the programs are "just for kids," the performing company reserves its best voices for adults and sends out singers whose training is not yet sufficiently advanced or whose talent will never progress to where they could sing for grownups. Without being aware of the finer points of the art, children can appreciate that what they are being given is second-rate or worse, and they have a right to be unimpressed. If you want your children to recognize quality when they hear it as adults, you have to start them off with it. Children's operas suffer musically in many instances when a lone piano must represent the rich color of a full orchestra.

Another mistake is selecting the wrong opera. Children must understand what it's all about. There are stylistic conventions they must adapt to, and this they can do—but an incomprehensible story on top of them is too much for most audiences, which sit in silent misery or rebel openly. In many operas for adults, the plots involve seduction or prostitution, murder, adultery, jealousy, and other assorted crimes and passions. When these operas are reduced to an hour for an audience of young people, the tendency is to eliminate or disguise elements of the story that the boys and girls shouldn't know about. The lengths some adapters will go to are absurd to avoid letting it be known that Traviata is a high-priced call girl and that Carmen isn't even high-priced. What happens in the opera makes little sense after cuts have been made, for either time's or Bowdler's sake. If for whatever cause cuts destroy the story, it stands to reason the opera should not have been selected for young people in the first place. They should be "introduced to opera" by a story that can take it, or they should go with their parents to a performance for adults that is not mangled through being hacked to bits.

Whether a child attends an opera for children or one for grownups, understanding the language is crucial to enjoyment. There are those rare children whose love for this kind of music is so intense that only the music matters, but the majority want to know what's happening every bar of the way. I've seen children sullen with hostility sitting uncomprehendingly through some of the world's most glorious music, sung in Italian, French, or German. Sometimes, in abbreviated versions, a narrator summarizes in English the action between arias and explains what the foreign-language aria is about, but children still resent being excluded from full knowledge of the words.

I'm aware of the controversary raging about whether operas for Americans should be performed in English, regardless of their original language. And I've sat through operas sung in English of which I couldn't catch more than one word in a hundred. My conclusion, reached after watching who knows how many tortured audiences of children, is that opera for them has to be in English. If, as adults, they will be willing to attend opera sung in the original language, that's another matter, but at least let them not have language as one more block to their pleasure in music. As to the incomprehensibility of sung English, this, it seems to me, is merely a matter of competence, not of principle. As audiences, once indifferent to acting, now demand credible performances as well as acceptable voices, so they will demand—and get—intelligible enunciation if they insist on it.

When, as is commonly done, a narrator bridges the arias, the results are disastrous. Everything about the story that would interest a young audience is chopped away to leave room for arias which seem to go on forever.

Opera, whether for young audiences or mature ones, should be a full theatrical experience. If it's less than that, the audience is defrauded of what eye and ear should absorb.

With the permission of Jack Leskoff, a colleague in the area of children's theater and my occasional writing collaborator, I quote his review of a children's performance of *La Bohème*, which he titled:

Making Children Hate Opera

An example of making children hate opera was presented at the Metropolitan Museum of Art by Boris Goldovsky Saturday afternoon, November 20. The choice of opera was Puccini's *La Bohème*, a work which every cultivated adult of our society knows so, ergo, children must be taught to appreciate this double love story also.

Youngsters are receptive to love stories if other factors are dominant—the broad humor of *The Barber of Seville*, the fantasy in *Le Coq d'Or*, the whimsy of *The Love for Three Oranges*, or the magic of Stravinsky's *Le Rossignol*. When will well-intentioned grownups realize that for children the story line must outrank the musical line in importance or at least equal it? Not in *Bohème*.

At this performance the children were asked to listen to aria after aria of lovely singing while watching a reduced cast in an almost static concert version of the score. Since the four personable players were in modern dress (Musetta in a pants suit), Mr. Goldovsky reminded the audience that the action takes place a long time ago, when there were no antibiotics. To emphasize this further, Rodolfo sat waving a quill pen at a modern table. Movable plain-painted wooden flats were the only scenery. There was no attempt to utilize lighting to enhance the production—not even to darken the stage somewhat while the lovers groped about the floor searching for the key after the candle flame had blown out.

Mr. Goldovsky made some odd comments:

"Good girls always say 'no' a few times before they say 'yes.' "

"She sings a waltz which is a little like a waltz because it is in three-quarter time."

"Mimi is going to die, so if you feel like crying, cry."

Applause should come at proper intervals—the end of a scene or the end of an act. Mr. G. believes in perpetuating the questionable practice of applause at the end of arias. He encouraged the children to applaud after each, cuing the audience and breaking whatever continuity and mood remained to the opera.

But the real trouble (and offense) of this production was its editing. By restricting the singers to the four major characters, Mr. Goldovsky eliminated those portions of the story which might have been of interest to the young audience. (E.g., the controversy with the landlord in Act I, the café crowd scene of Act II, the mock duel and mock bullfight of Act IV, as well as Colline's singing farewell to his overcoat.) The youngsters sat through one hour and twenty minutes with admirable restraint and unenthusiasm. Since there was no intermission, Bravi to them.

This was a pleasant concert for adults who remember the operatic action and who are emotionally moved by the familiar themes. Those adults enjoyed it whose memories could supply the missing orchestra (Mr. Goldovsky's piano was the only accompaniment), complete cast, scenery, costumes, lights, and action. For them, the singers were Mimi, Rodolfo, Musetta, and Marcello. But for the fledglings, the performers were merely attractive singers. The children were polite—after all, what else could they be with more than a third of the audience composed of escorting adults? But it's going to be tough giving these children *La Bohème* again when they mature.

I saw the same performance, and I echo Mr. Leskoff's opinions. His space didn't permit him to make a point which grated on me—Mr. Goldovsky's patronizing, grandfatherly address to the children.

Of all the operas for children I've seen, two stand out clearly as being on all counts superior to the rest. Both, as it happened, were by Rossini. The *Cinderella in Italy,* referred to earlier, is one. The other is *The Barber of Seville,* as produced by the Metropolitan Opera Studio, an adjunct of the Metropolitan Opera. I saw this opera first at the Brooklyn Academy of Music, where it played before school groups from the third grade through high school. As presented, it ran about an hour and forty-five minutes, including an intermission. If I remember correctly, the orchestral music was taped and the voices were adequate—in some instances, very fine. The set was opulent, having a two-story staircase, a charming living room with spinet, etc. The costumes were rich in fabric and color and added visual dash to match the spirited singing and the action. The audience stamped and whistled its approval. The second occasion on which I saw this same company's presentation of *Barber,* with other singers this time, was at a Children's Theatre Conference Showcase. About twenty-five minutes of it were given as the first item on a full day of excerpts that included a couple of musical fairy tales, a cowboy story, and other material of obvious appeal to boys and girls.

Several classes of schoolchildren had been invited to sit in the first rows of the theater so that the adults behind them could observe their reactions to the productions being showcased. I spoke afterward with two of the teachers who had escorted classes, since the teachers had on the way home taken a survey of their pupils' preferences. I should have expected the cowboy story to be first. It had a fistfight and other strong action. Or perhaps they would have liked best a rock production with a contemporary background. I've noticed that children often say they like best what they saw last; earlier experiences tend to blur in their memory. But with these children—"culturally deprived," from a poor "socioeconomic environment" in the "inner city"—all but two or three voted strongly for *The Barber of Seville.* "The music was nice." "The lady in the shiny pink dress sang pretty." "The drunk soldier was funny." "I liked the man with the fat belly." "They had a nice house." What the children were saying is that this presentation was a full theatrical experience in a sense that no other was that day; the performance was highly professional, the music was even more sparkling than the physical production, the story line was clear, with enunciation the children could understand, the comedy was funny and pertinent, and they were involved in every aspect.

Why should ten-year-old children, two-thirds of whom were black, respond to a love story of long-ago Spain? Because it was presented with no concessions to quality by reason of the audience's age. Because it respected not only the audience but the story and music, and because the performers respected themselves too much to give less than their best to any audience. If more opera were offered of such quality and in such spirit, more children would be enthusiastic about opera in their maturity.

ANIMATION

Mentioning animation to some parents and other critics of TV is the same as waving the proverbial red flag at a bull. They launch a tirade against the violence of the animated cartoons, or their idiocy, or whatever other irritant to the adult viewer is foremost at the moment. These fulminations miss the point. Animation is merely a medium which can be used to say virtually anything, just as puppetry is a medium, or dance, or "live" films. If TV employs the medium to express violence or inanity, animation can't be blamed. The fact that many animated cartoon programs have been replaced by "live" programs which no more reflect peaceful cooperation or intelligence is testimony to that.

Where animation can be blamed is that so often it's poor animation. The days are gone when the Disney Studios, Warner Brothers, and other large Hollywood companies could profitably turn out fully animated cartoons, in which all figures and their backgrounds moved naturally, and the aim was to imitate life. This treatment has become too expensive given current costs and marketing procedures, and the aim now is to get the message across with as little animating as possible, and, therefore, as little movement. Instead of having an animated figure stand, shift his weight, look around, raise his arm, adjust his leg, and call out, as would have been the case earleir, now the figure stands woodenly, raises his arm, and moves his eyes and his mouth only. This is a visual shorthand, the conventions of which children adapt to swiftly. Such limited animation is ground out by the mile at the Hanna-Barbera factories in their series with Yogi Bear, Huckleberry Hound, the Flintstones, the Jetsons, etc., etc. Inasmuch as these studios use the same voices in most of their products, it becomes simple to pick out Hanna-Barbera cartoons after you watch and listen for a while. The contents of these cartoons and their limited animation technique are no better or worse than most of their competitors.

The Charlie Brown animation specials, while limiting animation to a degree, are more artistic products visually than the Saturday-morning kiddie fare. The animation for the Dr. Seuss specials, taking their inspiration from drawings by the doctor himself, are more imaginative than most, and quite clever.

Under the classification of animation, people lump not only animated drawings but stop-action photography with puppets, cut outs, etc. They've all been tarred with the same brush, and just as unfairly. One can't hold a medium responsible for what is done with it by those whose aims are less a product expressing ideas, emotion, or beauty than making a buck in the lucrative TV marketplace.

Why so much animation on TV? Because children love it. I've watched year-old children in a room with the television on pay no attention to programs with real actors, but focus on the set when a cartoon appeared. They couldn't have had any knowledge of what the plots were about, but there was obviously some comprehension of what the linear characters were doing that was missing when they watched live people on the screen. I've wondered whether this might have something to do with the way children's eyes develop. A cartoon can be easier to see. All extraneous detail is eliminated from the frames. The viewer's eye is focused on the essentials only—the moving mouth, the opening hand, the swinging foot. The animation brings the eye in close to concentrate on that which is important, doing much of the eye's work, sparing the brain the necessity of sorting out what it sees. Nothing, no matter how decorative, even shadows, is included to confuse the eye unless it has to do with the action. In some respects, the limited animation so much in use today is as much for the lazy eyes of the viewer as it is for the pocketbook of the producer.

Non-television animation, as is turned out in smaller studios in this country and abroad, can reach heights where it can be called art. Sometimes whether animation is limited or otherwise isn't a factor. What matters is that those who produce these animated films—whether lyrical, cynical, comical, or deeply tragic, or in combination—have something to say, in a medium they respect, to other people they respect. It comes down to intent, then. Animation, like other forms of production, can be theater or kiddie show. It's sad that so much of what our children see falls into the latter category.

PUPPETRY

In some respects, puppetry on the stage is very like animated drawings in film or on television. Here are artificial creatures, endowed with life through the magic of theater, in which the viewer may believe for the duration of the production. Puppetry is successful to the degree that it is convincing. If the puppeteer manipulates his little people in such a way that they are imbued with the illusion of life, if they move in a world scaled to their being and consistent with it, the physical production is satisfactory, even thrilling. As for what they do—the content of the presentation, story, or vaudeville routines—this is subject to the same rules any other theatrical production should follow.

Whether the puppets are hand, rod, shadow, mask, or stringed, children can identify with them more immediately than with living actors. Perhaps the scale has something to do with it, but whatever the reason, most girls and boys are at once at home in the world these little figures establish. Perhaps, as with animated cartoons, the simplicity of most puppets relative to real people is a factor, but because children love puppets so, they should be entertained by *good* puppetry. A marionette, walking across the stage, should plant his feet as firmly on the "ground" as if his strings were not supporting his weight. A hand puppet, manipulated from below the stage, should not have the puppeteer's arm come into sight to demolish the effect of the puppet operating on its own. The illusion is all. The voices should be clear and differentiated so that it's always evident who is speaking, and business should not distract from the main action.

Puppetry is becoming more and more a mixed-media form. Several kinds of puppets may be used in one production. Rear-screen projections may create special stage effects. Live actors are used—not just speaking from in front of the stage, as Fran does to Kukla and Ollie, but irrupting onto the stage as a genie or a giant.

The presumption is common that puppets are just for children, but this isn't so by any means. It is the content of a puppet play that defines the age of its audience, just as in any other medium of entertainment. A puppetry play can be warm and gentle and nonthreatening for three- and four-year-olds, or it can be as brassily raunchy as Wayland Flowers's nightclub act. One of the kindest lessons we can teach our children is that they needn't outgrow puppetry with their first set of teeth. It can offer a wide range of theater adventures whether the boys and girls participate in them across a stage or through a TV screen.

IDENTIFICATION OR RECOGNITION SHOWS

There may be another name, but this is how I think of these shows, most of whose impact is dependent on the audience's ability to recognize the characters around whom a production is built. There are at least three that have played the New York area in the past several years, and gone on to tour the country: *Disney on Parade, H. R. Pufnstuf,* and one whose name escapes me, which featured Yogi Bear, Fred Flintstone, and other Hanna-Barbera cartoon characters. The Disney shows are the most opulent and the most heartlessly plastic. The Pufnstufs are the noisiest and the most vulgar, and the Hanna-Barbera, the tackiest.

In the Disney production, characters well known to audiences make an appearance, to wild ovations from children and adults alike. Mickey Mouse, Donald Duck, Pluto, and Herbie the Volkswagen come out to take their bows as stars. Sometimes that's mostly all they do—walk around and wave. Sometimes they're incorporated into little skits. These figures are part of a lavish production that may feature Peter Pan or other Disney characters flying from ropes or trapezes, and some all-out production numbers repeating dances from *Mary Poppins,* for example, or another successful film. Of all the recognition shows, this is by far the most professionally slick. Except for one or two segments (e.g., a scene from *Alice in Wonderland* that fills the arena with girls costumed as butterflies, waving soft, silken wings, or the *Poppins* chimney-sweep dance, in which the men display their own flesh-and-blood faces), the entire production is glittering hard, sterile, and sterilized. Mickey and his animal friends are people with huge plastic heads covering their own, and an invisible mesh for them to see and breathe through. All their songs and jokes come not from them, but from the sound system on a tape, while the jaws may or may not move in synchronization. Even where the faces show, when they "sing" they mouth words that have been recorded from the original film. There is little that is truly live or soft, like real skin. It's impossibly sanitized, as only artificial or lifeless forms can be. To a member of the audience unfamiliar with Goofy or Disney's Seven Dwarfs, the numbers in these revues would be meaningless. Few segments can stand on their own feet as entertainment without the audience's presumed familiarity with the characters.

Disney on Parade, as I have seen it in several instances at Madison Square Garden, is hard sell for the line of Disney-affiliated products. The ways in and out of the auditorium are lined with hawkers pushing Mickey Mouse balloons, toys, T-shirts of Disneyland and Disney World, books, you name it.

Only the parent with a will of iron can pass through with pocketbook intact, without succumbing to weeping children who want everything they see.

The Pufnstuf shows feature characters from the Saturday-morning kiddie TV programs in which his honor the mayor and the Lidsville people(?) star. In addition to WitchiPoo and the other grotesques, they regularly include campy versions of Frankenstein's monster or other creatures of mock horror in some old burlesque routines that have been updated and laundered for young audiences. Their master of ceremonies is usually a boy actor or singer the children know from a popular film or from TV appearances. The program uses strobe lights and any other startling attention-demanding devices as gimmicks, and leans heavily on slapstick and forays into the audience to build up spurious excitement. Their clowns tend to have balloon breasts and raucous voices. The show's conclusion is always a rousing flag-waving number with everyone on stage whooping it up patriotically, and this is supposed to make us forget whatever came before that bored us or turned us off.

I've seen only one of the Hanna-Barbera shows, and that was sadly amateurish. Characters from the animation series' stable each had a fifteen- or twenty-minute routine in the spotlight, emceed by a host who worked unremittingly for audience enthusiasm. The same small handful of actors climbed out of one set of plastic-headed costumes and into another while the emcee was killing time onstage. The youngest children, whose only concern was to identify their TV favorites, were pleased enough, but it was a disaster for anyone else.

When an ice show comes to town it usually has "something for the kids." Sometimes Snoopy, from the *Peanuts* comic strip, skates on, shakes hands with himself like a boxer, and skates off, to wild applause, and it seems to satisfy. In one instance, a major production number was built around a sketch that included characters from a well-known group of commercials paid for on the air by a cheap nationwide fast-food chain. Inasmuch as the food chain also had a large advertisement in the ice show's program, the surmise is inescapable that the eatery had an investment in the show, conditions of which included the segment featuring characters identified with it in the public mind and a story line that made no bones about it. Inclusion of this number is morally reprehensible. An audience that pays its money to see an ice show has no intention of purchasing as well the dubious privilege of a ten-minute glorified commercial for hamburgers. No matter that the children might have enjoyed recognizing their "friend" from TV—the producers had no right to collect tickets from the public and make a deal for a flagrant selling job to the public and combine them in one operation.

Building episodes around commercial figures is very different from creating a number based on fairy tale characters, as circuses and other spectacles do. When there is a parade of Mother Goose or magic story people passing by, it becomes a legitimate game for the children to guess that here comes Humpty Dumpty, or Little Red Riding Hood, or the Three Little Pigs, or Little Miss Muffet. But if a playlet involving these creatures is put on for the youngest audience, it's only viable when it can be understood without prior knowledge of the characters.

RODEOS

Rodeos have been a traditional family entertainment in which children cheer for their favorite bronc-buster or bulldogger, and admire the skill of the men and women contestants who are the performers. I doubt whether young people would be so enthusiastic if they had any appreciation of the sickening cruelty underlying much of what they see.

Most bucking horses are not the wild horses they are pur-ported to be. They are "inspired," by means that are inhumane to an almost unimaginable degree, to put on a performance that will give the riders a chance to demonstrate their proficiency. Electric prods to their genitals as they are forced into the arena are among the mildest means of obtaining the action that riders and public demand.

The steers are forced down when their muscles are twisted agonizingly. The "sport" of calf-roping and tying has been popular for generations despite its actually being the chasing of a terrified baby animal, which is caught by a rope, brutally knocked off its feet, and bound, with speed of the operation being the only concern. I have been roped in fun on many occasions, and I can assure you that it hurts. Torn muscles and broken bones are the least these helpless animals have to expect.

Young audiences should be reminded of what we discussed earlier in the context of hurting the feelings of those who come to be amused: a joke is a joke only if all concerned find it funny; a game is a game only if all concerned enter into it voluntarily and no one is harmed.

RADIO AND RECORDINGS

Although the golden days of radio are long past, public and noncommercial radio stations here and there broadcast shows for children as part of their regular programming, and another few put them on as specials from time to time. Radio has always had one great advantage over television, cinema, and the stage in that the listener's imagination is uninhibited. In the other media, the eye binds the audience to details of someone else's fancies. Where only the ear is involved, the mind can invent fancies of its own. The ear hears that Cinderella is the most beautiful girl in the world, wearing the loveliest of garments. No sight can possibly equal *your* concept of what Cinderella looks like. The casting director's "beautiful" and the costume designer's "loveliest" could add up, for you, to someone you wouldn't take to a cat fight. In a horror story, no visual image can compete with the undefined horror in your mind, no science fiction bug-eyed monster hold a candle to your internal visualization.

Some parents and grandparents may remember the Nila Mack *Let's Pretend* fairy tale dramatizations on Saturday mornings. In almost all stories they hewed to the original in their important aspects. Children loved them because they gave the imagination a structure on which to build without hindrance. *You* knew what Prince Charming looked like better than anyone else, or the fearsomeness of Jack's giant, and because these were *your* mental images they worked for you, satisfying deeply your need for the tale's relevance.

There's so little of this kind of radio magic for today's boys and girls that the appeal to the ear alone can best be found in tapes and records of literature for young people. Sometimes this literature is dramatized, sometimes read well by a good actor, but it evokes the same kind of response from children. Most of the standard fairy tales as well as folklore and myths from other countries can be found in excellent recordings. These aren't always inexpensive, but many libraries have a wide selection of children's records which may be listened to on the premises or taken home like books.

Not stories alone, but music is available to children. Recordings of *Peter and the Wolf* are popular, and so are folk songs and contemporary compositions of many kinds.

How do you judge which recordings are good? Just as you would evaluate anything else—partly on technical proficiency and partly on content. Your librarian may be of help to you, and several magazines, usually before Christmas in time for gift-giving, publish their recommendations. There's no substitute for hearing with your own ears, however, and the pleasure of a creatively stimulating aural experience is one that can be shared easily with your children.

One of the inventions of our time that I consider a mixed blessing is the transistor radio. Agreed, there's no substitute for it in a power failure and it brings news and music to all persons in almost every imaginable place. I wonder, though, whether young audiences take advantage of the wide range of music offered or whether most children tune most of the time to the popular forms. What readily available transistors have done is to make boys and girls unacquainted with silence. So many don't seem to know how to move without being hooked by ear to the little box that has them hypnotized. I think, too, it would be a good idea if radios and phonographs carried a warning like cigarette packages that too high sound levels are dangerous to one's hearing and health.

PREPARATION AND FOLLOW-UP

Not every performance your children attend needs to have the way paved for it. Most of the casual entertainment they see is self-explanatory and well within their ken. In fact, my objection to much so-called entertainment is that it provides no challenge to curious, growing minds. It does children no harm to reach a little beyond easy comprehension—whether for stimulating ideas that are new or for unfamiliar vocabulary that the production's context makes intelligible.

There are times when you may want to have a comfortable, informal chat with your young people, however, before they attend a performance of a kind that's strange to them. Or you may go beyond talking. You might take them to a museum where there are pictures or models of something in the production that will excite their desire for it.

Are you taking your children to their first concert? Then why not learn what the program will be and play records of the musical selections a few weeks before the great day. A degree of familiarity with the music may increase their anticipation. You could share any curiosity-piquing facts about the music, its composer, the performing artists, or the concert hall. Even better, if you're lucky enough to number among your friends a musician your children admire as a person, the artist might demonstrate in a one-to-one relationship the skill required to play good music.

For a trip to the opera, not only might you play recordings; you could go into detail about the libretto. If the ending is a surprise (as in *Help, Help, the Globolinks!*), you won't want to give it away, but knowledge about the story, presented lightly, could make children want to go more instead of less. It's important that they understand and accept operatic conventions if they are to enjoy opera fully. You might want to go into some of the history of opera as an institution that would have a bearing on their pleasure.

Gilbert and Sullivan operettas require more preparation than at first thought would seem likely. They are very much the product of the Victorian era and their scripts are filled with references that had meaning for the audiences of their own times, but not much for us without explanation. The accents of a British troupe won't make comprehension easier unless your young people have a prior grasp on the intricacies of the plots. It's well worth the time to make these explanations, because children love the nonsense and the music once they're over the initial hurdles. Boys and girls tend to accept the satires as straight comedies. When they're of an age to appreciate how the naval system of advancement is being derided, they'll have even more fun with *Pinafore*. With *Patience,* you might point out the similarity between Bunthorne's lovesick maidens and the swooning, shrieking groupies who follow rock stars today. You could also point out where G & S missed the boat completely, as in *Princess Ida,* a mockery of women's liberation that backfired. One of the songs jeers that woman will be man's equal only when we land on the moon—a joke on both scores in the late nineteenth century. Feeling privy to inside information on these operettas, children enjoy them all the more.

For musicals, on film, or as revivals on the stage, you don't *have* to talk about the Nazi takeover of Austria before World War II for *The Sound of Music;* the rancher-homesteader conflicts for *Oklahoma!;* the introduction of Western ideas into Southeast Asia for *The King and I;* or the Russian pogroms and other persecutions of the Jews for *Fiddler on the Roof.* You don't have to, but those musicals will be more memorable if young people can place them in the context of history and see them as part of a larger pattern.

Background information on plays may also interest your children. Molière has several plays that adapt well for young people. Chekhov's *The Marriage Proposal* and a host of other classics provide opportunities for broadening horizons.

Incidentally, many children have a dread of the classics, and if you have any problems in your household, you might call to their attention that books and theater pieces that have endured for centuries, even millennia, as with Greek drama, have lasted because they speak about the human condition in terms that are as moving now as when they were first conceived. If this sounds too high falutin, just say they've lasted because people still enjoy them.

If you're taking young children to see a fairy tale presentation, they'll like to go over the story again before they see the show. It might be a good idea to caution them that some dramatic liberties may be taken so that if the play doesn't conform to the story in all details, they won't be too disappointed.

We've already mentioned, in Chapter 15, that children new to dance should be given to understand how the body is the dancer's instrument. If the dance has a plot, you could talk about it, or you could discuss the culture an ethnic dancer might be demonstrating.

Something to beware of is overpreparing children to where all the fun, all the spontaneity of the event disappears. If they suspect that from your standpoint this is primarily an educational experience and not for their amusement, they may dig in their heels and refuse to go, or go grimly determined not to enjoy themselves.

You may want to take or send your children to a show you're convinced they'll enjoy, and they may balk. Even when there's nothing else they'd rather do, they've picked up the notion that they won't like it. Their reasons may not strike you as valid, but the kids are adamant. It's no good dragging them forcibly— that's no way to start off a happy afternoon or evening. This, then, is the time for all good parents to be underhanded. I don't mean to bribe the children, or to lie to them—merely to build up the event in terms that will make it seem attractive, even though those terms may be unorthodox. This is fair only when you're certain the children will find the show truly pleasurable. As we mentioned earlier, children who don't want anything to do with a ballet about a doll-maker may want to see a mad inventor and his robots. It's the same difference.

I remember when my son was about ten or so, I wanted him to see a *Ruddigore* by a good Gilbert and Sullivan repertory company. He had adored *The Mikado* and *The Pirates of Penzance,* but he wouldn't have anything to do with *Ruddigore.*

The title signified nothing to him, even when I explained it meant "red blood." So I told him it was science fiction, which was his consuming interest at the time. I went into some of the background not readily comprehensible to a non-Briton, but put the emphasis on the ghosts and the curse. He went to *Ruddigore* and it became one of his favorites.

A year or two later, when Shakespeare in the Park produced *The Comedy of Errors,* I thought this would be a good introduction to the bard. "No," my son said. "Absolutely not." Shakespeare was highbrow and dull, and difficult to understand. Everybody knew that. So a day or two later I picked up my copy of Shakespeare and laughed aloud as I read to myself. My son wanted to know what was funny, and I read him some of the earthier passages not usually explored in school, and explained what they meant. He changed his mind about going. I arranged a picnic on the grass before the performance, to make a gala occasion of it. The production was a superb one, and my son laughed till his sides hurt at all the "dirty" jokes. Not only did he relish every innuendo, but he felt superior to the adults who didn't. The result was that he developed a passion for Shakespeare and other classical theater which has endured.

I'm not holding these examples out as models, merely as ideas that could possibly be adapted to situations in which your children are unenthusiastic about something you want them to go to. However, this approach demands absolute honesty afterward. If it turns out that the children were right and the show was a bomb, it's no good trying to pretend everything was a rip-roaring success that your children didn't appreciate. All you can do is apologize and admit you were mistaken and they were entitled to dislike it.

A visit to the local movie house or drive-in is routine to many children and one they don't get excited about. It's much more special when it's an annual trip to a downtown theater or a circus or some other attraction available only occasionally. A play in the school auditorium may not be anything to thrill them, but a play in a big theater is a big deal.

When you're taking your children to some such event, you want them to enjoy it fully. You also want to be able to enjoy yourself. Basic to this is not tiring the children out by trying to cram too much into one day. If outings of this sort are rare, the temptation is to try to fill every moment. The age of the children and their familiarity with the theater or circus are factors in how much they can take without fatigue and irritability. If a trip to another city is entailed, the car or bus or train ride in itself is exciting to a small child. The ride and the show and an ice cream cone are enough. When the child is older or the trip nothing special, then you may be able to preface the matinee or evening performance with a restaurant meal. But remember, if a child isn't used to eating out, the bustle and scale of a large restaurant, and the concentration on a menu with a large selection of mouth-watering goodies, can be a pleasantly wearing experience. However, if you want to keep the budget down, most children are just as happy, if not more so, with a hamburger and French fries or a slice of pizza. If you'd like to squeeze an hour's shopping in for yourself, dragging the children along, be flexible. See what shape the children are in. The more intense their gratification with the show, the sharper the letdown can be afterward. The exhilaration that may be buoying up the boys and girls may be covering an emotional exhaustion which may burst through at any moment in an irrational explosion of temper or a flood of tears. There are still the trip home and, possibly, dinner, and by that time overtired children can be impossible for you and for themselves. You know how much they can take, so don't push it.

It can happen that children don't have too much to ask about a performance until after they've seen it—like the ten-year-old boy who was so affected by the Hallmark program on Galileo. The child who might not have been interested in Nazis before *The Sound of Music* now can't wait to learn as much as possible. This is the time when you might well be successful in arousing their minds and in learning what they're thinking about. Children don't always like to reveal what has stirred them. They might not be ready to discuss their reactions, so don't turn this into a question-and-answer probe. For one thing, the children may resent it, and for another, you're not likely to find out anything. Children have an instinct for telling adults what they want to hear—a form of self-protection the race probably developed from time immemorial. Teachers know this, and parents, and any other adults who deal with children.

In Leningrad I attended a performance of a favorite Russian tale, *The Little Humpbacked Horse.* It's not overstating it to call the production stunning. The plot was about an old rogue of a king who assigned impossible tasks to a sharp young man, who managed to do as he was ordered with the help of his little magic horse. During the intermission, the charming American woman who was our leader and translator spoke to a few of the children in Russian, asking how often they went to the theater, whether they came alone, whether they selected their own plays to see, and that sort of thing. She passed the information along to us and established a warm rapport with the boys and girls. She volunteered to ask the children any questions our group had. A professor of drama said, indicating a girl of eight or nine, "Ask her what she has got out of the show." Our leader did so, and the little girl, deadpan, answered promptly, "We learned we must be honest at all times."

I loved the answer, and the girl. The play had nothing to do with honesty. It was exactly what any smart child would have told any teacher anywhere in the world.

Should you watch what your children watch, go with them

to the movies and the theater? I couldn't all the time. My son would look at TV programs and go to movies without me when I had other commitments, but I did try to share with him as much of his entertainment as I could so that we could talk about what we'd seen together. If something sparked his imagination, I'd find a book on the subject and read him a page or two from it, or perhaps just leave it lying around for him to come upon by himself. He has been a valuable education for me. His comments have become remarkably penetrating and illuminating, and I should have missed a great deal if we had not had some of our discussions based on this sharing.

17. Bringing Theater to Children

All over the United States public and private organizations are importing professional theater companies to perform for the young people of their communities. The adults engaged in sponsoring live entertainment are doing this because it would not otherwise be available to their young children and they consider theater to be basic to a child's education. But there is another reason—live entertainment is the only form over which parents can exercise any degree of control. Here you as a parent are responsible for the production you bring through your organization into your child's school or church or community center —you, not a manager whose theater is part of a chain that shows whatever films are delivered; not a TV station that airs whatever its network broadcasts.

If you want to bring live theater to your children and you've never done it before, there are aspects of running such a project you should be aware of so that your investment of time and energy will yield maximum results. But first—how do you decide whether to operate a theater project in your community? Before you become too deeply involved, you need to know that you have the following:

- A clearly defined objective and agreement on the aims of your children's-theater project.
- Personnel to run the project.
- A production or productions.
- A theater.
- An audience.

If your circumstances are such that you will be charging no admission or merely a nominal amount, then you'll also need money.

Possibly the most important of the requirements listed are the first and the last. Working through an organization, you and it must be in agreement about what you both want. Good theater for children, yes. But what else? Is it also to be a fund-raiser? Are you willing to lose money by buying more expensive shows and charging smaller admissions than will cover your costs? Do you want to involve the community at large in a common project for more harmonious relations? Do you want this project to remain entirely within your own group? Do the volunteers want to work to make the project succeed or are they merely looking for something to do that's more creative than bridge or mah-jongg? Are they really interested in the children or do they want "glamor" jobs and prestige without the donkey work that is always part of any enterprise? It's a good idea to think this through and be precise about what you want to do and why you're doing it.

Now, regarding the audience that is to be the beneficiary of this theater project: where are the children coming from? Are they pupils of the school where the shows will be put on? Are they sons and daughters of members of a large social or charitable organization? Are they the children of a church or synagogue congregation? Are they the public? If they are pupils and the school will assist you by encouraging them to attend your productions, you are practically assured of selling out your house. If the members of the charitable or religious organization will buy tickets for their children, and there are enough of them to fill your auditorium, you will have no problem there. But if you must go out into the community and sell to the public without the backing of the schools and the churches, etc.—and by backing I mean more than lip service, I mean buying tickets —you may find it much harder than you anticipated to make a go of the project. You may be wildly enthusiastic about theater for children and conclude that other parents will also want for their children the benefits an intelligent, carefully selected program of live entertainment can offer. Unless you are prepared for overwhelming apathy on the part of a large sector of the public, you may be numbed when it dawns on you that they don't give a damn. They may decide to buy tickets for their children if they have nothing else to do at the time your shows are scheduled, but you can't count on it. What this comes down to is that if your audience is ready-made, you can do very well without too much hard work; if you have to acquire an audience through an intensive public relations campaign, so much effort may be required on the part of all the volunteers that although you still may do very well for the children, it may not be worth the sacrifice to you and your organization.

A children's theater isn't a one-person project. As suggested above, without the enthusiastic support of several responsible and energetic individuals plus the backing of your entire organization, the operation is too large to tackle. Later in this chapter, we'll go into setting up committees and their functioning, and this will aid your comprehension of the work that needs to be done and the persons to do it.

Of course, you need a theater. We detail this later, but primarily you have to decide whether you want a smaller theater that will be more intimate or a larger one that has the potential for more income. This may not be a matter of choice: you may have to use your school auditorium or church basement or whatever facilities your organization already has.

Finally, you need a production that will live up to your ideals for your children, be compatible with the stage on which it will play, and be within your budget.

What else do you need? Insurance, and the protection of the police and fire departments. Also, if you are in an area dependent on private transportation, a parking lot.

As to money—such items as postage or theater permit or lease may have to be paid for in advance, but charges for the production are customarily paid from receipts immediately after the performance, as are stagehands' fees and tips for janitorial services. Insurance premiums are usually not paid until the event has taken place.

Let's think about some of these points in more detail, along with the procedures to follow for a successful theater project. Once you have discussed it fully with your organization and obtained a promise of sufficient dependable cooperation, you're ready to go ahead.

The organization must decide whether the project is to be a one-shot event or a series of performances which will, if successful, be continued into the future. You may find there is almost as much work to do in selling one show as in selling a series. The main difference from the standpoint of organizational labor is that ticket-takers, ushers, etc., will be called back for additional performances. A series offers advantages to you and to the children that one show can't provide. Presenting several productions in a season gives you the opportunity to furnish a combination of different kinds of theater experiences to the children. It also offers possibilities for working out an average budget, which will let you bring in more expensive shows than you might otherwise afford, since these can be offset by low-budget productions. In addition, a series is mostly sold in advance, not always the case with single tickets. Selling seats in advance ensures a cushion in the event the weather is bad on a performance day. When a ticket has been paid for ahead of time, people are inclined to ignore rain or snow and go to the theater.

Your membership as a whole will also have to decide when performances will be presented: Saturday mornings? Saturday afternoons? Sunday afternoons? After school? At assembly?

The membership should then create an executive board for the project, answerable to the membership, and empowered to transact whatever business is necessary, including the setting up of various committees.

ORGANIZATION

To repeat, unless you're planning a one-shot production, a successful children's-theater project is too large an operation to be run by one person. For a permanent children's theater of more than one show a season, the heart of your project will be an executive board composed of a core of dedicated, durable volunteers.

In setting up this board, some decisions must be made about its structure. Is the board to consist of a revolving panel of parents who will be active while their children are in elementary school and lose interest when their boys and girls go on to higher grades? Is the board to be composed of permanent "citizens" not necessarily connected directly with your organization: parents, grandparents, teachers, librarians, etc., whose concern is not related to specific children? Judgment and competence in running any enterprise are developed with experience. An annual turnover in personnel, usual in PTAs , doesn't give the participants enough time to develop abilities to the highest level of efficiency. But since their own children are involved, parents are frequently ardent and intelligent workers for the relatively short period their cooperation is sustained. "Citizens" who are concerned with children generally can give stability; they become more valuable with each year's experience—more knowledgeable in running the mechanics of the operations and more perceptive in the selection of productions than a parent who has never seen a children's show before. I'd recommend a combination of parents and "citizens" as the nucleus of a good executive board.

Another decision is necessary. Will you have a small, relatively arbitrary board or a larger one, more democratically structured? Both types of boards are answerable to the total membership, and there are pros and cons for each. The small board makes its decisons quickly and stands or falls by the results, without having to spread credit or blame over more members. It can operate efficiently, albeit high-handedly in the opinion of some. It can incur the rancor of those who don't agree with its policies but who can't get on the board to affect them. A larger, looser board can also be efficient, but it stands the chance of getting snarled up in internal politics and wrangling. Interminable hours can be wasted while the opposing factions it may divide into split hairs. The trick is to learn what the minimum number of doers is for effectiveness that will keep the whole membership behind you. It's easier to add someone to the board if need be than to drop any who are unnecessary or counterproductive. When it comes to management of a specific project like children's theater, I'm in favor of starting small with a tight board and adding no more than you must to get the job done.

What are the functions of the board? Once the entire organization has decided to proceed with putting on theater for children, and laid down policy as to series, weekend, after-school, or school-time performances, etc., it is the board that implements these decisions. The board is responsible for the business of the project. It appoints committee heads, inviting those heads, at its discretion, to become members of the board for the time the committees will function.

Board meetings can be regular or called as needed.

The first year or so there will be some groping or floundering for the best systems, but when the board feels it has established a good modus operandi, it should prepare a manual of procedures as a permanent guide, subject to amendment if better methods are subsequently developed. Such a manual is invaluable in maintaining continuity over a long period. From time to time even the most dedicated board members may have to be replaced, and the manual will to a degree summarize their wisdom and experience for the next generation of members.

PROGRAM SELECTION COMMITTEE

This committee is the keystone of your children's-theater project. It establishes standards for the productions you import and in selection adheres as closely as possible to them. While stability of personnel is important for all committees, a minimum turnover is of outstanding value here. The judgment of its members must be nurtured through the seeing and evaluating of many productions, and there is no substitute for this experience.

As its title implies, this committee either recommends to the executive board the programs to be booked, or it determines the selections, depending on the authority the board has endowed it with. When it has previewed a production worthy of its consideration, the committee asks about the cost of the show and whether it has any special requirements (e.g., minimal stage dimensions, piano onstage, etc.). Only one person from your committee should be authorized to discuss these business aspects with the producer or company manager.

How, with no background in children's theater and no connections, do you go about finding worthwhile productions? One way is to contact other organizations to learn who the agents are with whom they do business. If you find a good agent with an adequate number of attractions, who concurs in your standards and comprehends the limitations of your theater and any problems peculiar to your audiences (e.g., language difficulties, socioeconomic background), you have a treasure indeed. But agents aren't necessarily conversant with your requirements and they may be more concerned with selling you what they have than with what you need.

Another method is to scour your area to look at touring shows for children, and if you like the caliber of the work, question the producer about other material in his repertory. Besides productions presented in schools, churches, etc., don't overlook the possibility that plays may be offered by departments of education, recreation, parks, mental health, and so on, and these may be of interest to you.

Throughout the country from time to time, agents, individual producers, or associations of producers put on "showcases" of children's entertainment to which buyers—or sponsors, the classification into which you now fit in the children's-theater scene—are invited. In New York City alone there are two such major showcases each spring. Over a period that may run several days, the sponsor is able to preview substantial excerpts from some two dozen musicals, puppet shows, straight plays, etc. Sponsors, feel these showcases are important enough for them to attend. For information about the major showcases, write to:

PACT [Producers Association of Children's Theater], 98 Riverside Drive, New York, N.Y. 10024.

Still another way to learn about individual productions or showcases is to check with the nearest regional office of the Children's Theatre Association of America for what is available in your territory. Headquarters for the Children's Theatre Association are at 1029 Vermont Avenue, N.W., Washington, D.C. 20005. Your state council or commission on the arts may also be able to let you know what is available locally.

Regardless of how you make contact with a producer, by far the best procedure is to see the show you are booking before you commit your organization to it. Further, it is preferable, ideally, to have the entire committee see each show so that when you compare notes you will all know what the others are talking about from direct knowledge. Granted that this is not always possible, every effort should be made to see for yourselves whether the show is correct for the age of your audiences, whether the treatment and theme are worthwhile and contain nothing contrary to your views, whether the cast and physical production are truly professional. . . . It would be easy to rely on the glowing recommendations of agents and producers, but let the buyer beware. Every show is the greatest in the world according to those who have a financial stake in it. Also be mistrustful of lavish praise from school principals or other organization heads. They may be sincere, but their opinions of quality may not be yours nor worth the paper they're written on.

I'd suggest that each member complete an evaluation form for every show previewed, if there is to be any objectivity in the previewing. This form should be a guide to the member, not a straitjacket. I've noticed that when members turn in essay reviews only, one often obtains a clearer picture of the previewer than of the production. An essay review is welcome, but it should be in addition to, not instead of, the standard evaluation form. In the Appendix are two forms drawn up by a committee of Region 14, Children's Theatre Conference (now the Children's Theatre Association of America), on which I served. I offer them as examples of forms you may want for yourself. They were designed to be completed by persons who are not necessarily theater professionals, and there is room for essays if the previewer wishes to comment at greater length.

The committee can eliminate from further consideration any production that doesn't satisfy your quality requirements or is too expensive for your budget. The productions that remain must be evaluated further. Is the age range appropriate? Is it otherwise suitable for your audiences? Can your theater and your personnel accommodate the needs of the production? In a series, will the production enhance a balance in theatrical experiences for your children? (For example, in a series of six shows, you wouldn't want six musical fairy tales. You might want to include, say, a puppet show with a folklore theme, a drama based on American history, an ethnic dance company, a modern dance or ballet with a contemporary story line.) Above all, is the production respectful of your children, and all that this implies?

When you have hammered out your selections and possible alternatives, you then take them to the executive board if approval is necessary, and the booking committee takes over. In a small organization with limited personnel available, the duties of the booking committee may be combined with those of the program selection committee. However, in a large organization, which may be supplying shows for a great number of schools, churches, etc., the booking is too demanding a job and should be separated from that of selection.

Before we go on to the booking, there's one other extremely

important service the program selection committee could provide. This is to educate the board and the members of the organization's body to understand what good theater for children is. Most members will have seen perhaps one or two children's shows only. They will judge the success of a production by how much noise the children make, how fast the action, and how loud the songs and comedy. At least one general meeting a year could be devoted to a speaker, or a panel of specialists in some aspect of entertainment, psychology, or education, to help the membership appreciate that there are other values. Where membership changes annually, as in a parent association, the new people have no background in entertainment for their children and this educational program should be an ongoing activity of the program selection committee.

A training program can serve another vital function. Out of it will come recruits for the entire theater project. Those recruits who demonstrate the most understanding of your aims and the most responsibility can be invited onto the program selection committee.

BOOKING COMMITTEE

As suggested above, if only one series of shows is planned and one sponsoring unit involved, someone from the program selection committee can be designated to contact the selected producers or agents and firm up arrangements. However, the booking committee may be a large and complex entity in itself if it is booking for a county school system of many units. . . . I offer here a setup for an elaborate structure; a simpler sponsor should ignore what isn't applicable to its functions.

The booking committee receives from the program selection committee or the executive board a list of approved productions and the prices for them as agreed by their producers or agents. The booking committee then sends to all its sponsor units a questionnaire asking them to list their available playing dates throughout the season. In other words, if the policy is to put on the shows on Saturday afternoons, the committee lists all Saturdays and the unit indicates those that are possible according to its own schedule. The booking committee also encloses a full roster of the productions with detailed descriptions. The unit then returns the form to the committee, indicating its preferred playing dates, the preferred productions for each date, and alternate choices.

Incidentally, there are some days when it's not a good idea to present your productions. Mother's Day is one, and the Saturday immediately preceding it, when the children will be busy shopping for gifts or putting the finishing touches on homemade presents. On Halloween many children want to go out trick-and-treating. Families tend to go off together over the Thanksgiving holidays or a three-day weekend. The Saturday before Easter, parents may be dragging their boys and girls out for last-minute shopping. And check with the schools before making your schedule final so that your attractions don't conflict with any important activities that may lose you the students.

The booking committee adjusts the preferences of the units to avoid conflicts, such as scheduling a production to be in two places at the same time. The committee then sends each approved producer a list of the dates the units have available, a letter of agreement or request for the producer's contract, and an inquiry into the producer's requirements for setup time, props, etc. . . . Is a mike needed? A piano? A table and chairs? A pitcher of water? A ladder? Help in loading and unloading? The unit must know what the producer needs; the producer must know the dimensions of the stages and whatever else his production calls for. The booking committee is the liaison. If unit and producer cannot meet each other's requirements, a production must be substituted that will work in the given circumstances.

On receiving the producers' replies, the committee confirms to the units the schedules of performances and the requirements. The committee may supply the units with publicity materials (posters, etc.), approval forms to be signed by the parents, lesson plans, tickets, or whatever else has been agreed to.

A week before the performance the booking committee or the unit, depending on the understanding, checks travel information with the producer and verifies requirements. Committee or unit makes any down payment to the producer (though usually no down payment is called for) and the balance to the company as agreed on conclusion of the performance.

The booking committee supplies the units with any necessary forms for reporting on the production's quality and the audience's reaction, as well as miscellaneous comments and a financial statement. The committee then compiles these reports and statistics for the executive board.

Theater projects of this sort are often run entirely by volunteers, but if there is any paid personnel, the booking committee is the place most in need of full-time, reliable services. If a hundred or more performances are scheduled for a season, it is virtually impossible to handle the detail involved without a full-time individual. Only if one or two companies bring the same production to each unit and there is minimal negotiation about playing dates can this detail be avoided.

Under Ways and Means, block booking and tour booking are discussed. These, if approved, are frequently the province of the booking committee.

WAYS AND MEANS COMMITTEE

This committee handles the financial affairs of the children's-theater project, and as a practical matter, any money business not involved with previewing or booking can be turned over to it. In addition to being involved with budgeting the operations, the ways and means committee may be directly responsible for renting the theater, arranging insurance, and so on.

The budget's expenses will include salaries, if any, to your personnel (including taxes, insurance, pension, incidentals) and other administrative expenses (office rent, telephone, postage, stationery, miscellaneous supplies, office equipment and furnishings, etc.). Much if not all of these costs are often absorbed by a parent organization or they may be defrayed by supporters as contributions. As a rule, such expenses for a small operation are nominal. Printing of tickets and posters and other public relations material can add up to a sizable amount, but they need not. Tickets may be designed by a volunteer and cranked out on a mimeograph machine, and other material can be made up inexpensively. Theater expenses are rent, permit, or other cost of use of the building and its facilities; insurance; purchase and rental of additional equipment, such as curtain and sound or lighting systems; gratuities to custodians; and cost of (or contributions to charity for) police and fire protection. Again, there are circumstances under which the auditorium may be used without charge; it may be fully equipped; tips may not be called for; insurance may be provided with the building; and you may not be expected to make a gesture to the police and firemen. What else could be charged to the project? Miscellaneous expenses: public relations (travel, luncheons, etc.), contingency allowance, and most important, the fee for the productions themselves. It is necessary that all this be reckoned early in the plans for the project, since until you know what the expenses total, you won't have any idea what you need to charge in admissions or raise elsewhere to keep from going into the red.

The ways and means committee must also estimate the income from the project. Admissions are the first thought. The price of a ticket is determined by the expenses plus consideration of your policy as a sponsor (make a profit? break even? subsidize a loss if this is the only way to give the children what you want for them?) divided by the number of seats (minus seats reserved for press and guests). The maximum gross income is the number of seats times the admission price. This must realistically be modified by allowing for some seats to be unsold and by establishing a reserve for sales or entertainment taxes, if you are liable for them.

Auxiliary income is possible: contributions by individuals, other organizations, and businesses; additional efforts of your own sponsoring organizations (cake sales, etc.); sales of advertising space in programs; and sales of candy or soft drinks to children before and after the show. This last idea is frowned on by as many as approve it. There are the parents who don't like their boys and girls to buy junk food (very hard not to do when the others are buying); clean-up squads resent the condition of the house after the performance; the players don't like the disturbance when candy or a paper cup rolls away and its owner institutes a noisy search; and most theater-lovers would like young people to be able to appreciate the stage without having to eat.

It's possible to provide good theater and cover expenses without auxiliary income if you can *sell out enough seats* and *the house is large enough* to hold a sufficient number of seats, the *ticket price is high enough* to cover expenses and low enough to attract audiences, and *the production price is reasonable.*

Now, you may have no choice about your theater. It may be the only one you can get or the only one without prohibitive expenses. Therefore, in many instances, there is a fixed limit on the number of seats available. Economics may determine how much you can charge in your territory. Other expenses may be fixed. There is one area of negotiation open, and that is the cost of the production. If you are having one performance only, you have nothing to negotiate with. But if you will be having more than one performance the same day, or several productions over a specified period from one producer, you may be able to obtain a reduction for the subsequent performances which will bring down the average cost. Some companies charge less to perform on weekdays than on weekends; others work the opposite way. If you can accommodate your schedule to theirs, you may find a saving.

There are other ways of bringing down the cost of the production in some instances. One is to arrange block bookings, either for the various units of your own organization or in conjunction with other organizations in your area, where the bookings won't compete with yours. For example, you may set up a dozen performances with one producer for your own after-school programs in the public school system; then you may enlist the cooperation of six parochial schools. The saving over what one performance would cost can be prorated for all participants. Another way is to help a producer arrange a tour. Particularly if the producer must come a long distance and travel expenses are a major share of the cost to you, you can work with him to involve other organizations outside your immediate area which could still be included in a tour. The performances these other organizations would book, when added to yours, could make such a tour much more attractive to the producer and reduce substantially the amount you would have to pay toward travel costs.

The ways and means committee must predetermine how to handle a loss if that is the net financial result of a children's-theater project, or decide, with the approval of the board, what to do with any profits. Should profits go into the general coffers, be reserved for future children's-theater programs of a costlier nature, be used to purchase lights, curtains, or other equipment to improve the theater?

If the general membership has decided on a program that can't be supported by the size of the theater, the price of tickets, or home-grown efforts of budget balancing, then the ways and means committee must put its foot down firmly or include securing of major funding from another source as one of its responsibilities. It is possible to obtain funding in some states from education departments, councils on the arts, etc., but this is definitely a case where you don't count your chickens prematurely. Funding of this order can take a long time to set up, sometimes more than a year, so don't commit yourself to spending before you're guaranteed this income.

PUBLIC RELATIONS COMMITTEE

You may or may not need a public relations committee, depending on two factors. The first is audience acquisition. If your tickets will all be taken as soon as they are available to your school, charitable organization, or whatever, a simple announcement to your members or notice to the principal and teachers by your executive board will suffice. However, if you anticipate that a hard sales campaign to the public will be necessary to sell out your house, a committee to handle the campaign is essential. The second factor is the purpose of your children's-theater project. If all you want to do is provide your boys and girls with good entertainment, no public relations activity is necessary. On the other hand, if along with good theater for your young people you want prestige for your organization, better community relations, or public acknowledgment of thanks to individuals and organizations, then you need one or more persons whose job it is to tell the world.

Your public relations committee, if you have one, should make it its business to see that word of your project reaches whoever should know about it. Naturally this includes the newspapers and your local radio and television stations. Speak with your news editors to learn what kind of story will interest them, the way it should be set up, deadlines, etc. Find out what free community news spots you may utilize. Make it clear that yours is a nonprofit venture and you will obtain a higher degree of cooperation.

If you decide on a campaign of posters and other informative printed or sketched material, check with the booking committee to learn what is on hand and how to contact the producers directly for additional attention-getting story material. Arrange with members of your organization to distribute fliers or put up posters in libraries, supermarkets, laundromats, or other places where children or parents are most likely to see them.

Arrange with chambers of commerce and fraternal organizations to have your speaker at their monthly luncheons, to enlist their support in purchasing tickets to be given in their name to underprivileged or handicapped children, helping you publicize your work, etc.

Your library may be willing to put on an exhibit in conjunction with your productions: books on the colonies if your play is about the American Revolution, or books and paintings on cats if the story is *Puss in Boots.* . . .

You may want to contact the parents' associations of other schools to have them take a quota of tickets for their own children, or speak at one of their meetings about the value of your enterprise.

You yourself, with your knowledge of your own community, will be able to devise public relations programs that could be better than anything an outsider could suggest.

TICKET SALES COMMITTEE

Unless ticket sales are handled by the public relations people, a special committee will be needed. If tickets are being sold in the classrooms, permission must be obtained to enter and transact business with the children directly or through the teacher. Tickets must be counted out and distributed. Money must be collected. Some projects prefer to set up a table in the hall where the children may buy their tickets. Notices must be posted or read to the school by the principal. All this is the responsibility of the committee. If tickets are to be distributed to parents at a membership meeting, some control must be exercised over distribution and payment. Collections, with records, are turned over to the ways and means committee.

PERFORMANCE DAY COMMITTEE

On performance day, there can be no skimping on the number of volunteers if a smoothly functioning event is to take place. Your people must arrive at the theater, school auditorium, etc., *early*. A member of the committee arrives an hour or two hours before the show—whatever is designated—to meet the producer, show him where to park and which entrance is nearest the stage door. If arrangements have been made for your volunteers to help unload scenery, they are waiting at the appointed time. The rooms the producer will need (including washrooms) are unlocked, and so is the tuned piano if one is called for. Either your stagehand or the company's stage manager is ready to work the lights and curtains, depending on your agreement. Your stagehand will have checked the lights to make sure all the bulbs and outlets work, and the stage manager is notified where the outlets are. The stage floor is clean—washed but *not* waxed. And even though it's not required by contract, it would be thoughtful if you provided coffee or soft drinks and sandwiches for the company. They may have been traveling for hours; they are in a strange town with neither the time to stop off at a restaurant nor the knowledge where to find one near the premises. Your thoughtfulness will be appreciated and it might be reflected in a better performance.

Your box office will be set up near the door, with change in coins and bills, ready to handle gate admissions. You may have a desk at another entrance clearly marked for reservations or special servicing. Your ushers will be stationed inside the house, at least one for each aisle if the tickets are general admission. If the seats are assigned, you'll need additional ushers to help the audience find the proper places. Other ushers should be stationed at steps leading to the stage and at exits leading backstage, to prevent boys and girls from wandering into forbidden territory and getting hurt, or vandalizing or making off with the properties of the production or personal belongings of the players.

If tickets have been sold to children only and admission is general—except for some seats reserved for handicapped children, press, or other special guests, which are roped off—children are free to sit where they wish on a first-come-first-served basis. If adults as well as children have tickets, the ushers may have no particular seating problem *if* your house floor is steeply raked or you have tiered seats with rows sharply angled, so that children in the back rows can see easily over the front ones. But if the floor is flat or the tiered seats are not banked enough to provide good visibility, we suggest the ushers seat the children in the front rows and the adults in the rear or along the outer fringes on the sides so that they don't block the view of the little boys and girls behind them. If any children are afraid to be separated from their parents, they may sit on their parents' laps or sit next to them in the rear.

It's the ushers' job to keep a reasonable amount of order for safety's sake and to let the audience enjoy the performance without distraction from rowdies. But the ushers should remember they are present to help the audience, not to serve as drill sergeants. If children laugh spontaneously or respond when participation is solicited, the ushers are unnecessarily officious when they stalk up and down the aisles shushing everyone.

Once the audience is seated in good order, unless some situation arises that demands the ushers' presence, they should make themselves scarce, not stand in the middle of the aisles like sentries, interfering with the view of the children behind them. There's something the ushers should not participate in or tolerate, which I've seen on too many occasions: members of your organization standing in the back of the house discussing, while the performance is in progress, how many tickets were sold, why Mrs. So-and-So failed to report for duty, and other business. They can be a worse distraction than any number of disruptive children, and they set a sorry example of courtesy. Sitting in an audience where this goes on, I wonder how we can expect good manners of our children. The ushers should be at least as firm with the grownups as they are with the children. If they come up against a situation they can't handle, they can turn to their friendly policeman—who will be assisting with parking, providing box office protection, and keeping obstreperous teen-agers from crashing the show and demoralizing it— to order the troublemakers out. If it's necessary to oust someone, or to request that a parent remove a crying child, refund the admission in full, unless the performance is virtually over.

One factor that will reduce the ushers' problems is not allowing the children into the auditorium too early. Sometimes young people line up at the door, ticket in hand, over an hour before curtain time. If the weather is mild, they can be kept outside in the schoolyard, or a park, if available. If the weather is too inclement, they can be detoured into a gym, possibly, until a half hour before curtain, at the earliest. Keeping them in their seats for an hour before the show will only tire them and make them fretful, not to mention interfering with the stage manager, who may still be setting up or checking sound levels or doing any number of other tasks he may not want the audience to witness. Some sponsors feel they solve the problem of early arrivals by admitting them to the auditorium and inviting them to a community sing or some other activity to occupy them until the curtain rises. I don't like this, either. If the children are to have an hour's entertainment before the show proper begins, the edge will be taken off their pleasure in the production they came to see and it will be an anticlimax. Parents must be notified not to drop their children off at the theater too early, and if they learn you mean it about not admitting them, they will abide by your rules for subsequent performances. It would be helpful to parents also if you would post prominently the time the performance will be over so that they'll know when to pick their children up.

All kinds of unexpected difficulties arise when one deals with children, so your committee should make preparation for trouble. Have a first-aid kit handy, and although chances of a serious accident or illness are remote, know where to find a doctor in a hurry.

Always have a responsible member of your committee prepared to stay late, if necessary, after your people have helped the producer pack up and seen him on his way and the theater is closed. There may be a child hanging around waiting for parents who have not arrived, and you just can't go home, leaving him there. Someone must keep an eye on him for a reasonable length of time, and then if no one comes for him, he can be turned over to the police for further care.

Is this all the help you need? Not quite. From time to time someone should check the boys' and girls' washrooms to see that everything's as it should be, and you may want to have someone make a little welcoming speech to the children and special guests. A *short* welcoming speech.

Before the company leaves, if the contract requires you to pay the stage manager in cash, the money is paid from box office receipts and a receipt obtained. The receipt and whatever money is left, less the amount advanced to make change with, if this was lent by a member, are turned over to the ways and means committee as soon as possible. Otherwise, a check is mailed by the designated committee to the producer or agent, as specified.

If it is part of your deal with the theater that you will clean up, your squad of volunteers goes to work as soon as the audience leaves. Otherwise, the auditorium is turned over to the custodial staff.

After the performance, when all records have been brought up to date by the performance day committee, reports are filed with the booking committee, ways and means, or whoever requires them.

Now you know what personnel you need, and what their duties consist of. You know your audiences, and productions have been selected and booked. It's time to discuss the theater in which your programs will play.

Let's look at the ideal theater for children's presentations—an imaginary one, because nothing's perfect. Better-than-average acoustics and sight lines are a prime consideration. Any child, particularly a young one, becomes frustrated, restless, and eventually unmanageable if his or her view is blocked by other children, adults, pillars, or whatever. It follows that "flat" floors are not to be recommended, except in special situations, and that a "raked" or sloping floor is preferable. The size of the theater should be suitable to the production and the audience, since a little boy or girl forty or fifty rows back or two balconies up has only a remote connection to the happenings onstage and the players. If overwhelmed by a vast auditorium, the audience loses the immediacy that is the unique characteristic of the living stage.

A comfortable, separate seat should be provided for each child, one that is fixed to the floor. If a seat can be pushed around, be assured it will. And if a child spots a group of buddies crowded together on a bench, he will squeeze in between them, regardless. Formal seating encourages decorum and enables the children to concentrate on the presentation with minimum distraction.

The theater should be carpeted. Why? Children will scuff their feet, drop things, and make untimely entrances and exits. Much of the resulting disturbance can be absorbed by padding underfoot.

Windows should be nonexistent or be curtained so that it's possible to darken the house completely.

Aisles are free, safety exits numerous and clearly marked.

The temperature of the auditorium should be on the cool side, but not cold. This will go far toward keeping the audience alert and comfortable.

Washrooms should be conveniently located, without intervening steps on which a child in a hurry can trip.

And, for the convenience of the patrons, the ideal theater has ample parking facilities close to the entrance.

Now, what does the ideal theater offer the production? A spacious stage with a full complement of draperies. A cyclorama backdrop. A flexible and complete lighting system. Good, sound flooring—wood, if possible, clean and free of splinters and protruding nails. Equipment and room for flying sets and props. Ample wing space. And, although they are not built into the theater, a skilled stage crew.

The ideal qualities of our theater don't stop here. Provision must be made for the performers: special dressing rooms for men and women, affording the cast privacy for costume changes and assuring the safety of their private property. Chairs, tables, and lighted make-up mirrors. Wash basins, including or adjacent to washrooms with more elaborate facilities. All this near the stage and not accessible to the public.

It goes without saying that all parts of the theater are spic and span and in good repair.

In this ideal structure it's possible to put on any kind of entertainment. In reality, however, although the ideal theater for children may exist, I've never seen one in this country. Does this mean that without splendid facilities you must abandon the thought of a children's-theater project? Not at all. It means you must fully understand the limits deviations from the ideal impose on *your* theater and adjust accordingly.

Obviously, in a hall that can't be darkened entirely, you must choose a production for which this is not important. No black-light effects or magic tricks dependent on utter darkness. With an auditorium seating fifteen hundred, you can't bring in a small-scale, "intimate" performance. By like token, with a postage-stamp stage, you can't present twenty ballet dancers.

Some limitations, like the lack of carpeting, are of minor consequence and can be compensated for to a degree by having the ushers wear rubber heels. Other considerations, like flat floors, are basic problems and will largely determine the kind of productions you import. For example: If it is difficult for children beyond the first rows to see the stage, it would be better to present a hand-puppet show, where the puppet stage has a high floor, than a marionette show, where the puppet floor is relatively low.

Recognition of the difficulties is a first step toward adjusting to them. They can be ignored only to your sorrow. Fortunately, most professional touring companies are realistically geared to meet and beat the challenge of the imperfect theater. It's possible to select many fine productions that can adapt themselves to your theater's limitations without sacrifice. Remedy those defects you can. Choose a production that doesn't demand the impossible, and on with the show!